KU-069-137

Leeds Metropolitan University

17 0424915 2

Nationalist Politics in Europe

Nationalist Politics in Europe

The Constitutional and Electoral Dimensions

James G. Kellas
Emeritus Professor of Politics, University of Glasgow, UK

© James G. Kellas 2004

All rights reserved. No reproduction, copy or transmission of this publication may be made without written permission.

No paragraph of this publication may be reproduced, copied or transmitted save with written permission or in accordance with the provisions of the Copyright, Designs and Patents Act 1988, or under the terms of any licence permitting limited copying issued by the Copyright Licensing Agency, 90 Tottenham Court Road, London W1T 4LP.

Any person who does any unauthorised act in relation to this publication may be liable to criminal prosecution and civil claims for damages.

The author has asserted his right to be identified as the author of this work in accordance with the Copyright, Designs and Patents Act 1988.

First published 2004 by
PALGRAVE MACMILLAN
Houndmills, Basingstoke, Hampshire RG21 6XS and
175 Fifth Avenue, New York, N.Y. 10010
Companies and representatives throughout the world

PALGRAVE MACMILLAN is the global academic imprint of the Palgrave Macmillan division of St. Martin's Press, LLC and of Palgrave Macmillan Ltd. Macmillan® is a registered trademark in the United States, United Kingdom and other countries. Palgrave is a registered trademark in the European Union and other countries.

ISBN 0–333–62046–1

This book is printed on paper suitable for recycling and made from fully managed and sustained forest sources.

A catalogue record for this book is available from the British Library.

Library of Congress Cataloging-in-Publication Data
Kellas, James G.
    Nationalist politics in Europe : the constitutional and electoral dimensions/James G. Kellas.
        p. cm.
    Includes bibliographical references and index.
    ISBN 0–333–62046–1
        1. Nationalism – Europe. 2. Nationalism. 3. Europe – Politics and government. I. Title.

JC311.K429 2004
320.54'094—dc22   2003062247

10 9 8 7 6 5 4 3 2 1
13 12 11 10 09 08 07 06 05 04

Printed and bound in Great Britain by
Antony Rowe Ltd, Chippenham and Eastbourne

LEEDS METROPOLITAN
UNIVERSITY
LIBRARY

1704249152
CV-B
CC-61535
22/05.21·4·05
320.54094 K

Contents

Acknowledgements

Among the many people who have helped me over the years in my study of nationalism in Europe, I should like to mention Professors Bill Miller and Brian Girvin at Glasgow University, and M. Jacques Leruez, of the Centre d'Études et de Recherches Internationales, Paris. The last has kept me fully informed about Corsica.

Introduction

The need for another book on nationalism might appear to be doubtful, in view of the very large number which have been published in the last ten to fifteen years. However, most of these have been written by philosophers, historians and sociologists, not political scientists. What a political science approach offers is a focus on political contexts and political behaviour. In the case of nationalism, that means especially looking at states and their relationships with nations, nationalist political parties and political organisations, and the votes for nationalist parties and propositions. That is what is offered here.

Another difference is that, unlike most works on the subject that treat of nationalism as a general subject, this book takes each country in Europe separately, and for each describes the historical context, the constitutional system and the results of elections. That means that the focus is on states and nations, and on nationalists as political actors, especially in elections. For convenience, a common scheme is adopted, so that each country, or group of countries, can be compared easily with the others. Such a strictly factual treatment is rare in the social sciences, but is necessary if the argument is to be based on detailed comparative information. For example, a discussion on 'right-wing' nationalism in Europe must be based on the actual results of elections, as well as on emotive reports of 'racism'.

In politics, violence and emotion do count, most especially in nationalism. But votes count for more today. The results of elections and referendums determine the fate of nations, as well as the might of states and armies. For example, most nations have achieved independence or autonomy in recent years as a result of peoples' votes. A democratic route to nationhood has largely replaced the use of force. That is because international legitimacy is now based on democracy, not empire.

To assemble a mass of facts and figures of this kind, modern sources have been used. In particular, these are web sites, press reports (also partly on web sites), and large-scale dictionaries, almanacs and encyclopaedias. Many are sourced during the book, but web sites are too numerous and ephemeral to be of much use as literary sources. The reader with access to Internet will soon be able to find these or equivalent sources.

Even so, there are many gaps, which no doubt exhaustive research would have filled. Some readers will be able to fill them for themselves. Political science has no databases comparable to those of the natural sciences, but it has improved greatly in recent years. Of course, any work of this kind goes out of date almost immediately as far as the latest information is concerned, but the updating should be easier when the sources are indicated.

While the end result is at first sight a jumble of statistics, the lessons for European politics are clear. Nationalism is as important as 'integration', and voters have loyalty to their nations more than to the European Union or any supranational body. That does not mean that they reject the EU or supranationalism entirely, but they put them in second place to the interests of their own nation. Immigrants and 'asylum seekers' are suspect everywhere, and the large increase in their number recently has given rise to voting for parties of a virulent nationalist, even 'racist', character. While racism and nationalism are not the same thing, racists are indeed nationalists when they seek to display their racism by a national flag. Nationalists are racists if they attribute racial characteristics to themselves and to foreigners. This makes it difficult to draw a line between a race and a nation. There is more racism as well as more nationalism in Europe now than there was 10 years ago. But there is also more 'integration'. The two may be connected, but that is not clear. The upsurge in immigration is more linked to political upheaval beyond the EU, leading to movements of people from the dangerous and poor zones of the world to the peaceful and rich zones. Nationalism rises when that happens, for nations are essentially long-term bodies that try to preserve themselves from threats from outside. They do absorb incomers, however, in time.

The future for Europe is thus a mixture of nationalism and supranationalism. That is not new, but what is new is the democratic underpinning for both. The new nation-states, national autonomies and language rights have been voted in. So has the 'ever-closer' EU, at least since direct elections and referendums came into use. The voters have spoken, and they have not rejected nationalism in favour of supranationalism. Rather, they have supported it where it was denied, for example, by empires and Unions. This is still the 'age of nationalism'.

1
States and Nations

If one examines an historical atlas of Europe,[1] one can see at a glance how the boundaries of states have constantly shifted over the years. The earliest territorial jurisdictions were those of what we call tribes or clans, which soon shade imperceptibly into kingdoms and principalities. From the Roman Empire to the European Union (EU) larger schemes of political union have taken place, which have competed with the claims of the smaller tribal/ethnic/national settlements. The distinctions between tribal, ethnic and national do not concern us at this point, but the distinction between nation and state is crucial. A nation is defined by its national identity, national territory and culture, national consciousness and nationalism, while a state is defined solely by its status in international society. States are thus easier to identify than nations, even if there are problems there too.

The contemporary map of Europe is the result of centuries of evolution, but also of very recent events. It shows 44 states from Iceland to Russia (Map 1.1) ('the Atlantic to the Urals'),[2] not counting such contentious 'independent states' as the 'Serbian Republic of Bosnia and Herzegovina' (*Republika Srpska*), the Transdniester Republic, Chechnya or the British colony of Gibraltar in the Iberian peninsula. One sign of statehood is membership of the United Nations (UN), but that is not necessary. Of the 44, one (the Vatican City State) is not a UN member, and 15 became members during and after 1990. Of these new members, those of the former USSR had been included in the membership of that state, but two (Ukraine and Belarus, formerly Byelorussia) had been admitted separately in 1945 under the deal with Stalin. These were UN members, but not states as normally understood. Russia (a new member) can be considered the successor state to the USSR. Moldova (formerly the Moldavian Republic of the USSR) was admitted in 1992. Before 1993,

3

EUROPE IN 1914
showing 20 states
+Ottoman Empire-in-Europe

Omits
1. Andorra
2. Liechtenstein
3. San Marino
4. Vatican City
5. Monaco
6. Malta

NORWAY 7
SWEDEN 8
UNITED KINGDOM 3
DENMARK 9
THE NETHERLANDS 20
BELGIUM 19
GERMAN EMPIRE 6
LUXEMBOURG 18
FRANCE 4
SPAIN 2
PORTUGAL 1
ITALY 5
RUSSIA 11
AUSTRIA-HUNGARY 10
ROMANIA 16
MONTE 12
SERBIA 14
BULGARIA 17
ALBANIA 13
GREECE 15
CASPIAN SEA
BLACK SEA
OTTOMAN EMPIRE

Map 1.1

the Czech Republic and Slovakia had been represented by Czechoslovakia; Slovenia, Croatia, Bosnia-Herzegovina and the Former Yugoslav Republic of Macedonia were represented by Yugoslavia before 1992. The Federal Republic of Germany (West Germany) and the German Democratic Republic (East Germany) had been separate members of the UN since 1973, and joined together as Germany in 1990, which was then admitted to the UN as one member. Switzerland joined the UN in 2002.

Apart from states there are substate regional political units within federal and devolved states, such as Catalonia in Spain, Flanders in Belgium and Corsica in France, and Scotland, Wales and Northern Ireland in Britain. While not UN members or states in international law, they have some autonomy, and some international status. Many are national in character and these owe their political status to nationalism.

Larger in territory than states are supranational or international bodies such as the EU (15 states), the Commonwealth of Independent States (12 of the 15 former republics of the USSR), and the Council of Europe (43 members, including formerly non-UN member Switzerland, and a non-European state, Cyprus (but only the southern or ethnically Greek 'Republic of Cyprus')). Cyprus and Turkey are both applicants for membership of the European Union, so could be considered in effect European. The Organisation for Security and Cooperation in Europe (OSCE; until 1995 called the Conference on Security and Cooperation in Europe or CSCE) has 55 members, including Canada and the United States, and the Asian Republics of the former USSR. Yugoslavia has had its membership suspended from 1992 to 2000. These organisations are confusingly also called 'regional' in the literature on international relations. To the extent that they have independent powers in their own right or in some majority combination of votes of their members, substate regions and international organisations represent an alternative source of political power to the states of Europe and to the political force of nationalism.

So much for states, regions and international organisations. What about the nations of Europe? These are not so easy to find. The historical atlases contain maps showing the divisions of Europe into languages, peoples and religions. Today we would also call 'peoples' nations or ethnic groups. In 1994 *The Times* published a *Guide to the Peoples of Europe*,[3] and a quick glance at the contents reveals 101 separate entries for these 'peoples', with some entries covering a group of peoples. So there are clearly more 'peoples' than states in Europe, even if not all 'peoples' are generally called 'nations'. It is rare to find a map of Europe which shows the 'nations' of Europe, independently of the states or regions.[4] To do so would of course be a highly controversial and political statement, as nations are the basis of nationalist claims, whereas peoples have no corresponding political doctrine, unless it is democracy with 'minority rights'. Political nationalists hold that states are legitimate only to the extent that they are 'nation-states', which clearly many are not. By superimposing the cultural divisions on the political divisions we can see at once that the two sets of lines do not often coincide. Perhaps only Iceland in Europe is a completely national state.

So nations and states usually have different boundaries. That is a political problem, since it seems that some (most?) people want the political and national divisions to coincide. This is not the place to enter into extended anthropological discussion, but it looks as if the possession of common ethnicity, coupled with a common territory, is the normal basis of political community, at least today. Nations (as defined here) are not usually single ethnic groups or even peoples, rather a wider grouping based essentially on long-term residence in a common territory with a shared culture.[5]

The problem of matching states to nations became more serious when the idea of nationalism took root generally in the nineteenth century, and self-proclaimed 'nationalists' became central to the politics of Europe. The nationalists combined with liberals and democrats to proclaim that the coincidence of national and state boundaries was essential to 'freedom', and to 'democracy'. Before this new wave of nationalism was current, there had been in some states a general correspondence of nation to state, and a kind of nationalism had always existed in Europe. But now the problem was more acute, as nationalists, liberals and democrats stressed the mobilisation of the whole nation in pursuit of the establishment of a nation-state.

The main political difficulty for this kind of nationalism is that nations do not have boundaries in the same way as states. Nations are generally biologically, culturally and territorially defined (homelands), while states are based on territorial jurisdiction and political power. The maps show the cultural divisions, such as language, ethnic and religious boundaries, but despite these apparent boundaries, the lines are in reality blurred. There is usually a mix of languages, ethnicities and religions within any one territory and state, although the proportions of mixing differ from place to place. Sometimes there are cultural–national enclaves, and at the border between cultures, nations and states there may be a grey area where national identities are mixed, although other borders are strongly divisive. Sometimes the different nations are apparently randomly mixed away from the borders, in isolated villages, regional pockets of nationality, and, in modern times, within cities. To explain the origins and contemporary character of all these differences is extremely difficult, yet crucial to the operation of nationalism in different contexts. Over time, the cultural and national divisions have been more enduring than the political divisions (e.g. many languages have survived the numerous political changes over the last thousand years, and have persisted in much the same territories). But there *have* been changes to the nations of Europe over the years. People have moved about, voluntarily or involuntarily, and have intermarried, so that their children are a mixture of the original ethnicities. Many changes have also occurred to languages, religions and nations. These changes often engender nationalism, as the original inhabitants of territories resist migrants and cultural change through forced assimilation and discrimination. Conversely, expanding nations assert their dominant nationalism.

The nations of Europe cannot be clearly identified, and placed on maps in the way that states can, even if these states seem to have changed even more from one historic map to the next in chronological order. At any particular time, state boundaries have the backing of international law, and their boundaries in the atlas are usually definite (if not necessarily agreed to be legitimate), while cultural divisions are difficult to determine, and have only uncertain political support in institutions or governments. Nevertheless, the languages of Europe have frequently been mapped, and one is provided here (Map 1.4 on p. 22). Cultures are weakly supported in international law, but the 'right of peoples to self-determination' and the protection of minorities is part of such law. The implementation of this right and protection is secondary in international law to the maintenance of the sovereignty of states.

Yet the relative political importance of these different divisions does not correspond to their status in maps or in international law. Nations may be (and usually are) more powerful in the long run than states, and have altered or destroyed these states completely, or in part. An example is the Austro-Hungarian Empire, which was largely dismantled by nationalism and the First World War. At the same time, states can alter and destroy nations in the short run (rarely for ever), although that is more unusual. Poland, for example, was partitioned between Prussia, Austria and Russia in the eighteenth century, but was resurrected in 1918. So there is a constant, dynamic relationship between nations and states. This is essentially based on political power.

States have been involved in nation-building – that is, moulding 'subjects' into 'nationals' with a common national identity and culture – using

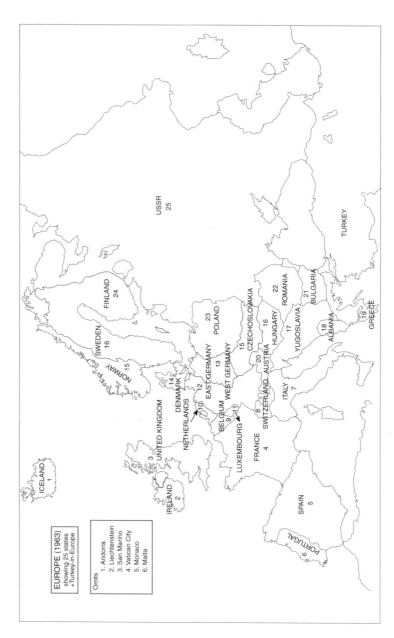

EUROPE (1963)
showing 25 states
+Turkey-in-Europe

Omits
1. Andorra
2. Liechtenstein
3. San Marino
4. Vatican City
5. Monaco
6. Malta

ICELAND
1

IRELAND
2

UNITED KINGDOM
3

NORWAY
15

SWEDEN
16

FINLAND
24

USSR
25

DENMARK
14

NETHERLANDS
12

BELGIUM
9

LUXEMBOURG
10

EAST GERMANY
13

WEST GERMANY
11

POLAND
23

CZECHOSLOVAKIA
15

FRANCE
4

SWITZERLAND
8

AUSTRIA
20

HUNGARY
16

ROMANIA
22

ITALY
7

YUGOSLAVIA
17

BULGARIA
21

ALBANIA
18

GREECE
19

TURKEY

SPAIN
5

PORTUGAL
6

Map 1.2

their superiority in political power. But they have also been subject to challenges to that power from nationalist pressures coming from below. These are also forces for nation-building, often in opposition to the states' nation-building. State nation-building started in medieval times, as monarchs sought to identify themselves culturally and ethnically with their subjects, and turn their kingdoms into one politically loyal and national, community.

States are more performance-related in their popular appeal than nations, which tap a primordial well of ethnicity, language, traditional habits, and, above all, loyalty to a national territory (homeland). The nationalist question is an old one: how to match political and national boundaries. But it is only a political priority in certain circumstances, and anti-nationalists (in contemporary Europe these are Enlightenment-style universalists, socialist internationalists of the old school and new-style European Unionists and Federalists) may deal with it by attempting to control the circumstances which favour nationalism, or by ignoring it altogether. The latter strategy is unlikely to work for long, as nationalism is now persistent in Europe, and needs to be satisfied, at least up to a point. People everywhere want to be ruled by people of their own nation in their own national territory, and object to rule by foreigners. This is related to the universal appeal of democracy and nationality today, but it is also a much older feeling. Only by changing the perception of the nation – the 'us' of 'us and them' – to include all the inhabitants of the state, or to give each nation equal status, can existing multinational states satisfy the demands of nationalism. The former may be achieved by nation-building so that previously distinct nations come to form one new nation. The latter may be engineered by a careful integration of separate nations within one 'consociational' or consensus democracy which retains the nations as building-blocks of the state, but with no nation dominating the other(s). Otherwise, the dominated nations will try to substitute their own 'nation-states' for these states.

If all the inhabitants of each state truly constituted a 'nation' as well as a 'state' then nationalism would in theory be satisfied. But unfortunately this condition is almost never realised, from the fact that most nations do not have clear boundaries which can become the basis of homogeneous nation-states. So most nations have to live with other nations in the same states. Even if all nations had their own states, with no non-nationals present (an unlikely scenario) that might not be the end of nationalism. For nationalism is also associated with predatory raids on the territories of other nations, with annexations, colonisations and so on. This 'territorial imperative' is very ancient or primordial, as survival, community and politics is based on a viable territory, even if that means expansion and grabbing someone else's territory. In this way, nationalism may shade into imperialism. So it is not clear that the establishment of the nation-state can always satisfy the claims of nationalism in its own terms.

Nationalism which is imperialist can be seen in many places in Europe today: for example, that of Britain (in Gibraltar and Ulster); France (in Corsica); Russia (in Chechnya, and the 'Near Abroad' of the former USSR), Romania (in Transylvania), Serbia (in Kosovo) and so on. But imperialism is not included in the doctrine of nationalism *per se*. The claim that the nation and the state should be coterminous does not justify the takeover of other nations' territory. If that happens, it is not surprising that there is a reaction from the attacked nation, which shows the 'genuine' (doctrinal) nationalism. The takeover may have happened long ago, with the effective reaction to it delayed till now. We are now seeing nationalisms in Europe against states whose territories have been the same for centuries. Nationalism, unlike most international law in Europe, does not give legitimacy to 'historic boundaries' if these are not national. Ireland claimed (and won) national independence in 1918 after centuries of British rule, and many other new nation-states are newcomers to the historical atlas. It is difficult to find Euskadi (the Basque Lands), Catalonia, Chechnya, Estonia, Latvia, Romania, Slovakia or Slovenia, on any map before the nineteenth or even the twentieth century, at least with names and political boundaries that correspond with these states or regions today. Even Germany and Italy are names which appear only sporadically in historical atlases. But that has not diminished their nationalism, or that of the most recent 'nation-states', and may even have strengthened it. For their nationalists are likely to claim that their absence from the map is not because they did not exist but because their nationhood was suppressed in the past, and must be redeemed today through statehood.

Another well-founded indictment of nationalism relates to its 'exclusive' nature. Citizenship is defined in national terms, and non-nationals may be excluded from it, as is usually the case in Germany, whose citizenship laws are based mainly on German ancestry. If the 'nation-state' does have resident non-nationals (and Germany now has seven million 'foreigners' in its territory) their position is precarious. If they are given citizenship, they may be made aware that they are not first-class citizens in political and cultural terms. They constitute a 'national minority' who do not relate to the state in the same way as the majority or the 'titular' nation, which may actually be a numerical minority. I do not know of any such cases in Europe at present: Latvians come closest, with 52 per cent of the population of Latvia in 1988, but because of strongly exclusive citizenship laws since independence in 1991 this proportion has risen to over 55 per cent, as some non-Latvians have left. There may be no legal discrimination against the 'national minorities' in a state (although there often is), but there is usually cultural and psychological discrimination. To be a national minority citizen in a nation-state is to be an anomaly in terms of nationalism, for according to that everyone should ideally live in his or her own nation-state.

Nations and states are thus interdependent in nationalist politics, although 'state' can be interpreted broadly. When nationalists claim 'the right of national self-determination' they do not know in advance what political unit the nation will determine for itself. Nationalists generally claim nation-statehood, but nations and even some nationalists may settle for less, perhaps for some form of autonomy in a federal or devolved system, or in a more advanced 'consociational' democracy. Some 'nationalists' may accept a multinational state, if there is considerable national autonomy. So many Welsh, Catalan, Basque, Breton and Corsican nationalists or 'autonomists' stop short of claiming statehood, and have settled (at least in the meantime) for federalism or devolution. Flemish and Walloon nationalists have gone further, and have set up a power-sharing 'consociational democracy' in Belgium.

It is important to notice here that most of the secessions which have been attributed to the 'extremes' of nationalism have in fact come about reluctantly, after the failure of states to concede sufficient concessions to the nationalists. Thus the failure of the British state to deliver home rule for Ireland led to its secession in 1918. Gorbachev's inadequate response to the demands of the Baltic republics for sovereignty within the USSR in 1991 led to their declarations of independence the following year. Similarly, Yugoslavia broke up when Milošević's government in Belgrade refused to recognise the confederal, multi-party electoral and liberal-economic aspirations of Slovenia and Croatia in 1990. Instead, Serbia (with Montenegro) imposed Belgrade's will on them at a special Communist Party conference in January 1990, provoking their walkout. Serbia resisted democratisation by hanging on to communism and set out to dominate the federation by excluding non-Serbs from the federal presidency, and then denying its authority altogether (March 1991). Belgrade had already shown the Slovenes and Croats the kind of Yugoslavia it had in mind when it imposed its rule on the autonomous provinces of Kosovo and Vojvodina against the will of their inhabitants

LEEDS METROPOLITAN UNIVERSITY LIBRARY

(July 1990), who were mostly ethnically distinct from the rest of Serbia. All these events provoked the secession of Slovenia and Croatia from Yugoslavia (June 1991), followed by Macedonia (September 1991), and Bosnia-Hercegovina (March 1992). Czechoslovakia broke up in 1993–94 when the Czech Government refused to compromise with the Slovak Government on its differing views on the economy.

In each case, the nationalists did not at first seek secession, but had it forced upon them by the central or larger state's intransigence. Conversely, the governments of Spain, Belgium and France have so far shown some sensitivity to the claims of moderate Basque, Catalan, Flemish, Walloon and Corsican nationalists, thereby avoiding secessions.

The EU has moderated the nationalism of many sub-state (anti-state) nationalists, while at the same time it has strengthened the official (dominant) nationalism of state-identifying 'Eurosceptics'. The concept of the state, with sovereignty and exclusive legislative powers, seems less relevant under a supranational and quasi-federal Europe, where such sovereignty is frowned upon, even for large states such as Britain, France and Germany. All the EU states have found that their sovereignty is threatened, or even superseded, by EU legislation, in some matters at least, and that a more consociational multinational political system has taken the place of the traditional international system. So in the interaction between state and nation, the power relations have changed in the EU. Those nationalists in nations which do not possess their own states have lost some of their urge to achieve sovereign statehood, since that seems passé in a quasi-federal EU. Instead, they may accept regional status in a supranational 'Europe of the Regions'. That is more true of the Welsh than the Scots, and of the Catalans rather than the Basques. All these nationalists are 'good Europeans', more than the British, French and Spanish official (state) nationalists, who resist European encroachments on state sovereignty. EU federalists retain the states as constituent members, but with much reduced power. Some, like the sub-state nationalists, aim for a 'Europe of the Regions'. These regions would include those nations mentioned above whose political aims stop short of statehood. But for such national 'regions' even this limited aim is based on nationalism, not 'regionalism'.[6]

This book is about aspects of the constitutional and electoral aspects of nationalist politics in contemporary Europe, so history, philosophy and sociology are kept to a minimum. It is essentially a reference work for information on nations and nationalism in their constitutional and electoral aspects. This will certainly distinguish it from most books on nationalism. Even more unusually, there will be no extended discussion of the origins of nationalism, or of its moral 'rights and wrongs' (that it is considered politically right for the present time is another matter). There will be little on cultural nationalism concerning literature, music and so on, which is a subject in its own right. But language is central to contemporary European nationalism and citizenship. Economic nationalism will not be a focus. It is only where these forms of nationalism impinge on political nationalism – on the claims to national territory and national political power – and on the operation of national self-determination, that they will be discussed here.

The main sources of political power in the world are held by states (by which we mean the governments of these states for the time being: 'states' as actors in international and domestic politics only exist in the form of governments, albeit that there is much talk of enduring 'national interests'). That states have a monopoly of territorial jurisdictions and legitimate domestic power and violence is a truism of traditional political and legal theory, although it has been modified by some aspects of international law and the operation of supranational institutions. Even so, the prime suspects in any case of domestic or international power-wielding and thus wrongdoing must be the governments of states. These have it in their power to provide for justice and the well-being for all the citizens in their territory, more than anyone else. Their failure to do so is usually what leads to nationalism. For example, when one state invades and annexes the territory of another, or seeks to dominate a nation in a state by using state powers in a discriminatory fashion, it is inviting a nationalist response from the oppressed nation. As we have seen, this can lead to secession. Here, we can sympathise with nationalism, and attribute blame to the state for acting contrary to the interests of nations beyond its borders; or within a multinational state, for acting contrary to the interests of its dominated or 'colonised' nations.

Such a multinational state would have to act very carefully to keep all its constituent nations happy. It would have to respect their national identities, cultures, autonomy, and give them a share in central government and so on. This can be done, but the record shows that dominant nations in multinational states tend to act as if the entire state was theirs. Their governments are of course concerned to retain their power. Their statism is actually an 'official nationalism'. Thus England has tended to dominate Britain, to the discomfort of nationally conscious Scots, Welsh and Irish; so has France with regard to Bretons and Corsicans. To blame sub-state nationalists for their reaction against domination is to take the side of the dominant power, which is usually itself a nation with its own nationalism.

Nationalist political behaviour has many forms. At its most unattractive it is of the most primitive and brutal kind. Terrorism, aggression, discrimination, 'ethnic cleansing' and genocide are nationalist strategies which cannot be excused, even if they can be explained and sometimes seen as 'rational' actions. They do not occur in all nationalisms and, even in those which have displayed these features, only in special circumstances. It is the duty of students of nationalism to try to explain what these circumstances are, and how they can be transcended. Again, we should beware of accusing only nationalists for bringing about such a sorry state of affairs. What they do is usually a reaction to the action of states (although these too may be acting nationalistically), or to the actions of international forces and organisations. We can see this clearly in the case of former Yugoslavia. Here a complex interaction of political forces, reaching from local warlords all the way up to the UN is involved, but with states (old and new) playing the crucial part, rather than nationalists. These states created the historic legacy of national conflict, failure of the state, and so on, and their actions today perpetuate the conflict. And who can solve the mess? Again, all the political forces together, not just the 'nationalists', whoever they are, but also (especially) the states, and more recently, international bodies.

Each example of nationalism in Europe today tells a different story, but Europe today provides a common, democratic context for nationalist politics. It is essential to have a scientific methodology to study nationalism, and a theory to guide enquiry. A brief recapitulation of the essentials of this methodology and theory follows, but readers should look at my earlier book (Kellas, 1998) for a fuller discussion.

It is first necessary to define the concepts and terms used, and to construct a taxonomy of nationalisms. Three distinct concepts will be used to analyse nationalism in general: (a) national identity and identification (the former subjective or self-assessed, the latter allocated by someone else, usually the state); (b) national consciousness beyond mere identity, mainly in the forms of ethnocentrism (i.e. favourable feelings and actions regarding one's own nation and unfavourable feelings and actions concerning other nations); (c) nationalism in its three forms, cultural, economic and political. Here, political nationalism is the focus. Political nationalism is itself divided into three forms: official, social and ethnic. The first appertains to the state, and may be called patriotism when expressed by the citizens, and official nationalism when operated by the government of the state. The second (social or civic nationalism) calls for the state to be formed on the basis of the nation, which is a subdivision of the state in nearly all cases (except Iceland?). That nation is open to all who adopt its social and cultural norms. The third (ethnic or exclusive nationalism) restricts members of the nation-state to members of an ethnic nation, defined by descent and common culture, and regards non-ethnic citizens as different from ethnic nationals. All these terms and concepts are not just academic: they tell us how nationalism operates in each type. The politics of nationalism differs considerably between these types.

Another typology which helps to explain nationalism relates to the differing contexts in which nationalism operates. The simplest, and most satisfactory context from the point of view of nationalism is a homogeneous nation-state which, as we have seen, is however rarely found; perhaps the nearest in Europe are Iceland and Denmark. Then there is the case of the nation which is dominant within its own state, but that state is actually a multinational state, not a nation-state (the English in Britain, French in France and so on). Third, there is the nation which has its own state, but that state is regarded by nationalists as incomplete, as a significant part of the nation lives outside it. Nationalists may then claim that all co-nationals be united in the one nation-state, especially if these live just across the border (e.g. Russians in the Baltics, and Hungarians in Slovakia and Romania). This is called irredentism. Fourth, a few non-dominant nations in Europe are so scattered among different states as to be make a claim for nation-statehood practically unrealisable. Such nations are the Roma (Gypsies) and Sami (Eskimos). Fifth, there are sub-state 'dominated' (according to nationalists) nations such as the Scots and Welsh in Britain and Basques in Spain. These nationalists seek secession or home rule. Lastly, and here nationalism should not really be present at all, is the case of a multinational state in which no nation or nations dominate. Switzerland seems to fit this type, although in fact German-speakers are a clear majority there, and Belgium ought to do so also, as it is supposed to be a power-sharing 'consociational' democracy. However, Flemish and Walloon nationalists do not see it that way, for they claim that Belgium is not so much consociational as dominant-national in type, no matter that both nationalisms claim that the other nation is dominant. These differing contexts largely determine the claims and characters of the nationalisms found there, even if all nationalisms share some common features.

These common features are also contained in the theory of nationalism presented here. This states that nationalism results from the fear that the nation is threatened by another nation, in one or more of the cultural, economic and political fields. The answer of political nationalists to the fear they have and the threat they see to their nation is to gain control over its territory and the institutions of political power, especially the state. To this end, they require that the nation must make up the majority of citizens within the nation-state, and not be a minority. If that is not possible, the members of the nation must have the controlling interest and power in the state as against other nationals, or at the very least an equal share with other nations in the state through power-sharing along consociational lines (that includes federalism or devolution).

Nationalists may also seek to expand their power into the territory of other states and nations. In the case of expansion into other states, if this is done to bring co-nationals within the fold of the nation-state, then this can be considered nationalism, otherwise called irredentism. But in the case of expansion into the territory of other nations, this amounts to colonialism or imperialism, even if is based on the same fear of domination as nationalism within the state. Now the nation wishes to survive and prosper by expanding its territory or economic and cultural power. In essence, political nationalists are power-seekers who wish to control the state or national region, and build up the power of the nation in the state and beyond its boundaries. In the state they base their political claims on the interests of the nation rather on the interests of some other constituency such as an undifferentiated majority of citizens, or a social class, or a sectional interest such as a church, trade union movement, non-national region or promotional group (e.g. Greens or feminists). Beyond their own state, nationalists base their politics on opposition to anything which seems to them to threaten the 'national interest'. This can be the activities of other nations, states or international organisations such as the EU or UN.

To test for the strength of nationalism in any case, and to explain it, it is necessary to find out the amount and strength of exclusive (as opposed to dual, triple and so on) national identity, and other forms of national consciousness. This will help to explain the causes and strength of nationalism. It is also necessary to discover the political circumstances which give rise to nationalism. This means looking for patterns of national domination and subordination in state–nation relations and international relations, and how members of the different nations react to these. Fears of domination, especially as states change in territory and forms of regime, usually spark the fires of nationalist movements. But so too does the nation's desire to defend itself from and to dominate other nations, through territorial expansion and other ethnocentric policies of the nation-state. Fear and aggression are of course related, for aggressive behaviour is often the result of fear and the widely accepted idea of the 'survival of the fittest'. Here, survival concerns the nation, not just the individual. Compared to other competitive political ideals, nationalism is transcendental and collective rather than based on the lifespan and interests of individuals. It matters in nationalism what happened before and what will happen after the lives of the members of a nation. In this, nationalism resembles religion, and indeed it taps much the same emotions.

Nationalists may be converts from other ideologies, especially transcendental ones, and even from other nationalisms. For example, communists can become nationalists, and British nationalists can convert to Scottish nationalism. They usually do this when their original ideology or nationalism collapses in terms of political power, and their adopted nationalism is seen as instrumental to achieving political power for themselves and their nation. They choose nationalism rather than class politics or something else as the instrument to achieve power because in these circumstances nationalism is the most powerful political force.

In politics there are politicians (activists and leaders) and others (the people, or the masses). These correspond to the distinction between political 'nationalists' and others within the same nation. In each nation 'nationalists' and 'nationalist parties' display different political behaviour from the mass of the nation, just as politicians in general are different from other people in political behaviour. Each section influences the other, but each has its own agenda. In brief, the political elite seeks control of the state, and the people generally seek a more diffuse satisfaction from the outcomes of the political system. Nationalists aim to establish nation-states or national governments, while members of the nation may not be so concerned about that. It is difficult to say which is more 'nationally conscious' (i.e. ethnocentric) in general: the politicians (outside the smaller group of nationalists) or the masses. It could be either. That can only be found out from looking at different examples.

In some cases, the elites are propelled to nationalism by popular pressure (the former communist leaders in the Baltics seem to fit this type). In other cases, that section of the elite which is nationalist is the vanguard in promoting national consciousness and nationalist voting in the nation (Czechs and Slovaks). Western European nationalists are more of this latter kind, although non-nationalist politicians in democracies are very sensitive to nationalist electoral successes, and will introduce concessions to nationalism in order to keep their seats. One obvious variation between East and West is the context of the collapse of communism in the former, and the long-term existence of liberal democracy in most of the latter (but not Germany, Italy, Spain and

Portugal). Communist and fascist systems did not allow for the political expression of nationalism through nationalist voting, while the western democracies did. When the authoritarian systems were opened up to competitive voting, the voters forced the old-style politicians to convert to nationalism in order to get elected, although new nationalist politi- cians also emerged, usually hesitantly.

In the west outside Spain and Portugal (but these are included as liberal democracies after the late 1970s), the voters have had the opportunity of voting nationalist for a long time, but most have not given nationalist parties majority support. In Europe, only in Belgium, Catalonia and the Basque Country can it be said that nationalist parties (including national autonomist parties) have now achieved a majority position. For the rest, the nations await conversion to the nationalist parties.

In this book the aim is, first, to establish the historical context for con- temporary nationalism in each state, and then to describe the constitu- tional and electoral dimensions of these nationalisms. A conclusion is drawn for each case, and a general theoretical interpretation is made, providing in some cases a prescription for action. Cases of nationalism are examined in geographic sequence, from western Europe to the boundaries of Europe in the east (i.e. from the Atlantic-bordering states in the west to the Urals in the east).

Information is not equally available for each case of nationalism, and in some cases hardly at all. In an ideal 'scientific' analysis the data nec- essary to establish that a theory is correct (or not clearly falsified) would be available and comparable across the cases. That is not possible for nationalism at present, and may never be possible.

It is well known that the social sciences rarely, if ever, fulfil the strin- gent conditions of other scientific enquiry, although that is not for lack of trying. The study of nationalism is if anything in a worse position in this respect than other areas of political science. The relevant data on nationalism are not as easily obtained, and are not clearly comparable across countries. Here, what data are available will be used as 'exemplars' for cases where the data are not available or not found. So (for example) if it is in the available data that single national identification is strongly correlated with voting for nationalist parties in one nation, the hypoth- esis is that this will apply to other nations, even if no data about these is available or found. When such data become available and used, then the exemplar can be verified or rejected.

A well-known snag in comparative enquiry is that the concepts used may not 'travel' from one country to another. Thus, the concepts (or is it just the terms?) 'nation' and 'ethnicity' may mean different things in

Chechnya and the Czech Republic, or in Slovakia and Scotland. But then again, the concepts might mean the same thing, even if the terms differ. The aim here is to provide something *systematic* to shed light on what is happening in Europe today with regard to nationalism. Let us then theorise that nationalism is important in conditions of predominantly exclusive subjective national identity (and weak multiple national identity), when the territory or existence/health of the nation is in some way threatened. Invasion of national territory by another nation (e.g. annexation, immigration), and state discrimination, 'internal colonialism' or other domination of one nation by another will lead to nationalism (latent or overt).

The capacity for nationalism to challenge the existing order is strongly related to the strength and policies of the central state power, the actions of other influential states and the international order generally. It is also the result of effective nationalist leadership and political organisation, giving rise to widespread support in the nation. Regime change, whether because of war (victory and defeat), revolution and counter-revolution, provides a strong opportunity for nationalism to defeat the state.

The cure for political conflicts arising from unsatisfied nationalism is of course the antidote to the symptoms which caused the conflict. In most cases, this means granting national self-determination through a democratic vote. In cases where a nation-state is not the appropriate solution (but these are rare today) the democratic answer is to engender a less exclusive national identity in the people of the affected nations, and to put an end to state discrimination and domination by one nation over another, through minority rights, power-sharing among the nations in the state and guarantees by international organisations in a manner perceived to be equitable.

A discredited antidote to nationalism is to restrain or suppress all national identities apart from one; and for that favoured nation or power elite to dominate the state completely. That would destroy the capacity of the subjected nations to challenge the state, and with it their nationalisms. The result is the dominance of one nationalism, state nationalism, although it might also be democratic in a purely majoritarian sense. It can only succeed if the central power sustains itself militarily and economically, and the international environment does not prevent it following its policies. The USSR under Stalin fulfilled this condition, and its break-up was the result of the collapse of the Soviet state, partly because of the changing international environment. The democratic solution to the national problems of the USSR would have followed the non-authoritarian alternatives suggested, but the Soviet state did not do so, and its successor states are still not doing so with regard to Chechnya and some other nations.

There are elements of tautology in this theorising, and of being 'wise after the event'. But there are also distinct and clear parts to the theory which can be based on the evidence, and tested against the outcomes. If something has happened which completely and consistently flies in the face of the postulates, then a new theory is needed. Without a theory of any kind, we are left with a mass of undigested information and unexplained events. We ought to have more to go on, if we wish to make some sense of it all.

In the chapters which follow, there is a separate treatment of nationalism for nearly all the different states of Europe (see Maps 1.3 and 1.4).[7] This is preferred to a thematic approach, in which particular themes of nationalism are illustrated by examples drawn from different countries. However, in each chapter a thematic pattern is followed in that there is first an account of the historical context from which contemporary nationalism is derived. Second, a description of the constitutions of these states where these impinge on nations and nationalism is given. Third, electoral nationalism is described, with as full a description of election and referendum results as is available in current web sites and encyclopaedias and other sources. Finally, there is a conclusion on the politics of nationalism in the area, with a discussion on what seems an appropriate mode of conflict resolution, whether secession, devolution/federalism, consociational democracy, the status quo, stronger centralisation and so on.

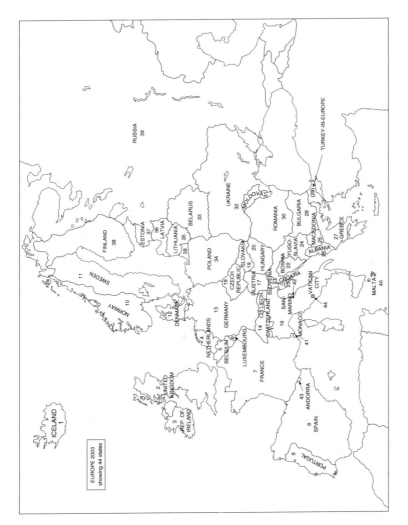

EUROPE 2003
showing 44 states

ICELAND 1

REP. OF IRELAND 3

UNITED KINGDOM 2

NORWAY 10

SWEDEN 11

FINLAND 38

DENMARK 12

NETHERLANDS 4

BELGIUM 5

LUXEMBOURG 6

GERMANY 13

FRANCE 7

SWITZERLAND 14

LIECH. 15

MONACO 16

ESTONIA 37

LATVIA 36

LITHUANIA 35

BELARUS 33

POLAND 34

CZECH REPUBLIC 18

SLOVAKIA 19

AUSTRIA 17

SLOVENIA 21

HUNGARY 20

CROATIA 23

BOSNIA 22

SAN MARINO 42

VATICAN CITY 44

ANDORRA 43

SPAIN 8

PORTUGAL 9

MALTA 40

RUSSIA 39

UKRAINE 32

MOLDOVA 31

ROMANIA 30

YUGO-SLAVIA 24

BULGARIA 28

MACEDONIA 25

ALBANIA 26

GREECE 27

TURKEY-IN-EUROPE 29

Map 1.3

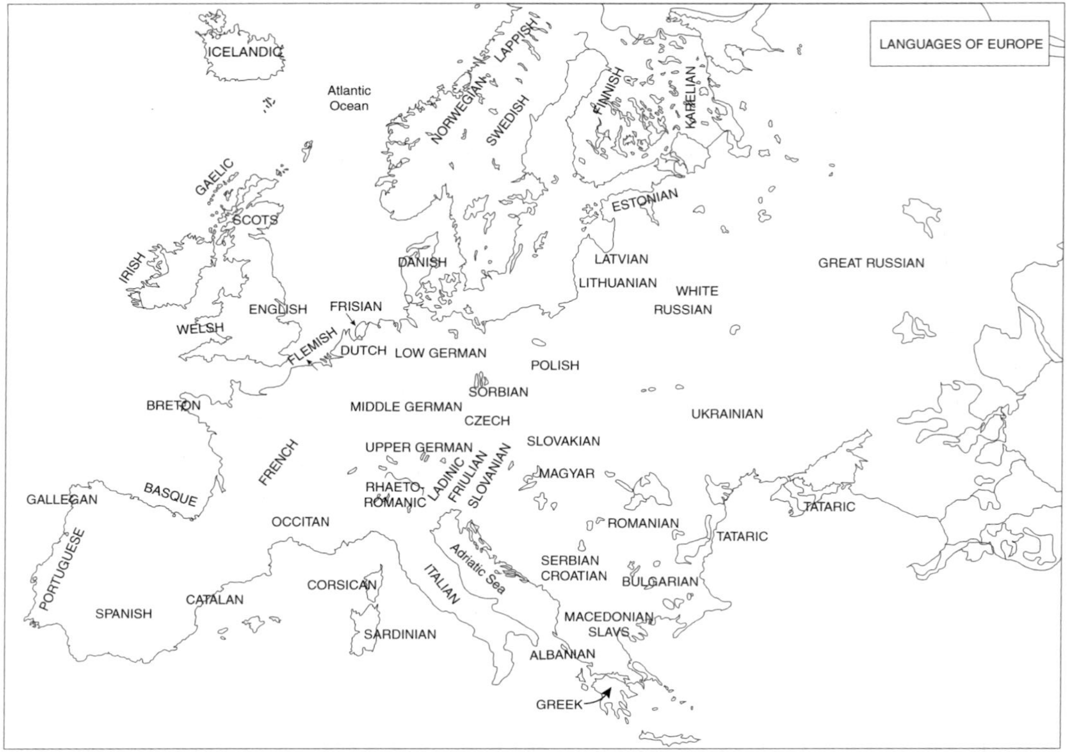

LANGUAGES OF EUROPE
ICELANDIC
Atlantic Ocean
NORWEGIAN
LAPPISH
SWEDISH
FINNISH
KARELIAN
GAELIC
SCOTS
IRISH
ESTONIAN
DANISH
LATVIAN
LITHUANIAN
WHITE RUSSIAN
GREAT RUSSIAN
ENGLISH
FRISIAN
WELSH
FLEMISH
DUTCH
LOW GERMAN
POLISH
SORBIAN
BRETON
MIDDLE GERMAN
CZECH
UKRAINIAN
UPPER GERMAN
SLOVAKIAN
FRENCH
LADINIC
FRIULIAN
SLOVANIAN
MAGYAR
RHAETO-ROMANIC
GALLEGAN
BASQUE
OCCITAN
ROMANIAN
TATARIC
TATARIC
PORTUGUESE
SERBIAN CROATIAN
BULGARIAN
Adriatic Sea
ITALIAN
CORSICAN
CATALAN
SPANISH
MACEDONIAN SLAVS
SARDINIAN
ALBANIAN
GREEK

Map 1.4

2
The British Isles

Historical context

The British Isles consist today of two states (the United Kingdom of Great Britain and Northern Ireland – Britain in short; and the Republic of Ireland/*Poblacht Na hÉireann/Éire*), and at least four nations (England, Scotland, Wales/*Cymru* and Ireland). Claims are made by Cornish nationalists that there is a Cornish nation, and by Manx people that there is a Manx nation. Many inhabitants of Orkney and Shetland deny that they are Scottish: instead, they claim to be Norse (they were ruled by Norway until 1469), and they never spoke Gaelic. The Gaelic-speaking parts of Scotland today (the Western Isles, Skye and some parts of the western mainland), despite their language difference with most of Scotland (which is now English-speaking) identify with Scotland in national terms.

Manx (Isle of Man) identity is Norse and Celtic, and the Channel Isles have Norman French origins. They are not part of the United Kingdom (they do not send MPs to the British Parliament), and have for long possessed extensive self-government. Today they are tax havens, with a special relationship to the European Union (EU). Despite a large number of incomers, much of the original cultural and ethnic identity is retained. Although there is occasional conflict with London, which maintains sovereignty over the islands as over colonies, there is no separatism or nationalism.

Cornwall and Orkney and Shetland, on the other hand, are integral parts of Britain, but both have strong regional identities and regionalist politics. There is also a weak Cornish Nationalist Movement. Cornish and Orkney/Shetland regionalism is expressed mainly through the (British) Liberal Democratic Party at parliamentary elections, which has consistently won seats there. At local elections the Cornish Nationalist Party (*Mebyon Kernow*/Sons of Cornwall) (founded 1951) and the Orkney and Shetland Movement have had some representation. The latter stood for the UK Parliament in 1987 and secured 14.5 per cent of the vote. But the Scottish National Party (SNP) did not stand in that election in Orkney and Shetland.

None of these parts of the UK displays strong political nationalism, which is here defined as support for national self-determination, with significant electoral support for nationalist parties or for organisations which aim to establish either independence or autonomy stronger than devolution or federalism for their nations. Non-nationalist state-wide parties other than the Conservatives today espouse a kind of 'home rule' (devolution in the case of Labour, and federalism in the case of the Liberal Democrats) but attempt to do this on largely non-nationalist grounds. Of course, the distinction between nationalist, non-nationalist and regionalist is to some extent arbitrary, but in politics non-nationalist and regionalist parties are usually at pains to stress that they are not nationalist, while nationalists object to their nation being called a region. In part this is because nationalist and non-nationalist parties are in electoral competition with each other, but it is also because of ideological differences between them regarding nationalism.

In the British Isles there is 'official' or state nationalism, and unofficial nationalism comprising social and ethnic nationalisms. The official nationalism is supportive of the British and Irish states, while the latter seek to supplant these with new nation-states or national polities. However, the picture is complicated since official Irish nationalism has until recently sought to change the British and Irish states by incorporating Northern Ireland (part of the British state) into the Republic of Ireland. Since 1998, the Republic of Ireland has accepted that the people of Northern Ireland must consent to any change in the national status of the North. Nevertheless, there is a residual irredentist nationalism in the Republic.

The balance between the two forms (official and unofficial) of nationalism in the British Isles is different today from what it was 30 years ago. For the forces of disintegration in the British state are stronger now, with the rise of Scottish and Welsh nationalism from the mid-1960s, and the nationalist campaign in Northern Ireland since 1969. There is also a clearer English nationalism today, mainly in opposition to the EU and to non-white immigrants, but also more distinguished from British nationalism, since it excludes the non-English nations of Britain in its desire to promote and protect the English nation. So far, there is no English nationalist party to promote an English nation-state.

British nationalism is weaker today than it has been since the eighteenth century.[1] It is found in all state-wide parties, and there is an extreme racist form in a few fringe parties such as the National Front and the British National Party. The Unionists of Northern Ireland are British nationalists of a kind since they are 'loyal' to the British state and opposed to the claim of Irish nationalism that Northern Ireland should join the Republic of Ireland. But Ulster Unionists oppose London-based official nationalism if that does not serve their interests in Northern Ireland. The Ulster Unionists are split into several parties, the main ones being the ('Official') Ulster Unionist Party (UUP) and the Democratic Unionist Party (DUP). Irish official nationalism is represented by Fianna Fáil (Soldiers of Destiny) and Fine Gael (Tribe of the Gael) both of which have shared in Irish Governments. Unofficial Irish nationalism is mainly represented by Sinn Féin (Ourselves Alone), which contests seats in Northern Ireland as well as in the Republic. In Northern Ireland itself, the Social and Democratic Labour Party (SDLP) is the main nationalist party in terms of votes, closely followed by Sinn Féin.

So there is a complex set of nationalisms in the nations of the United Kingdom and the Republic of Ireland. The other parts of the British Isles mentioned (the Channel Isles, the Isle of Man, Orkney and Shetland) have weak or non-existent nationalist parties or movements, and will not be discussed further.

Before 1922 the British Isles (excluding the Channel Isles and the Isle of Man) comprised one state. Irish nationalism destroyed that state and split it in two: the UK and the Irish Free State (from 1937, the Republic of Ireland, or Éire). Most explanations of Irish nationalism are based on the effect of the religious and cultural differences between Ireland (a largely Catholic country, at least outside Northern Ireland) and the rest of the British Isles. This sociological approach, while largely correct, ignores the inconvenient fact that many Irish nationalists up to and including Charles Stewart Parnell (1846–91) were not Catholics but Protestants. What is more important in accounting for Irish nationalism is the effect of the *ethnic* distinction between the Irish and the other nations of the British Isles. This distinction exists not only between the Irish nation and the nations of Great Britain but within Ireland itself, for a settler population from Great Britain was introduced in the seventeenth century to Ulster which has ever since been the cause of ethnic conflict. Religion alone might not have brought about this conflict if the ethnic and other conditions had not been present as well. The ethnic difference might even have been a sufficient condition on its own, but it was made doubly divisive by the disastrous policies of the British state, for social and political discrimination was practised against anyone who was not in communion with the Church of England. That policy applied to Roman Catholics and Protestant non-conformists alike, but was in effect directed mainly against the Irish people, who were overwhelmingly Catholic. The political discrimination included exclusion from the monarchy, Parliament and even the parliamentary vote. The last two, but not the former, were repealed by 'Catholic emancipation' in 1829. Despite that, an extensive range of social and economic disabilities on the Catholics continued.

This policy was fatal, for Catholics came to see the British state and British loyalists in Ireland as opposed both to their religion and their nationality. The Protestant non-conformists, on the other hand, who are descended from the seventeenth-century settlers, identify mainly as British, which ethnically they are. Their national identification with Britain modified the sense of discrimination which they too felt in relationship to the English Establishment. In fact, they needed the British state to protect them from the hostile Irish. They form a majority of the population in the north-east, and for them, as for the Catholics, religion and nationality are inextricably connected.

Religion may be a necessary condition for Irish nationalism, and for Ulster Unionism, but it was not a sufficient condition. That condition was the long-term discriminatory and exploitative policy of the British state towards those who, through their ethnicity and religion, identified themselves as 'Irish'. Political discrimination by the state against particular nations (even if these are not targeted as such, but through religions, languages, economic opportunities and so on) is the explanation for any nationalism which is directed against the state. A big change since the 1970s has been the gradual decline of all official discrimination against Catholics in Northern Ireland, and a strong policy of positive discrimination in their favour in matters of employment, Catholic education, the use of the Gaelic language and so on.

The refusal of the British Government and Parliament to implement Home Rule in 1914 and even in 1918, and the execution of the 'Easter Rising' leaders in 1916, led quickly to the total wipe out of all but the secessionist nationalists (Sinn Féin) in the south of Ireland at the election of 1918. The devolutionist nationalists of the Irish Parliamentary Party had been undermined by the British Government's actions, and the Irish example shows once again that states are responsible for secessions as much as nationalists. After a period of armed struggle between Britain and Ireland, independence came in 1922, but without Northern Ireland, which was allowed to exercise its own self-determination. The boundary between the North and South was not that of the historic

Ulster, which contained nine counties, but a boundary separating six predominantly Protestant counties from the rest of Ireland. This left a Catholic minority amounting today to over two-fifths of the Northern Ireland population, whose nationalism was Irish rather than British. This conflict of nationalisms remains to this day, although greatly modified by the political settlement of 1998.

The 'Stormont' Government and Parliament in the North from 1922 proceeded to discriminate against Catholics as London had done in the past, only more so. Ulster Unionists called it 'a Protestant Parliament for a Protestant people'. In local elections office-holding Catholics remained largely excluded by franchise restrictions and the gerrymandering of constituencies. There were other forms of discrimination against Catholics in housing, employment and in expressions of Irishness, such as displaying the Irish flag and speaking Gaelic. It was not until the 1970s, when the devolution system was suspended and Westminster enforced civil rights legislation, that political discrimination was ended, although the right to share in government outside a few local authorities was still denied to Catholics. 'Power-sharing' between Catholics and Protestants in the Executive of 1974 was brought to an end by the Ulster Workers Strike. After that, Catholics could not trust the Protestant majority to treat them as equals, until the 'Good Friday Agreement' of April 1998 inaugurated power-sharing between the parties and the reconvening of the Northern Ireland Assembly (1 July 1998). This was accompanied by a cease-fire by the Irish Republican Army (IRA) and by some Unionist military groups. Most significantly, it involved the Republic of Ireland in the running of the affairs of the North, through various 'North-South' and 'East-West' bodies, and in the repeal of its claim to jurisdiction over the whole of Ireland.

Even so, Irish nationalism is still unsatisfied today, and other militant groups, both nationalist and Unionist, have continued the fight. While at elite level there is now peace, at the grass roots level there is as much tension as before. Belfast remains physically divided into Catholic and Protestant sectors, education is segregated, and the symbols of Irish and British nationality (e.g. flags) are omnipresent. The British Army is still present, though with a lower profile than before. The Royal Ulster Constabulary has been reformed, and is now the Police Service of Northern Ireland, with a policy of recruiting Catholics and a new symbol.

Most Catholics in Northern Ireland regard themselves as Irish rather than British. However, perhaps a third or more wish to stay in Britain (see below), so for this group Irish national identity does not mean a demand for Irish as opposed to British citizenship. But they would like to see a constitutional and political 'Irish Dimension' in Northern Ireland. The Ulster Protestant elite still represents the Catholic community as disloyal to Britain, and itself as the only 'Loyalists'.

Irredentism is no longer the main feature of Irish nationalism today, for practical politics and a changing set of priorities in the Republic have prevented the unification of Ireland. In very recent years other, less clearly nationalist, formulas have been adopted to satisfy the claims of Irish Nationalists and British Loyalists. These formulas modify classical nationalist claims to an Irish nation-state and seek to convert Unionist Loyalists to various complicated proposals involving a form of dual sovereignty of Ireland and Britain over Northern Ireland, with power-sharing between parties representing the two communities in a Northern Ireland legislature.

Yet classic Irish nationalism is still strong, especially in Sinn Féin and the IRA, but also in the SDLP, for these all demand the political unity of Ireland, even if the last under John Hume now stresses the rights of people not territory. For their part, Loyalist nationalists oppose the unification of Ireland as a threat to their British national identity and citizenship. While Irish nationalists in both the Republic and in Northern Ireland support the Irish unity claim, in the 1990s this irredentism was modified by the acceptance of the right of a majority of the people of Northern Ireland to determine which state they wish to belong to. As a majority of these people wish to stay part of Britain, total incorporation into an Irish nation-state is practically ruled out for the present. But so is total incorporation into the British state, for the minority (variously called Catholic or Republican or Nationalist) does not accept that.

The policies of the British and Irish states, and of the United States, have an additional impact on Irish nationalism and Ulster Unionism. So too does the context of the changing EU, to which all of Ireland, north and South, belongs. Britain has changed from a resolute Unionism defying Irish nationalist irredentism to a virtual concession of the nationalist case. This started with the 'Anglo-Irish Agreement' of 1985, involving the Republic of Ireland in the affairs of Northern Ireland in an Intergovernmental Conference. Later, Britain denied having any 'selfish strategic or economic interest in Northern Ireland' and will abide by a majority vote there which wishes to secede (the joint Irish–British 'Downing Street Declaration' of 15 December 1993). This short (12 paragraphs) Document was later (22 February 1995) 'clarified' by a longer (26 pages) joint 'Framework' document (*Framework for the Future*) supplemented by a 12-page document on a Northern Ireland Assembly and Executive (*A Framework for Accountable Government in Northern Ireland*). All these showed how far the British Government had moved towards accepting a united Ireland, and disengaging from Protestant majority rule in Northern Ireland.

Ireland also changed from irredentism without conditions to supporting a joint authority over Northern Ireland with Britain and a new-style Belfast Government. Article 2 of its Constitution, which claimed that 'The national territory consists of the whole island of Ireland, its islands and the territorial seas' and the similar Article 3 (see Constitutions, below) were repealed by amendments made in December 1999.

The United States was indirectly present in this 'peace process', with President Clinton's Administration, the Democratic Party and the Irish American Lobby putting pressure on Britain and Ireland to settle, backed up with economic incentives. The former US Senator George Mitchell played a vital role as go-between and facilitator in the 'peace process' from 1995. This eventually led to the IRA cease-fire and the 'Good Friday Agreement' of 10 April 1998, inaugurating a complex set of institutions in Belfast, London and Dublin.

The EU, while not a party to the negotiations, is important, since both Britain and Ireland are members. In a quasi-federal EU without frontiers, the divisions between North and South in Ireland look anomalous, and the increasing recourse for citizens to European Courts (including the Council of Europe's Court of Human Rights) shows that a quasi-state structure for Europe is developing in which European citizenship has meaning alongside state citizenship, especially in the fields of civil rights. Most importantly, the new European focus of the Republic of Ireland has diverted attention away from Belfast to Brussels. Ireland's national destiny was now as much on the continent of Europe as at home, and the transformation of Ireland from a relatively backward economy to a 'tiger' economy gave the country a confidence which it had never experienced before.

The case of Ireland opens a large number of conceptual as well as political questions. Just what do all these identities, communities and nationalisms mean, and what do they amount to in political terms? Is this the solution at last to the violent forms of Irish nationalism experienced in Northern Ireland and even in England (terrorist bombs), and the equally violent reaction from the British Loyalists in Northern Ireland?

Irish nationalism is the most difficult case of nationalism to analyse in the British Isles today, for two reasons. First, Northern Ireland is a deeply divided society whose divisions tend to reinforce each other rather than to cross-cut. Thus, religious, educational, class and political divisions between the two 'communities' tend to coincide. Intermarriage between Catholics and Protestants has historically been very unusual (4 per cent of marriages in 1989), but is now on the increase, as indicated by the increase in the percentage of marriages celebrated in a Registrar's Office from 7.1 per cent in 1971 to 25.2 per cent in 2000.[2]

On top of that is the unresolved claim of Irish nationalists (but not now the Irish Constitution) to a nation-state based on the whole island of Ireland. As we have seen, a long history of discrimination and conflict continued right down to the recent past. But the latest period since 1998 has shown that the traditional claims of both Irish nationalism and Unionism can be modified, when circumstances are favourable. These circumstances are the changing political context and the fatigue felt by the extremists on both the Nationalist and Unionist sides. There is also increasing public alienation in Northern Ireland from these extremists. On top of all this are the changing policies of the British and Irish states, and the general context of the integrationist effects of the EU.

In comparison, the other nationalisms in the British Isles (excluding for the present British official nationalism) are relatively peaceful and straightforward to analyse, although they have some similar features to Irish nationalism. Scottish nationalism claims independence for the historic Scottish state (merged with England in 1707 by the Union of the Kingdoms and Parliaments). There is no irredentism, and no deeply divided society with separate national communities, although not all the population identifies itself as Scottish: around 90 per cent do. Yet over half of these combine a Scottish with a British national identity. The nationalist claim to an independent Scottish state, articulated by the SNP, relies for its fulfilment on achieving a majority vote within Scotland, either for the SNP itself (not an absolute majority of voters, but of seats in Parliament) and/or in a referendum on independence. The SNP would combine both methods, but is unwilling to act outside the British constitutional procedures. The Scottish Parliament might consider holding a referendum on independence, but under the Scotland Act 1998 the Union is a 'reserved' not a 'devolved' matter. Nevertheless, practical politics at a time of nationalist control of the Parliament would prevail over constitutional niceties.

No power-sharing arrangement is involved in Scotland, for Scotland is not seen as a 'divided' society, whether by religion, ethnicity or language. The SNP does not espouse 'ethnic' nationalism, rather the social or 'civic' variety which includes all residents as 'Scots' irrespective of ethnicity, if they apply for Scottish citizenship. Nevertheless, regional and political divisions within Scotland are recognised as a problem, and proportional representation has been adopted for the Scottish Parliament. Devolution or federalism satisfies many (around half) Nationalist voters but not the SNP itself, while in Ireland devolution for Northern Ireland has been associated with Unionism, not nationalism. Its present form is, however, as much Nationalist as Unionist, which many Unionists resent.

There are no paramilitary organisations of any significance in Scotland associated with either nationalism or Unionism, although some celebrated trials have taken place of members of the Scottish National Liberation Army, a tiny group of extremists who do espouse ethnic nationalism. Other ethnic nationalists have existed in the recent past in marginal groups called Scottish Watch and Settler Watch, but these were barred from membership of the SNP.

Welsh nationalism is somewhat more problematic than Scottish nationalism. Wales is more divided a nation than Scotland, because of the Welsh language and the presence of a large number (*c.*30 per cent of the total population, with more in some parts of Wales) of English people, who are usually seen by nationalists as hostile to Welsh national claims. For their part, the 'Welsh Welsh' (those Welsh people who speak Welsh) see themselves as more Welsh than non-speaking Welsh people, even if the latter are still Welsh. All Welsh nationalists see the Welsh as different in national identity from the English. The Welsh language is spoken by only a fifth of the population in Wales, and it can be used to exclude English-speakers in public employment and in social situations such as shops and meetings. So the divided society in Wales can be drawn on linguistic lines as well as national lines (these lines not coinciding in all cases). Welsh nationalism in the form of voting for Plaid Cymru (PC) ('The Party of Wales') is strongly associated with areas of Welsh-speaking, which means the north-west of Wales. Much of the energy of Welsh nationalism is devoted to promoting the Welsh language, while less of Scottish nationalist activity is concerned with the Gaelic language (spoken by under 2 per cent of the Scottish population). Even so, the SNP would make Gaelic one of the official languages in an independent Scotland (the others would be English and Scots). Plaid Cymru now accepts English as a 'national language' of Wales, but this is somewhat divisive among Welsh nationalists.

In contrast to their strong linguistic nationalism, Welsh nationalists in PC do not clearly claim independent statehood for Wales, even if they back 'full self-government'. This is very different from the SNP. Welsh nationalist aims are more communal and cultural, and today some PC leaders regard nationalism itself as outdated. They see Wales as a nation in a EU-based Europe of the Regions, not as a sovereign state with a seat in the UN. The SNP, on the other hand, demands full international status in the EU and the UN, even if it too can be heard to attack old-fashioned state sovereignty in the light of supranational developments in the EU.

While it is relevant to discuss the social and economic differences between Scotland, Wales and England, and to find out the nature and strength of national identities there, the effect of these on nationalism is not clear. The political strength of nationalism is more dependent on political factors than most writers on nationalism are prepared to admit. National identities, for example, are often activated by political discrimination or by changes in political regimes, and these alone do not give rise to political nationalism unless these conditions are met. But national identity is certainly a necessary condition for nationalism, and once it becomes exclusive and strong, it is likely to be a sufficient condition for such nationalism.

Unfortunately, describing and measuring national identity is difficult. Modern surveys have asked individuals questions about their national identity, but they are rarely comparable across time or countries. Many nations in Europe do not have surveys on national identity, so comparisons with these are impossible. In any case, they are not very useful as predictors of political events. Rather, it seems that political events can change identities as much as identities can change politics. Nevertheless, surveys on national identity are one source which must be used to find out about nationalism, and scholars who write about national identity without such data are less enlightening than those who do use surveys.[3]

Northern Ireland presents a very strong relationship between national identity and nationalism. Both of these correlate strongly with the religious divide between Protestants and Catholics. Thus, in 1989 Catholics identified as Irish (60 per cent in 1989) or Northern Irish/Ulster (27 per cent), rather than British (8 per cent). Protestants identified as British (68 per cent) or Northern/Ulster (26 per cent), rather than Irish (3 per cent). These identities were reflected in support for the political parties. Thus the Irish nationalist parties, the SDLP and SF, were made up of supporters who mainly identified as Irish (65 per cent and 73 per cent respectively) or Northern Irish/Ulster (26 per cent and 27 per cent). British identifiers were 8 per cent (SDLP) and 0 per cent (SF). The Unionist parties (the Democratic Unionist Party/DUP and the Official Unionist Party/OUP) identified as British (70 per cent and 71 per cent respectively), or Ulster/Northern Irish (24 per cent and 27 per cent). Irish identifiers were only 6 per cent (DUP) and 3 per cent (OUP). The cross-communal Alliance Party was 54 per cent British, 10 per cent Irish, and 28 per cent (Northern Irish/Ulster). Over the years from 1968, when the 'Troubles' began, Irish and British identities have polarised further in the two 'communities'. In 1968, 20 per cent of Catholics gave a British identity but in 1989 the figure was only 8 per cent. In 1968, 20 per cent of Protestants gave an Irish identity, but in 1989 that had dropped to 3 per cent, and has stayed low since then. However, a Northern Irish identity has become more popular with both Catholics and Protestant, and was given by 25 per cent of Catholics in 1989, compared to 20 per cent in 1986 and 1995 (no Northern Irish option before 1986), and Ulster identity attracted only 5 per cent in 1968 and 6 per cent in 1978, dropping to zero in Catholic working class in 1995.[4]

Scots were surprisingly similar to the English and Welsh in a 1979 British-wide survey.[5] Thirty five per cent were British in national identity, and 52 per cent were Scottish. 10 per cent said other, mixed; don't know. English replies were 57 per cent English and 38 per cent British, and Welsh were 57 per cent Welsh and 33 per cent British. Given that there is a Scottish nationalist movement but no obvious English nationalist movement, it is odd that the Scots were less 'Scottish' than the English were 'English'. But perhaps they do not need such a movement, as they are clearly the majority nation in Britain. The main threat to English national identity comes not from the non-English nations of Britain but from the EU. Thus English national identity is better tested in comparison with European identity. Here, the Eurobarometer and other surveys clearly show how low European identity is in Britain (but England is not given separately). The Eurobarometer of Spring 1990[6] found that 71 per cent of British respondents never thought of themselves as European as well as British. This was the highest figure for the 12 states which were members at that time (the next highest was another part of the British Isles, Ireland, with 67 per cent).

In the 1979 survey Northern Ireland Protestants were far-and-away the most British, with 67 per cent British, 20 per cent Ulster, 8 per cent Irish, and 5 per cent other, mixed. Roman Catholics in Northern Ireland were 15 per cent British, 6 per cent Ulster, 69 per cent Irish, and 10 per cent other, mixed, don't know. The clear contrast between Protestants and Catholics in Northern Ireland in terms of national identity is politically significant, but whether it is the cause or the result of Irish Nationalism and British Loyalism is not clear. Common sense might suggest the former, but in fact even these loyalties can change as a result of political developments. Thus, more Protestants identify as British than before, which relates to the threats they have perceived from the British–Irish agreements dating from the 'Anglo-Irish Agreement' of 1986. Catholics for their part are even less British than before. Another indication that national identity is fluid and influenced by the political context and by the questions asked in surveys comes from Scotland. The 1979 survey found that 52 per cent of respondents in Scotland gave their national identity as Scottish, with 35 per cent as British. From 1986 surveys[7] probed national identity further, with identical questions in each survey. Now the questions allowed for dual national identity (English/Scottish/Welsh and British at the same time) and for degrees of identity (exclusive, predominant, equal). Not only do these surveys show different responses from the 1979 survey, but they also show large changes within the short time scale of 1986 to 1999. Respondents were asked whether they saw themselves as 'Scottish, not British'. Thirty nine per cent did so in 1986, but only 19 per cent in 1992, 23 per cent in the 1997 general election, 32 per cent in the 1997 Referendum, and 32 per cent in 1999.[8] Surveys conducted during British general elections, give lower 'Scottish' identity than surveys conducted at other times. This is matched by the lower votes for the SNP for the British Parliament than for the Scottish Parliament.

Looking at the trend from 1992 to 1999, there is a marked rise in those professing an exclusive Scottish identity (from 19 per cent to 32 per cent), with a drop in the British 'as best choice' category compared to Scottish from 25 per cent to 17 per cent. Comparing Scotland with Wales and England, the 1997 survey reveals considerable variations between the nations of Britain in national identity. Combining the exclusive and predominant categories of national identity ('X not British' and 'More X than British') Scotland gives 61 per cent, Wales 42 per cent and England 24 per cent.[9]

Constitutions

United Kingdom of Great Britain and Northern Ireland/Britain

The British Constitution, in its relationship to nationalism, is less explicit than the constitutions of other European countries about the nature of the British nation and of the British state. No statements are made about the 'indivisible' nature of the nation, as in France, Spain and Portugal, and neither are there any ethnic criteria of Britishness as in Germany.

What binds the state together is not nationality but the Crown and Parliament. The monarchy is explicitly a Protestant one (Act of

Settlement 1700 and Act of Union 1707), a fact which irks many Catholics today. The 'Crown-in-Parliament' is sovereign, which means that there is no federalism or consociational democracy.[10] Nevertheless, the nations/regions of the United Kingdom other than England (Scotland, Wales and Northern Ireland) now have devolution, and Northern Ireland's devolution is of the consociational type.

There is nothing in the British Constitution to prevent the break-up of the state into separate nation-states or national regions, and the secession of Ireland (1918–21) showed how this could be done. After a period of conflict between the presumptive government of Ireland and the British Government, a treaty was conducted between the two to give effective independence to the south of Ireland (called the Irish Free State). However, this was 'Dominion-type' independence under the British Crown, and total independence did not come until the Irish Government declared itself a Republic in 1937 and the British state disentangled its citizenship from Irish in citizenship in 1949. Even then, Irish citizens were allowed to vote in British elections and have free entry to the UK. The reverse, however, was not true, and Irish nationality law is more exclusive than British.

The absence of British nationhood, as opposed to British 'nationality' (citizenship), allows Britain to be a multinational state, with separate flags, national anthems, official languages and churches. These are facts of political importance, since the different nations in Britain can legitimately claim recognition beyond that given in many other European states to their constituent nations. For nationalists in Scotland, Wales and Northern Ireland, this means the right of national self-determination, leading to either autonomy or independence. The Constitution, however, gives no procedure for achieving these ends other than by parliamentary legislation. Since the 1970s, however, referendums have been used in Northern Ireland, Scotland and Wales, to 'advise' Parliament on the wishes of these nations. No doubt, independence would also be subject to referendums, whether mandated by the British Parliament or by the governments of the devolved nations. It seems unlikely that today a fight would be put up to preserve the integrity of the British state, in the face of a majority vote to dissolve it in any of the non-English nations. This is one of the major changes in British politics from the period before 1945.

Citizenship[11]

British citizenship is based on three main forms of citizenship under the British Nationality Act 1981, which came into force in 1983. These are (a) British citizenship for people closely connected with Britain, the Channel Islands and the Isle of Man; (b) British Dependent

Territories citizenship for people connected with the dependencies; (c) British Overseas Citizenship for those citizens of the United Kingdom and colonies who did not acquire either of the other citizenships when the 1981 Act came into force.

British citizenship is acquired automatically at birth by a child born in Britain if his or her father or mother is a British citizen or settled in Britain ... A child born abroad to a British citizen born, adopted, naturalised or registered in Britain is a British citizen by descent ...

British citizenship may also be acquired: by registration of certain children who do not automatically acquire such citizenship at birth or who have been born abroad to a parent who is a citizen by descent; by British Dependent Territories citizens [etc.] ... after five years' residence in Britain (except for people from Gibraltar, who may be registered without residence); and naturalisation for Commonwealth citizens, citizens of the Irish Republic, and foreign nationals aged 18 or over. Naturalisation is at the Home Secretary's discretion: it requires five years' residence, good character ... the intention to have one's home in Britain thereafter and sufficient knowledge of English, Welsh or Scottish Gaelic, except for the spouse of a British citizen, who need only three years' residence and no language or future intentions qualification. Curiously, not all British citizens have the right to live in Britain under this law, unless they had the right of abode before 1983. Other British citizens require permission to enter and remain in Britain. Britain is probably the only state that excludes some of its own citizens from the home country. Nevertheless, dual citizenship is allowed, most notably in the case of Irish citizens born before 1949.

Republic of Ireland (1937, amended)

Preamble
In the name of the Most Holy Trinity, from Whom all is all authority ... We, the people of Ireland ... Gratefully remembering their heroic and unremitting struggle to regain the rightful independence of our Nation ... do ... give to ourselves this Constitution.

[*Article 2 (Territory)*
The national territory consists of the whole island of Ireland, its islands and the territorial seas.

Article 3 (Extent of application of laws)
Pending the re-integration of the national territory ... the laws enacted by that Parliament shall have the like area and extent of application as the laws of Ireland and the like extra-territorial effect.]

Articles 2 and 3 repealed, 2 December 1999

Article 6 (Language)
(1) The Irish language as the national language is the first official language.
(2) The English language is recognised as a second official language.
(3) Provision may, however, be made by law for the exclusive use of either of the said languages for any one or more official purposes, either throughout the State or in any part of Ireland.

Article 7 (Citizenship)
(1.1) On the coming into operation of this Constitution, any person who was a citizen of Ireland immediately before the coming into operation of this Constitution shall become and be a citizen of Ireland.[12]
(2) Fidelity to the nation and loyalty to the State are fundamental political duties of all citizens.

Citizenship law
Anyone born in Ireland is automatically an Irish citizen, and anyone whose father or mother was Irish at the time of the person's birth is also automatically Irish. A person whose grandfather or grandmother, but not his or her parents, was born in Ireland may become an Irish citizen by registering. A person born in Northern Ireland after December 1922 with a parent or grandparent born in Ireland prior to 6 December 1922 is automatically an Irish citizen. Persons born in Northern Ireland who do not meet this requirement may make a declaration of Irish citizenship on the appropriate statutory form.

Naturalisation: five years' residence in a nine-year period preceding the application date; but this may be dispensed with if applicant is of Irish descent, or has Irish associations, or is a refugee or a stateless person.

Dual citizenship: allowed.

Electoral nationalism

Britain

British nationalism
British nationalism is difficult to detect in voting behaviour because the 'British' parties are all to some extent British nationalists, that is, they defend the integrity of the United Kingdom both with regard to sub-state nationalism and the intrusions of the EU into national sovereignty. However, the Conservative Party since the leadership of Margaret Thatcher has acted much more nationalistically than it did under the

leadership of Harold Macmillan (1957–63), Sir Alec Douglas-Home (1963–65) and Edward Heath (1965–75). This is most clearly seen in the party's opposition to devolution (except for Northern Ireland), and to European integration.

Labour and the Liberal Democrats are devolutionist and friendly to European integration, but attack sub-state nationalism, in the case of Labour often virulently. This reflects the very intense electoral competition between Labour and the nationalist parties of Scotland and Wales.

The one party that is overtly British nationalist is the British National Party (BNP). This is in the family of extreme right-wing nationalist parties of Europe such as the National Front (FN) in France and the Freedom Party of Austria. Pro-white, anti-immigrant and state nationalist, it does not compare in electoral strength to its counterparts in the rest of Europe. For example, in the 1997 general election it only put up 57 candidates, winning 35 832 (0.1 per cent) votes. There was very little change in 2001 as shown in Table 2.1 (33 candidates, 47 129 votes (0.2 per cent)). Nevertheless, the BNP has pockets of support in areas of high immigration/ black population such as the towns of the north of England.

In the local elections of May 2002, the BNP won three seats on Burnley (Lancashire) council (it had only held one council seat before, in Tower Hamlets, east London, 1993–94). In 2002 it sought to present less of a 'street fighter' image and targeted middle-class as well as working-class areas. But it put up only a handful (68/*c.*6000) of candidates throughout England (no local elections were held elsewhere at this time).

Table 2.1   The BNP's top ten constituencies, 2001 (UK Parliament elections)

Constituency	% of vote	Votes
Oldham West and Royton	16.4	6552
Burnley	11.3	4151
Oldham East and Saddleworth	11.2	5091
Barking	6.4	1606
Poplar and Canning Town	5.1	1733
Dagenham	5.0	1378
Pendle	5.0	1976
Dudley North	4.7	1822
Bradford North	4.6	1613
Ashton under Lyne	4.5	1617

Source: see Cas Mudde, ' "England Belongs to Me": The Extreme Right in the UK Parliamentary Election of 2001', *Representation*, Vol. 39, no. 1, 2002, pp. 37–43.

The BNP hoped to benefit from the electoral success of Le Pen (National Front) in France, who almost simultaneously (April 2002) came second in the French Presidential elections with 17 per cent of the vote in the first round. But there was really no comparison in electoral strength, even if there is in partisan character. Despite their attempts to appeal to moderates, the BNP and the French National Front are associated with race riots and violence, some of the latter initiated by opponents. Of course, the BNP has no sympathy with sub-state nationalists such as the SNP or PC, and is much weaker electorally in Scotland and Wales.

In the English local elections of May 2003, the BNP advanced further, although it contested just over 200 of the 10 000 seats contested. In Burnley, a northern town with a large Asian population, it won the largest share of the vote and seven seats.

Scotland

The importance of national identity is that it correlates with other attitudes and with political behaviour, such as voting. The 1992 survey showed that degrees of national identity correlate with attitudes towards other nations (later surveys give similar results). Those with exclusive Scottish identity were more likely to say that there is a very or fairly serious conflict between Scots and English people, although this was just under half (48 per cent) of this group. Only 19 per cent of those giving an exclusively or predominantly British identity took this view. However, a large majority of all identity groups perceived some conflict between Scots and English; the highest score for 'no conflict' was 31 per cent among the 'British not Scottish Group' but they were only 3 per cent of the total sample. Additional questions on whether Scots like English people revealed responses which also confirm that the type of national identity relates to attitudes (the more Scottish, the less affection for the English). More to the point for political nationalism is the strong correlation between Scottish national identity and desire for independence for Scotland. 45 per cent of those with exclusive Scottish identity supported independence, but only 12 per cent of those equally Scottish and British, 10 per cent of those more British than Scottish, and only 4 per cent of those exclusively British. However, support for a Scottish Assembly/Parliament was more evenly spread across the identity categories (the range was 39 to 58 per cent). Surprisingly, the exclusively British group was 54 per cent in favour, and the lowest support came from the 'British more than Scottish' group. This probably means that the former group were English whose opposition to devolution cannot be taken for granted, while the latter are Scottish Unionists (but since only 3 per cent of all respondents gave this identity, they are a minority of Unionists, whose vote was 25.7 per cent in 1992). So another dimension enters to complicate the issue: party identification. Conservative supporters in Scotland constituted 58 per cent of the 'British not Scottish' group, and only 10 per cent of the exclusively Scottish group. Conversely, as one would expect, SNP supporters made up the largest component of the exclusively Scottish group, but only 38 per cent, with Labour supporters at 30 per cent.

From the detailed evidence available for the Scottish case, it is clear that national identity is strongly related to nationalism, but that dual national identity is also widespread and important. Less than half of the Scottish respondents claim to be 'Scottish, not British' or 'British not Scottish'. However, an exclusive or predominantly Scottish identity relates strongly to political nationalism, that is, voting for the SNP, desiring independence or devolution, perceiving a conflict with and disliking the members of another nation (here, England). So if national identity can be changed (and it seems that it can) this will be politically important, even if it is not a total predictor of attitudes or votes. Should more people identify exclusively or strongly with a nation, then political nationalism will also be stronger. So it makes sense for the SNP to increase the size of that group, if it can. But it is also possible for anti-nationalist parties to decrease that group, as the Conservatives seem to have done in 1992, but signally failed to do in the later 1990s. How parties can alter national identity is something of a mystery, and seems to be related to political contexts and events. In particular, regime changes or even changes of government affect how people see themselves in terms of national identity and nationalism, especially if they experience discrimination on grounds of their nationality or feel threatened that such discrimination will take place when regimes or governments change.

Having said all that, however, it is important to note that there is no one-to-one connection between claiming a national identity and claiming a national state or even devolution. Indeed, all the examples of national identity in Britain show a rather weak link between the two. Northern Irish Catholics are mostly united in their sense of Irish nationality but strongly divided in their desire to join the Irish Republic. Scots are divided in their strength of Scottish national identity, and even amongst those who claim to be exclusively Scottish, under half support independence. Even fewer Welsh identifiers want a Welsh state, or English identifiers an English state. So national identity must be treated with caution as an indicator of political nationalism, even if it is important.

In a democracy like Britain the obvious way to express political nationalism is through the vote, although minorities may not be able to achieve protection from majority rule in the ballot box. Thus in Northern Ireland, the Catholic minority is permanently outvoted by the Protestant majority, and in Britain Wales and Scotland are outvoted by England. So voting may not be enough. The majority has to be persuaded to respect the minority, and accede to at least its strongest wishes ('vital national interests'). If that does not happen, direct action will be resorted to and, in divided societies, violence. Northern Ireland represents this 'worst case scenario', because of its divided society and irredentism. Wales is another case with nationalist violence, because of the apparent submerging of the Welsh-speaking minority in the face of English immigration and political domination. But Wales, as we have seen, is doubly divided, within its own nation and between the Welsh and English. So the violence is confined to a tiny minority, and is shunned by PC and the Welsh Language Society. Scottish nationalism is almost entirely based on the ballot box. What holds it back is the Scottish people's reluctance to vote for the SNP.

Measuring nationalism by counting the votes of nationalist parties is an essential if incomplete method for assessing its strength. This method is used by political scientists, but not often by other writers on nationalism. As with surveys of national identity, data is needed if the study of nationalism is to advance. In a democracy votes ought to give a fair reflection of what parties the voters prefer, but even that simple conclusion may be partly unwarranted. The voters may be casting a 'protest vote' or a 'tactical vote', rather than a positive vote for the party. It seems that in Scotland and Wales the nationalist parties are often used in this way, so it is difficult to know from the voting returns which are 'nationalist' votes and which are not. Often the context of voting, whether it be a general election, a by-election, a local election or a European election, changes the voting behaviour of the elector. So it is found that SNP victories at by-elections are often followed by losses at general elections, and strong SNP returns at local or European elections are not matched by those at general elections. Plaid Cymru voting seems to be more consistent, but also more limited to particular areas of Wales where Welsh-speaking is strong. The Irish Nationalists, on the other hand, split between the 'constitutional' SDLP and the direct action Sinn Féin, are firmly based in the Catholic community, and do not get many 'floating voters', including 'protest' or 'tactical' voters, least of all from

Protestants. So their voting record does reflect the strengths of the different types of Irish nationalism.

The SNP dates from 1928 (then called the National Party of Scotland), but only came to prominence in electoral terms in the 1960s. Even then, its strength was limited to parliamentary by-elections and local elections. In 1974 it rose to 30 per cent of the Scottish vote with 11 seats in Parliament, then declined to two seats and 17 per cent in 1979 (see Table 2.2). In the 1992 election the SNP won three seats and 21.5 per cent of the Scottish vote (proportional representation would have given the SNP 15 seats). In the 1995 European Parliamentary Elections the SNP rose to 33 per cent and won two seats out the eight Scottish seats. That is the highest total for the SNP in any general (not by-)election. In the general election of 1997 the SNP won 22.1 per cent of the Scottish vote, and in the 2001 general election 20.1 per cent. In the meantime, however, there had been the first elections to the Scottish Parliament

Table 2.2   Scottish National Party in Parliaments

	% of Scottish vote	Seats
UK Parliament (71 Scottish seats to 1979; 72, 1983–2001)		
1970	11.4	1
1974 (Feb.)	21.9	7
1974 (Oct.)	30.4	11
1979	17.3	2
1983	11.8	2
1987	14.0	3
1992	21.5	3
1997	22.1	6
2001	20.1	5
European Parliament (8 Scottish seats: under PR from 1999)		
1979	19.4	1
1984	17.8	1
1989	25.6	1
1994	32.6	2
1999	27.2	2
Scottish Parliament		
1997		
Constituencies	28.7	7
Regional List (PR)	27.3	28
2003		
Constituencies	23.8	9
Regional List	20.9	18

in 1999, conducted under a two-ballot 'Additional Member System' of proportional representation. The SNP obtained 28.7 per cent at the first ballot and 27.3 per cent at the second ballot. This was clearly an improvement on the British election figures, even if it was somewhat disappointing for the Nationalists, who had been running at a higher level in opinion polls. The 2003 Scottish Parliament elections saw a drop in SNP voting and seats, to 23.7 per cent and nine seats at the first ballot and 20.9 per cent and 18 seats at the second ballot.

The SNP's electoral record is thus one of successive waves which rise and fall, combined with different results in different types of election. Scottish elections are the best for it, but it has never received a majority of the vote in Scotland, even those professing an exclusive Scottish identity (it got 38 per cent of these in 1992) or a Scottish 'forced-choice best identity' (24 per cent of these in 1992 and 25 per cent in 1999).[13] It is strongest in a few constituencies, mainly away from the cities. Paradoxically, Edinburgh, the capital of Scotland is poor territory for the SNP, and there is evidence that 'third party voting' goes either to the SNP or to the Liberal Democrats, but rarely to both in equal strength. So SNP voting may be a function of the party system as well as of positive nationalism. Moreover, and most surprisingly of all, surveys have shown that the SNP's policy of independence is not supported by all its supporters, and that those who do support independence do not necessarily support the SNP. In fact, about a third of each of these categories is deviant from what might be expected.

However, the support for independence has been steadily rising, and in the late 1980s and early 1990s has been roughly constant at between 30 per cent and 35 per cent, compared with around 20 per cent in the 1970s. Devolution (the Scotland Act 1978) was supported by 52 per cent to 48 per cent in the Referendum on 1 March 1979, on a 63.6 per cent turnout. The progress of the Act was blocked by Parliament for failing to reach the required threshold of 40 per cent of the votes of the entire Scottish electorate (the '40 per cent rule'). For about 10 years after 1979, the SNP and support for independence gained ground, while support for devolution stagnated. It then took off rapidly when Thatcher's government introduced the community charge ('poll tax') in Scotland. Now Labour supporters started to unite in favour of devolution, where previously they had been divided. A Scottish Constitutional Convention was established in 1989 with Labour, Liberal Democrat and Green participation, but without the SNP and the Conservatives. It eventually (1992) produced a blueprint for a Scottish Parliament, which was to be the model for the Labour Party's proposals.

Labour did not win the 1992 election, but the support for devolution grew even stronger in Scotland under Major's Government. Labour swept to power in 1997, and a referendum on devolution soon followed (11 September 1997). This time, the result was conclusive. On a 60.4 per cent turnout, 74.3 per cent voted Yes to the principle of a Scottish Parliament, and 63.5 per cent to tax-varying powers. With a much stronger Yes vote than in 1979, the divisions in Scotland did not show up as strongly as before. All the regions voted in favour of a Scottish Parliament within a range of 57.3 per cent to 79.4 per cent, although two (Orkney and Dumfries/Galloway) rejected the tax-varying powers. A survey[14] showed that Labour supporters were 66 per cent Yes, 7 per cent No and 27 per cent did not vote. SNP identifiers were 76 per cent Yes, 1 per cent No and 22 per cent did not vote. National identity discriminated between Yes and No voters, but not greatly. Scottish identifiers were 57 per cent Yes, 16 per cent No and 26 per cent did not vote. British identifiers were 46 per cent Yes, 26 per cent No and 27 per cent did not vote. English identifiers (a very small number) were 38 per cent Yes, 29 per cent No and 33 per cent did not vote. Respondents could opt for more than one identity.

Wales

Welsh nationalism can also be plotted by voting and surveys, and these show contrasts with Scottish nationalism. Plaid Cymru is electorally weaker than the SNP, but more consistent in its support. Like the SNP, it emerged electorally in the 1960s, but reached its first electoral peak in 1970 with 11.5 per cent of the Welsh vote, but no seats (see Table 2.3). Three seats were won in October 1974, and this number has stayed fairly steady since. In 1992 the Plaid won 8.8 per cent and four seats, and has kept four seats at every election since, though its vote rose to 14.3 per cent in 2001. Traditionally its strength has been in the Welsh-speaking parts of Wales (the north and west), but in 1999, at the elections to the National Assembly of Wales, Plaid broke through in the south, to Labour's great discomfiture. It now commanded 30.5 per cent of the Welsh vote, higher than the SNP's vote share in the Scottish Parliament elections (but it fell to 19.7% in 2003).

Nevertheless, the aim of nationalism on the Scottish model (independence) is much weaker in Wales, even within PC. Indeed, the philosophy of PC does not bear much resemblance to that of the SNP. It does not aim at achieving sovereign status for Wales in the UN and a

Table 2.3 Plaid Cymru (The Party of Wales) in Parliament and Welsh National Assembly

	% of Welsh vote	Seats
UK Parliament (36 seats to 1983; 38 seats, 1983–97; 40 Welsh seats, 1997–2001)		
1970	11.5	2
1974 (Feb.)	10.7	2
1974 (Oct.)	10.8	3
1979	8.1	2
1983	7.8	2
1987	7.3	3
1992	8.8	4
1997	9.9	4
2001	14.3	4
European Parliament (5 Welsh seats)		
1979	11.7	0
1994	17.1	0
1999	29.6	2
Welsh National Assembly (60 members)		
1999	30.5 (2nd vote)	17 (9 constituency seats and 8 regional seats)
2003	19.7 (2nd vote) 19.7	12 (5 constituency seats and 7 regional seats)

seat in the Council of Ministers in the EU. Rather, it looks to autonomy within the UK, and a place in a 'Europe of the Regions'.

The culturally and ethnically divided nature of Wales and its weak political (but not linguistic and ethnic) nationalism have been demonstrated continuously in modern times. The return of Labour to power in 1997 quickly led to a referendum on setting up a Welsh Assembly, the counterpart to the referendum in Scotland on setting up a Scottish Parliament. The result was unlike that in Scotland. On a turnout of only 50.1 per cent, 50.3 per cent voted Yes that there 'should be a Welsh Assembly'. Survey evidence[15] indicated that the divisions in Wales over devolution were much stronger than they were in Scotland. Labour supporters voted 34 per cent Yes to 24 per cent No and 42 per cent did not vote, despite the fact that devolution was Labour policy. Plaid Cymru, on the other hand voted 71 per cent Yes, 6 per cent No and 24 per cent did not vote. National identity correlated strongly with a Yes vote, with Welsh identifiers more than twice as much in support than British identifiers. There was also a strong regional polarisation, though not as strong as in 1979. Of those voting in Gwynedd, 84.3 per cent voted Yes, but only 33.3 per cent in Clwyd. This correlates with Welsh-speakers, who were strongly in favour. Given that abstainers tended to be No supporters, the 'Yes' result of the referendum in Wales was probably a false representation of majority opinion. Nevertheless, with no '40 per cent rule' this time, the 6721 votes separating the Yes and No votes was sufficient to bring about the legislation for the Welsh Assembly.

Ireland

Republic of Ireland

Note: all parties are in a sense 'nationalist' parties, since they all support the nationalist secession of Ireland from the UK (there are no 'Unionist' parties). Nevertheless, some are more nationalist than others, with Fine Gael ('Family of the Irish') (founded 1922) and Fianna Fáil ('Soldiers of Destiny') (founded by Eamon de Valera in 1926) the heirs to the original (founded 1905 to promote Irish independence). Sinn Féin which collapsed under the strain of the British–Irish Treaty of 1921, which accepted the partition of Ireland into the Irish Free State (Eire) and Northern Ireland (part of the UK, albeit with devolution). Here the progress of Sinn Féin in the Republic is charted (see Table 2.6), because of its extreme nationalism and its unique position in Northern Ireland politics as the only all-Irish party.

The electoral dimension to Irish Nationalism and Ulster Unionism is complicated by the changing nature of the parties there, with several Nationalist and Unionist parties over the years. This is unlike Scotland and Wales, where single Nationalist parties have been in existence since

Table 2.4   Social and Democratic Labour Party (SDLP)

year	% of Northern Ireland vote	Seats
Northern Ireland (12 seats to 1983; 17 seats, 1983–1999)		
UK Parliament		
1974 (Feb.)	22.4	2
1974 (Oct.)	22.0	2
1979	19.9	1
1983	17.9	1
1987	21.5	3
1992	23.5	4
1997	24.1	3
Northern Ireland Assembly (108 seats)		
1998	22.0	24

Table 2.5 Sinn Féin (SF)(to 1955 and from 1983)/'Republican Clubs'

Year	% of vote	Seats
UK Parliament		
1974 (Feb.)	2.1	0
1974 (Oct.)	3.1	0
1979	1.7	0
1983	13.4	1
1987	11.4	1
1992	10.0	1
1997	16.1	2
Northern Ireland Assembly (108 seats)		
1998	17.6	18

Table 2.6 Sinn Féin in the elections

Year	% of vote	Seats
UK Parliament (101 seats) (see Note)		
1918	47.0	72
Irish Parliament (Dáil) (see Note)		
1997	2.5	1
2002	6.5	5
European Parliament		
1995	3.1	0
1999	6.3	0

Note: In this election the Irish Parliamentary Party of John Redmond won 22.0 per cent of the Irish vote but only 6 seats. Sinn Féin decided not to take up seats in the Irish Parliament after most of its members departed to join Fine Gael (1922) and Fianna Fáil (1926). Nevertheless, it won four seats in 1957, losing them in 1961. In 1986, the party ended its policy of abstention from taking up seats, but did not win any seats until 1997, when it won 1 seat on 2.5 per cent of the overall first preference vote. In 2002 it more than doubled its vote to 6.5 per cent and won five seats. This was seen as a reward for its acceptance of electoral politics as opposed to the old direct action 'war' in alliance with the IRA.

the 1920s. Today the Irish Nationalists are divided between the SDLP (loosely called 'nationalists') and SF (loosely called 'republicans'). Nearly all the voters for these parties are Catholics, and the Catholic 'community' amounts to just over two-fifths of the Northern Ireland electorate of 1.2 million (c.480.000). In the Northern Assembly elections in 1998 the combined SDLP/SF vote was 39.6 per cent of the votes cast, a pretty accurate reflection of the number of Catholics in the country. The SDLP: SF ratio was 22 : 18 or 55 per cent : 45 per cent (see Tables 2.4 and 2.5).

SF is considered to be the political wing of the Irish Republican Army, and it rejects parliamentary representation in London. However, it does contest parliamentary elections. It lost its one seat of Belfast West in 1992. Local and European elections do not diverge markedly from parliamentary, because voters tend to be tied to their 'communities'. Under the single transferable system of proportional representation used in Northern Ireland for European Parliament elections, the SDLP came second in 1989 and 1994, and thus gained one of the three seats.

The Unionists or 'Loyalists' are split, mainly between the moderates of the UUP (34.5 per cent in 1992) and the more militant DUP, led by the Rev. Dr Ian Paisley (13.1 per cent). This gave the UUP eight seats and the DUP three seats in the House of Commons, with one other independent Unionist elected. The total Unionist vote dropped to just over 50 per cent in 1992 because some seats were contested by Conservatives, who took nearly 6 per cent of the total vote but no seats. These Conservatives represent the view that Northern Ireland should be fully integrated into Britain, something which the UUP rejects, since it favours devolution. As it happens, the British Conservative Government also favours devolution for Northern Ireland (but not for Scotland or Wales), along with an arrangement with Dublin. The Conservative Party leaders were reluctant to have their party contest Northern Ireland seats but were forced to do so through pressure at the party conference. The Labour and Liberal Democratic parties do not contest seats in Northern Ireland, which indicates that all the British parties have treated Northern Ireland as a place apart from normal British politics. This is significant in view of the context of Irish nationalism and its claim that Northern Ireland should be part of Ireland, not Britain.

The representation of Unionism at Westminster was important to the Conservative Government after 1992, since its small majority meant that it depended on Unionist votes to sustain its majority in European and some other matters. That is because rebel 'Eurosceptic' Conservative MPs deprived the Government of its majority in some votes. This naturally made the Conservative Government sensitive to the views of the Unionists on the constitutional question, even if it did not prevent the Downing Street Declaration of 1993 and the Framework Document of 1995, both of which are abhorrent to the Unionist parties. Similar situations have arisen in the past with regard to the Nationalist parties, and have forced the hands of British Governments to introduce home rule. Some Liberal Governments before 1914 were in this position with regard to the Irish Nationalist Party, and the Labour Government after 1976 relied on the votes of the SNP and Plaid Cymru, as well as on the Liberals. This advanced the progress of the devolution Bills, even if it could not ensure their success, since Labour rebels forced amendments to bring in referendums with the '40 per cent Rule', as mentioned earlier. Had the House of Commons been elected under proportional representation, the parliamentary strength of the Nationalist parties would have been much greater, and might have forced even the Conservatives to introduce devolution.

In the last two European Parliamentary elections the DUP, represented by Dr Paisley, has come first, and the Official Unionists third, which may indicate some voting across the 'communities'. To dig out what individuals think in Northern Ireland is more difficult than in other parts of Britain, as surveys are more unreliable. Nevertheless, the apparently hard division between the 'communities' is not entirely mirrored by responses to the constitutional options. In a Channel Four Television/Ulster Marketing Survey in February 1995 there was a substantial majority among both Catholics (69 per cent) and Protestants (84 per cent) for the creation of a Northern Ireland Assembly, and 44 per cent of Catholics, including a majority of SDLP supporters, supported ending the Irish constitutional claim to sovereignty over the North. Among Protestants the figure was 80 per cent.[16] In earlier polls (1988, 1990 and 1991) Catholics in Northern Ireland showed weak support for a united Ireland. In 1988 only 32 per cent of Catholics chose that option as the best, with a further 22 per cent considering it acceptable. In 1990 the total 'best option' and 'acceptable' figure had risen to 60 per cent, and by 1991 the proportion of Catholics supporting further integration of Northern Ireland with the UK (8 per cent) had dropped from the previous polls. Protestants are more united in their opposition to Irish unity than Catholics are in favour. Only 2 per cent of Protestants chose that as their first preference in 1988 and 1991, while 13 per cent said it was 'acceptable' in 1990.[17] Thus many Catholics apparently want to stay in Britain, and some even vote for non-Nationalist parties. In the politics of Northern Ireland, however, support for Republican and Unionist parties in elections is much more consistent and polarised than the polls on constitutional options would suggest. Thus, electorally Irish nationalism and Ulster Unionism remain opposed, and the only 'non-sectarian' party of any size, the Alliance Party of Northern Ireland, got only 8.7 per cent of the vote in the general election of 1992, and no seats.

More important to the 'peace process' is the political and communal strength of minor parties and paramilitary organisations on both sides of the 'sectarian' divide. Thus, SF, led by Gerry Adams, has through its links with the IRA been able to dominate the negotiations on a constitutional settlement, since an IRA cease-fire was high on the agenda and the British Government insisted on a surrender of IRA arms before holding all-party talks in Northern Ireland. Only Sinn Féin, it seems, could effect that cease-fire and such a surrender. On the Unionist side, the tiny parties linked to the Protestant paramilitaries have appeared out of nowhere to make their voice heard. Dr Paisley's DUP also seems on occasion to upstage the larger (Official) UUP. So counting majority preferences in surveys, or even votes in elections, does not produce a settlement when the parties are divided and some have other resources such as paramilitary organisations. Yet it ought to be possible (one might think) to construct a settlement out of the majority preferences of both Unionists and Republicans, with the backing of the British and Irish Governments. Such a settlement now seems more likely, but the power of the militant minorities and their leaders to obstruct remains. Some commentators do see this power fast diminishing because of the failure of both Nationalist and Loyalist organisations to achieve their ends by traditional means.[18]

England

English nationalism is as strong as the nationalisms of Scotland, Wales and Ireland, but it is not as easy to measure, or even to define. That is because it is usually synonymous with British or official nationalism. So the most clear manifestation of English nationalism is the defence of the British state, whether against nationalisms within Britain or against foreign states and international and supranational institutions such as the EU or the UN. In recent years, 'Eurosceptics', particularly in the Conservative Party, have represented this kind of nationalism. Both Margaret Thatcher and John Major warned of the dangers to British nationhood and culture from a more powerful EU, and their language is certainly that of nationalism. The debates and rebellions on the Maastricht Treaty Bill show how that nationalism can come to the surface and be important politically (the survival of the Conservative Government was at stake, and a Vote of Confidence was called). There were Eurosceptics and 'Maastricht rebels' in all the parties, but if there is an English nationalist party it is the Conservative Party. At the

Conservative Party Conference on 10 October 1995, the Defence Secretary, Michael Portillo, was loudly applauded when he attacked EU institutions and majority voting on a European defence policy. 'Don't mess with Britain!', he exclaimed, and he insisted that British troops would not be prepared to die for Brussels. The Prime Minister John Major, appeared to express his approval, and all the Government speakers moved towards hostility to European integration on that occasion. Jacques Santer, the President of the European Commission, called Portillo's speech 'grotesque and deplorable', which revealed a clear division between the nationalism of the Conservative Government and the supranationalism of the European Commission, which was generally on the retreat in the mid-1990s. Some Conservative backbenchers such as Tony Marlow combine Euroscepticism with opposition to devolution. Marlow shouted in a heated Scottish Question Time in the House of Commons on 13 November 1991 that England should have home rule if Scotland got devolution. Other English Tory backbenchers supported by interjecting, 'Speak for England!'.

Any challenge to the British state, whether from the EU or from nationalism and devolution within Great Britain, is resisted by English nationalists, and by British nationalists who are not English. The Conservative Party represents most of these nationalists, and no specifically British or English nationalist party as such has made much impact electorally. The FN and the British National Party may be considered British nationalist parties and both have been active in demonstrations and in other direct action politics (see Table 2.1 for votes in 2001).

These parties also represent a virulent strain of English nationalism directed against immigrants and residents who, even if citizens, are regarded as non-British. Those attacked are usually non-white, but any foreigner can be the object of nationalist hostility. Thus, even nationals of EU countries may be vilified. It would be a mistake to confine such nationalism to the fringe nationalist parties, for there is widespread nationalism and racism in England generally. This is reflected in the xenophobic behaviour of many English football fans and the anti-foreigner content of the tabloid press in London. Although many Scots, Welsh and English people are also ethnocentric and racist, the particular features of English nationalism relate to the identification of the English nation with the British state. There is usually no need for English nationalism to support an English state as Scottish nationalists support a Scottish state, for England already has a state, and can count on controlling that state in Parliament. Only when there is a 'hung Parliament' with non-English MPs holding the balance of seats will English nationalists lament the loss of English self-government. For many in England and abroad, England is Britain, and there is a 'Queen of England', an English Parliament, and Anglo-... relations with other states. Thus in 1985 the British Government made an 'Anglo-Irish Agreement' with the Republic of Ireland. So being British does not normally mean the sacrifice of Englishness. But if Englishness is threatened from within or without the British state then English nationalists seek a defence of their nation.

We have seen a general reluctance on the part of British people (around 83 per cent of whom are resident in England) in 1990 to identify as 'European', and in the 1979 national identity surveys quoted earlier more people in England identified as English (57 per cent) than people in Scotland identified as Scottish (52 per cent). British identifiers were 38 per cent in England and 35 per cent in Scotland. So an English as distinct from a British identity is strong in England. It is thus possible to isolate English nationalism from British nationalism.

Conclusion

The nationalisms of the British Isles share one thing in common: they all relate to the British state in some way or other. The English nation is most satisfied with that relationship, since it can usually rely on the state to represent that nation and support its interests. Only when the non-English nations appear to be capturing the state or to be subverting it do English nationalists start considering the possibility of a separate English state. So far, that view is confined to a few Conservative mavericks. More common among English nationalists is the defence of state sovereignty against the incursions of the EU and the defence of English national integrity against immigrants and citizens of non-English descent. Euroscepticism and xenophobia are widespread in England, and have been powerful influences on the policies of the British parties since the 1960s. Tight immigration laws have been introduced by both Labour and Conservative Governments, and Euroscepticism is strong in Parliament and in the English nation generally. It is probably more widespread in that nation than in the other nations of the British Isles, although survey evidence is difficult to come by. The non-English nations have of course the English and London Governments to direct their nationalism against, while the English usually have only Europe and immigrants (the United States is on occasion the object of English nationalist hostility, but that resembles a love–hate relationship within what at least the English regard as one family).

The other nations of the British Isles define their nationalism in relation to London Government and England. Their view of the European Community/Union is now more favourable than it was in the 1970s, probably because Europe has often opposed the British state and English nationalism. The non-English attitude to immigrants is hardly different from the English. Thus Welsh nationalists vehemently and sometimes violently oppose English incomers in Wales. So too does a section of Scottish nationalism represented by the tiny organisations, Scottish Watch and Settler Watch, but also by a more general opinion in Scotland that English people have 'taken over' too many cultural institutions, particularly in Edinburgh and Glasgow. In the Highlands and Islands, the fact that many English people have houses and enterprises is seen by some nationalists as detrimental to the survival of the indigenous culture. The SNP, however, distances itself from this ethnic nationalism, and so far there has been no political effect of anti-English feeling. This cannot be said of Wales, where ethnic nationalism is espoused by Plaid Cymru and many other Welsh people.

Irish nationalism is by far the most anti-English nationalism and is totally opposed to the British state's presence in Ireland. In the North there is both ethnic nationalism and social nationalism, with official nationalism in the South. Yet Irish nationalism could probably have been contained if the British state had not discriminated against Catholics, and had not opposed home rule until it was too late. When home rule came in 1922, it was not on the basis of total Irish autonomy but on the basis of the partition of Ireland. So Irish nationalism remained unsatisfied. That is still the situation. British Loyalism in the North provides its own nationalism, and when any two nationalisms compete for the same territory old-style nationalist ideology produces a recipe for conflict. Only now are new power-sharing solutions being tried, but the old nationalisms are also strongly in evidence. These demand that one nation be the victor in the disputed territory. That usually means stalemate, unless a forced solution is imposed.

So how will nationalism develop in the British Isles? It is stronger everywhere than before, as the constituent nations of the UK pull apart under the influence of the 'end of Empire' and the new appeal of EU. But the nationalist parties are not electorally as strong as this underlying nationalism would suggest, and British citizens are wary of secessions and even devolution. They have weighed the costs and benefits and have stayed largely neutral. Moreover, their national identities are largely not exclusive, but dual, especially in England, Scotland and Wales. Failures of the state and stupid discriminatory actions would tip the balance to the nationalist side. This applies to Ireland as much as to Scotland and Wales.

The somewhat low-key context for nationalism in the British Isles is more understandable when it is remembered that national identities are fairly fluid and a matter of personal choice, not imposed from outside. The exception is in Northern Ireland, where citizens are allocated to 'communities' based on religion and nationality, with physical walls dividing them in Belfast. It is no accident that it is there that nationalism is at its most violent and intractable. In England, Scotland and Wales, national identity is largely subjective while 'nationality' (meaning citizenship) is allocated by the British state. This leaves people a choice as to which national identity they may adopt, and lowers the salience of such identity in social and political terms. There is also a low salience of nationalist issues in politics and elections in Great Britain. Few people (under one-fifth usually) there put independence or devolution as one of the most important issues, compared with a majority choosing economic and social matters. Even SNP supporters put independence below unemployment and health.[19] But this too can change, and priorities depend on how the nations are treated by the state.

That leaves the English as the prisoners of the British state, facing the other nationalisms around them and the 'foreigners' in Europe and at home. By a process of elimination, home rule to the Scots, Welsh and Irish will give the English their own state or polity. No doubt the dominance of England in population and economic terms in the British Isles would soften the isolation it might now feel. But English nationalism, now clearly exposed as different from the nationalism of the multinational British state, would be more ethnic, more exclusive and probably more unhappy with its 'loss of Empire'. For the Scots, Welsh and Irish would no longer be ruled from London and would be aliens. The British nation would be completely destroyed in the absence of the British state, just as the Soviet citizenry vanished with the break-up of the USSR. Would the English now feel more free or, like the Russians, give some support to an aggressive nationalism which seeks to recover its territory and protect its co-nationals now living in the 'near abroad'? Or would the experience of Irish independence be followed in the cases of Scotland and Wales? For, after the initial fighting, the British state withdrew permanently from the new Irish state and is now on amicable terms with it for most of the time. As there are no 'Northern Irelands' in Scotland or Wales, this should be the pattern for the future if independence or devolution comes to the nations of Britain.

3
France

Historical context

The spread of nationalism has often been attributed to France. For the French Revolution was based on 'the sovereignty of the people' and popularised the ideology of national self-determination. In this ideology, the nation is given a special place alongside democracy. In fact, the two are made interdependent. Without a nation there can be no democracy, since it is the nation which constitutes the people who are given the right of self-determination. Democracy propelled nations out of feudalism into the modern era since it gave all the people theoretical control over the state. So while nations certainly existed before the French Revolution, according to many scholars they were not nationalist until then. Only when the aim of the 'sovereignty of the people' was combined with existing national consciousness did nationalism (in this view) emerge. After that, nationalism spread as a contagion throughout Europe and the world. For the 'modernising' force of capitalism, then taking off in Europe through the Industrial Revolution, became inevitably intertwined with the desire for national self-determination to produce nationalism. So economic and political forces combined to make nationalism the most important feature of European history after the French Revolution.[1]

Actually, there is much ambiguity about the part played by France and the French Revolution in the rise and spread of nationalism, and this ambiguity remains in French politics today. In 1789 it was not clear what was meant by a nation or a people, and whether France was either of these. A 'people' could perhaps mean any group of citizens who were members of the same state, while a 'nation' might be more limited and exclusive. In one interpretation, the French Revolution, with its

Declaration of the Rights of Man, was essentially universalist. But in another interpretation it was nationalist, since it gave the French people alone their first democracy, with their symbols of nationhood in the flag and national anthem, '*La Marseillaise*'. In fact, the Revolution can be interpreted as either nationalist or universalist, or both.

In the politics of present-day France, the division in the revolutionary tradition is still present. There are those who subscribe to the universalist view, and those who take the nationalist view. Universalists in French politics today tend to be on the Left, and have been declining in strength. The French Communist Party used to represent this strain, but it has recently (1980) attacked the high number of immigrants in Communist-run local authorities, and has taken direct action against immigrants in housing.[2] However, support for the Communists has declined from 21.5 per cent in the 1969 Presidential elections to a record post-war low of 6.8 per cent in 1988. It recovered somewhat in the 1995 Presidential election, with 8.6 per cent in the first round. After winning 38 seats in the 1997 National Assembly elections, the Communists joined the Jospin coalition government with one Council of Ministers member. In the 2002 Assembly elections, the Communists were reduced to 4.9 per cent of the vote in the first round, yet won 20 seats.

The Socialist Party also stands for universalism, or at least internationalism, and its representatives were President Mitterand and Jacques Delors, the former President of the European Commission. Both these Socialist leaders promoted European integration and distrusted nationalism, although since the 1970s the Socialists have promoted regionalisation[3] within France which is a concession to nationalism in Corsica and Brittany. At the referendum on the Maastricht Treaty in September 1992, the vote in favour was 51 per cent to 49 per cent against, an indication that the French people were reluctant to follow Jacques Delors' Eurofederalist policy and endorse a further loss of French sovereignty to the European Union (EU).

The nationalist legacy of the French Revolution is itself split into two tendencies. One tendency conflates the French nation with the French Republic (including both 'metropolitan' France and overseas 'non-metropolitan' departments, territories and territorial collectivities). This is the traditional constitutional view of France. To be French is to be a citizen of France, and until 1993 anyone born on French soil could be such a citizen (the *droit du sol*). In 1993 new restrictive immigration and citizenship rules were adopted (see below). In 1999, 5.6 per cent of the population were 'foreign nationals' (i.e. non-citizens), and this was down from 6.3 per cent in 1990. Similarly, the number of asylum applications was down from 54 813 in 1990 to 38 590 in 2000, when 17 per cent were recognised (15.4 per cent in 1990).[4]

French soil extends beyond 'metropolitan France', the France of the atlases, to all the overseas possessions of France. French citizens in the overseas departments, territories and territorial collectivities have the right to vote in French national elections for 22 Deputies who represent these areas in the National Assembly. The Senate includes 13 Senators to represent the overseas departments and territories, and there are also 12 Senators nominated by the Higher Council of French Abroad to represent French citizens overseas. In contrast, as we have seen, the British Parliament consists only of MPs and Peers from the United Kingdom, and excludes even the nearby Isle of Man and the Channel Isles. Overseas British territories are thus not included in the British state. In the first French view of nationalism, the constitutional view, membership of the French nation is open to all citizens of the French Republic, which stretches far beyond the boundaries of 'metropolitan' France, and is not based on common ethnicity.

Nationalism first enters when the French nation is seen to be under attack from other nations or states, and it is felt that it must be defended. In contemporary politics, this type of nationalism is most associated with Gaullism, which is derived from President de Gaulle's period of office (1958–68), but is perpetuated in the Gaullist Party, now called the Rassemblement pour la République (Rally for the Republic – RPR). De Gaulle was a French nationalist with an internationalist mission. He believed that France was 'the light of the world; its destiny is to illuminate the universe'. This extended to Quebec in 1967, when De Gaulle encouraged the French Québecois to secede from Canada ('*Vive le Québec Libre!*'/'Long Live Free Quebec!'). Thus his universalism was essentially based on French nationalism, and he was not a supranationalist or a Eurofederalist. He withdrew France from the North Atlantic Treaty Organisation (NATO) military command in 1964 and from July 1965 to the end of January 1966 France boycotted the European Economic Community (EEC). He resisted supranationalism in the EEC by refusing to let France be overruled when its national interest was involved, and insisted that any state could veto EEC policy if a vital national interest was deemed to be involved. He propounded the idea of a '*Europe des patries*' (Europe of homelands, or fatherlands) as opposed to the kind of EU being promoted by European federalists. This Gaullist tradition is still strong in France. In the 1993 National Assembly the RPR won more seats than any other party (247 out of 577), and in the Presidential election (2nd round) in May 1995 the Gaullist Jacques Chirac was elected President, albeit by a very small majority (52 per cent). However, he was soon faced with a hostile majority in the National Assembly as a result of the 1997 elections, when the Socialists won most seats (241) and the RPR was reduced to 134. A coalition of Socialists, Communists, Radical Socialists and Greens was formed, which had to 'cohabit' with the Gaullist President. This produced tensions between the Presidency and the Government of Prime Minister Lionel Jospin, when the latter inaugurated his attempt to pacify Corsican nationalists with a stronger form of devolution from 1999 to 2002 (see below).

Chirac, unlike the Socialists, followed the Gaullist tradition of promoting '*la gloire*' (national glory), notably in the resumption of atomic bomb testing in the south Pacific (September 1995). He maintained France's border controls, despite German acceptance of the 'Schengen' open frontiers zone which the socialist former President Mitterand had agreed to.

The Gaullist type of French nationalism is inclusive in that French citizens are not ethnically defined, and the French Republic and nation stretches beyond metropolitan France to the far corners of the globe. This view of the French nation received a near-fatal blow when most French citizens abroad decided it was time to leave France and set up their own nation-states. In other words, they had become nationalists in their own right. This was of course the same process of decolonisation which was taking place in all the European-centred Empires after the Second World War, but for France it was especially traumatic since most of these colonies had been regarded as integral parts of the French nation and state. The climax came when Algeria, with many French settlers and with Deputies in the National Assembly, broke away (1962). Paradoxically, it was the French 'official' nationalist, De Gaulle, who presided over, and facilitated, that secession. That must have changed his perception of the French nation towards one based on a more narrow 'patrie', continental France. The aftermath of Algerian independence is still present in French politics, since emigration from there of Muslims to France and of *pieds-noirs* (former settlers) to Corsica has produced tensions which have exposed a different kind of nationalism: the second nationalist tendency, which is exclusive and ethnic. In continental France this is anti-Muslim, while in Corsica it is anti-French.

In France this second tendency tries to establish who is 'really French', and seeks to maintain a France 'for the French'. It is thus opposed to immigrants, especially from the former Muslim French territories, mainly because these are not considered French in ethnicity or culture. In particular, the Muslim religion is regarded as un-French, especially in its visible manifestations such as the wearing of headscarves at state schools. This caused a major political issue in France in 1989, for it threatened both the secular character of French schools and French ethnic identity. The 'Headscarves Affair' went all the way to the Council of State, and an Education Ministry circular in September 1994 banned 'any outwardly ostentatious symbols whose precise effect is to separate certain children from the general rules of school-life'.[5] This episode came at a period when ethnic nationalism in France was rising, mainly as a result of complaints about immigration. Immigrants were no larger a proportion of the population than before (in 1990 they amounted to 3.6 million, or 6.8 per cent of the population, compared to 6.5 per cent in 1971 and 6.6 per cent in 1931; in 1999 they were 4.3 million or 7.4 per cent of the population), but they were now predominantly non-European, with around 3 million in 1999 of North African descent.[6] Moreover, they were arriving at a time when unemployment was rising, and pressures on housing were heavy. Algerian immigrants tended to concentrate in particular areas, while European immigrants were spread around.

The main proponent of ethnic nationalism in contemporary France is the *Front National* (National Front – FN), which is the most successful overtly all-French nationalist party in electoral terms (see below). Mainstream and other parties, especially on the Right, have come to support much of this tendency of nationalism. They too seek to restrict immigration, and they propound an ethnic French nationalism. But they now bitterly oppose the FN in elections, even if at first (in the late 1970s) FN candidates ran on the RPR lists in some places.

The effect of the FN in shaping French nationalism, and in influencing government policies was most clearly seen during the late 1980s when the socialists were replaced by the right-wing Government under the Gaullist Prime Minister, Jacques Chirac (later President). Chirac, when Mayor of Paris, had complained that France was suffering from 'an overdose of foreigners' whose 'noise' and 'smell' 'drives the French worker crazy'.[7] Chirac's Government changed the immigration laws under the *loi Pasqua* (1986), called after the then Interior Minister Charles Pasqua. This limited the issue of residency permits, and extended the categories of immigrants who could be expelled or refused entry. Next came the proposed reform of French Nationality Law. Apparently rejecting the *droit du sol*, the Government proposed to make French citizenship 'voluntary' for the children born in France to immigrants not themselves French citizens. They would now have to apply for French citizenship between the ages of 16 and 23, and might be refused if they had been in prison. 'Marriages of convenience' were also to be scrutinised to see whether they were genuine marriages. Strong opposition to these changes prevented the law from passing, and the Socialists did not proceed with it on their return to office in 1988. They also liberalised the immigration laws. But they would not give immigrants the vote, even in local elections. With the return of a right-wing Government in 1993, again including Pasqua, the tough immigration laws were re-imposed, with the aim of producing, in Pasqua's words, 'zero immigration', and the reform of the Nationality Code was enacted with a reduction in the age group for children of immigrants born in France who could apply for citizenship from 16 to 21, instead of 23. So the ethnic tendency of French nationalism was back in the ascendant.

Official (state) nationalism in France thus straddles the civic and ethnic tendencies of nationalism. The first is most obviously seen on the 14th of July (the anniversary of the fall of the Bastille), when the Revolutionary tradition is celebrated with the singing of '*La Marseillaise*' and the flying of the tricolour flag. This is intended to unite the French nation and raise national consciousness. No questions are asked about 'who is French?'.

The French language plays a special part in official nationalism, and this moves French nationalism somewhat towards the second, ethnic tendency. It has been estimated that the French language was spoken by only around half of the citizens of France until the latter part of the nineteenth century, but since the Revolution it has been a marker, and even a condition, of French nationality. In this view, any other language should not be spoken officially by a French citizen. This applies even to international meetings today! The policy is officially sanctioned and enforced by the French state, which makes the French language the only official language of France. In 1994 a law was passed to exclude non-French words from the French language, but the Constitutional Court supported the Revolutionary universalist tradition in this instance, and struck it down as an invasion of human rights. However, the French state must attempt to exclude non-French words in its own documents. The French Academy, a pre-Revolutionary institution (1635), is the state guardian of the French language, and French education is heavily biased towards grammatical and lexicographical studies and examinations. The competition from foreign languages, especially English, is resented by French nationalists of all kinds, and the General Agreement on Trade and Tariffs (GATT) trade negotiations have foundered on the issue of free trade in American films and TV programmes. The French Government has maintained a quota of non-French cultural products disseminated in France, and heavily subsidises the French film and TV industry. All this must be seen as exclusive ethnic nationalism within official French nationalism, which is otherwise relatively inclusive.

Constitution (1958)

Unlike British official nationalism, official French nationalism recognises only one nation (France) in the French state. Britain is officially a multinational state, but France is not. That does not mean that there are actually no historic nations other than the French nation in France, at least in the opinion of non-French nationalists, who claim to speak for their own nations. The most prominent politically today of these nationalisms is Corsican nationalism, but Corsica's claim to be a 'people' was denied by the Constitutional Court on 9 May 1991. The Court maintained that the French Constitution recognised only one people or nation, France, and that the Bill (*le statut Joxe*, named after the Minister of the Interior, Pierre Joxe) which intended to extend Corsican autonomy was therefore wrong to start with an article asserting the existence of a 'Corsican people', even as a 'component of the French people' (*'peuple corse, composante du peuple français'*).

The French Constitution[8] does have implications for sub-state nationalism, which have not been resolved.

Article 2 (State Form and Symbols)
(1) France is an indivisible, secular, democratic and social republic...
(2) The language of the Republic is French.
(3) The national emblem is the blue, white and red tricolor flag.

Article 3 (Electoral Rights)
(1) National sovereignty belongs to the people, who exercise it through their representatives and by means of referendums.

Article 4 (Political Parties)
Political parties... must respect the principles of national sovereignty...

Article 34 (Legislative Powers)
(1) All legislation must be passed by Parliament.

Corsica's claim to nationhood, to have official status for its language, to have its own flag and to exercise a veto over French legislation all appeared to fly in the face of the Constitution. Only Corsica has a 'Statute of Autonomy' (passed in 1982) and *le statut Joxe* was passed on 13 May 1991 once it had been altered to take account of the Constitutional Court's ruling. This law recognises the cultural identity of Corsica, and encourages the teaching of the Corsican language (similar to Italian) and culture.

In January 2002, the Court again struck down one clause of the legislation extending Corsica's autonomy (that giving the Corsican Assembly the right to amend national legislation in devolved matters). The government headed by Prime Minister Lionel Jospin had initiated moves towards a new devolution settlement in 1999, following increased violence on the island and a cease-fire on 24 December 1999. Later, there was a highly embarrassing episode for Paris, when the Paris-appointed Prefect in Corsica, Bernard Bonnet, was put on trial for of conspiring to set fire to a beach café. He was found guilty in January 2002 and sentenced to a year in prison. This put Paris on the defensive with regard to violence in Corsica. However, the Constitutional Court was not deflected from striking down a key proposal in the new devolution legislation giving the Corsican Assembly the right to amend laws passed by Paris in the devolved area. This offended against the French doctrine of state sovereignty and the supreme power of the National Assembly. Needless to say, the Corsican nationalists reacted with anger to this slight on their aspirations to be a separate nation within France.

The French state has in recent years accepted many (but not all) Corsican linguistic and cultural aspirations, even if the Constitutional Court has not accepted the nationalist claim that Corsica is a nation with its own 'people', and that the French 'nation-state' can divide up its sovereignty. We have already seen this question in the case of Britain, but Britain has in effect accepted that it is a 'multinational' state, and that devolution, while respecting the 'sovereignty of Parliament' has in the case of Scotland at least given the devolved parliament the right to amend legislation passed by London in devolved matters, subject to judicial review (Scotland Act 1998). On the question of the Corsican language, Jospin's devolution proposals would have made the teaching of Corsican mandatory in all schools, along with French, but with the right of parents to opt out of such teaching for their children.

Although the Right won in the elections of 2002, the new Government of President Chirac and Prime Minister Raffarin continued with the Corsican legislation, and indeed by 28 March 2003 had passed through the National Assembly and Senate amendments[9] to the Constitution which moved France more in a devolutionary direction. It was declared that the

Republic's organisation is 'decentralised', and that 'local' authorities (including devolved), would henceforth be called 'territorial', and would have the right to hold a referendum on any 'organic' law passed by Paris which affected them. This gives Corsica a right of veto on the devolution legislation, and removes the basis of the Constitutional Court's annulment of one clause in the previous legislation. Whether Corsica will endorse the new devolution Bill remains to be seen, for the claims of Corsica to be 'a people' and to determine their language laws remain in doubt. This is bound to lead to further alienation of all the parties in Corsica, which in the 2002 elections swung to the Left.

Brittany parallels Corsica in some ways, but politically there is now a great difference. For while Corsica has become more nationalist in electoral terms, Brittany has become less so. In cultural terms both have non-French languages, which are spoken alongside French. Breton is a Celtic language and is quite different from French. The Breton culture is also Celtic, and is nurtured particularly at the University of Rennes and by various nationalist organisations. As in Corsica, there is a strong sense in Brittany of being on the periphery of France, and of being economically deprived. But the French state and the EU have supported a strong regional policy which, along with concessions to the Breton language and culture, have reduced the strength of Breton nationalism, at least as far as voting for nationalist parties is concerned. The fact that Corsica is an island, and joined France relatively recently (in 1768, when it was acquired from Genoa) means that it is physically detached from 'the Continent' and sees itself as a colony.[10] Brittany, on the other hand, has been part of France since 1532, and its culture, while distinctive, is less securely based. The Breton language is less commonly spoken in Brittany than Corsican is in Corsica, and non-Bretons probably make up a larger proportion of the population of Brittany than non-Corsicans of Corsica, although the latter are only half of the total population there.

Other non-French nations (as defined by nationalists) in France are the Basques and the Catalans (both divided between France and Spain), and the Occitans. In French/Parisian political parlance, these are variously nationalists, regionalists and autonomists. In this book, the only regionalists as such in France are in Alsace, and even these have non-French (German) ethnic characteristics. The state boundaries in this area have been contested in modern times, in particular by Germany which (as Prussia) annexed Alsace and part of Lorraine in 1871 after it defeated France in the Franco-Prussian War. France's claim to Alsace-Lorraine was uncharacteristically not based on a community of language, for the Alsatians and some in Lorraine spoke (and speak) German. Instead, the claim seemed to hark back to the Revolution's inclusive nationalism's claim that a nation is based on self-determination. As Ernest Renan (1823–92), the French philosopher, put it in his famous essay, *Qu'est-ce qu'une nation?* (What is a nation?) (1882), a nation is a 'daily plebiscite' rather than an objective entity based on language, ethnicity and so on. This meant, when applied to Alsace-Lorraine, that the people there should decide which nation they wished to belong to. While it appears that the people of Alsace-Lorraine have indeed wished to be in France and not in Germany, their fate has been decided by power politics, not plebiscites. Thus, Alsace-Lorraine went back to France in 1919 after Germany's defeat in the First World War; Hitler annexed it to the Reich in 1940; and France regained it in 1944. Today, the FN has strength in the area, and it appeals to those who see a threat to their French national identity from immigration and European integration. The French state now seems secure in its German-speaking borderlands, and there nationalism is supportive of the state and not of secession, even if there is a small amount of electoral regionalism. The regionalisation of France in the 1980s has helped to satisfy regional demands and, for many people, the effect of European integration has been to soften the boundary between France and Germany as cross-border cooperation has developed. Moreover, the EU affords a guarantee to France that Germany will not again attempt to annex French territory.

Electoral nationalism

Today, the strongest nationalism in France in political and electoral terms is 'official' nationalism, in both the Gaullist and ethnic varieties. As we have seen, the Gaullists have since 1993 formed the Government along with their coalition partners the UDF (*Union pour la Démocratie Française*/Union for French Democracy) and since 1995 have occupied the Presidency of the Republic. One reason for the return of the Gaullists is an increasing hostility to the EU and to immigration, especially from North Africa. The Referendum on the Maastricht Treaty (20 September 1992) gave it a bare endorsement (51 to 49 per cent) and the *Eurobarometer* surveys chart increasing disillusion in France with the EU. The most pronounced nationalism of this kind is seen in the rise of the FN and the 'Anti-Maastricht List' of Philippe de Villiers and Sir James Goldsmith (*L'Autre Europe*/The Other Europe), although the two are not socially similar. The latter got 12.4 per cent of the vote and 13 of France's 87 seats in the 1994 European Parliament elections.

National Front/*Front National*

The National Front has grown steadily since its establishment in 1972 as the data below show in Table 3.1.

The Front does best in the towns of the Mediterranean, some suburbs in Paris and Lyons, and in Alsace and Moselle in Lorraine. It reached as high as 29.2 per cent of the vote in the 1998 regional elections in Provence-Alpes-Côte d'Azur. In the first round of the 2002 Presidential elections the Front's highest votes could be charted on a map of France,[13] showing its strength in the Mediterranean areas, a couple of departments in the middle-east and a broad swathe of departments in the north-east as far as Alsace (see Table 3.2). Paris, however, was

Table 3.1 The growth of National Front (since 1972)

Year	% of vote	Seats
Presidential elections		
(1st round)		
1974	0.7	
1981	did not qualify	
1988	14.4	
1995	15.0	
2002	16.95 (Le Pen)	2.4 (Mégret)
2nd round	17.95	
National Assembly elections (577 Deputies)		
1986 (under PR)	9.8	35
1988 (1st round)	9.8[11]	1
1993 (1st round)	12.5	0
1997 (1st round)	14.9	1
2002 (1st round)	11.3	0
2002 (2nd round)		
(37 contests)	1.9	0
European Parliament (87 MEPs)		
1984	10.9	10
1989	11.7	10
1994	10.5	11
1999	9.2[12]	5
Regional elections		
1986	9.7	137
1992	13.9	239
1998	15.2	273
Municipal elections		
1983	17	
1988	5.4	
1994	9.8	
1998	7.4	(*c.*2000 councillors, and control of 8 councils)

Table 3.2   The Front's performance in the
Presidential elections (2002)

Areas and departments	% of vote
Regions	
Alsace	23.4
Provence-Alpes-Côte d'Azur	23.4
Languedoc-Rousillon	22.3
Departments	
Alpes-Maritimes	26.0
Vaucluse	25.8
Var	23.5
Municipalities	
Orange	33.0
La Trinité	31.4
Tarascon	30.9
Wittelsheim	28.9
Wittenheim	28.9
Fréjus	28.8
Carros	28.3
Marignane	27.7

conspicuously weak (9.4 per cent/3rd) for the FN, with neighbouring
Seine-et-Marne stronger at 18.9 per cent (2nd). The highest scores in the
voting were given in Table 3.2.

For the best scores in the 37 seats contested by the FN in the second
round of the National Assembly elections (16 June 2002), see Table 3.3.

This was a remarkably poor showing for the FN, with many absten-
tions or switches to the Union for the Presidential Majority (Chirac).
Even so, there were no seats to lose, and the echo of the Presidential
election remained to haunt French politics, even if the threat of
electoral nationalism seemed to have past.

The Front's appeal varies according to the area, with the
Mediterranean/suburban vote based on anti-Muslim feeling, insecurity
and unemployment. While about half the FN vote comes from disaf-
fected mainstream right-wing voters, especially the Gaullist RPR, one-
third comes from new voters and the remainder from former left-wing
parties.[14] In the eastern borderlands, the immigration factor is less
obvious and the FN's nationalism seems more traditional and defensive
of France's historic national identity. Yet its anti-Semitic and pro-Nazi
utterances would appear to point to a sympathy with Hitler's Germany,
when Alsace-Lorraine was part of the Reich.

Table 3.3 FN's performance in the
National Assembly elections

Regions	% of vote
Orange	42.4
Marseille (7th)	36.9
Dunkerque-Ouest	35.8
Marseille (4th)	35.2
Mauberge	35.2

The electoral support for the Front rose in the 1990s, reaching 10–15 per cent of the French vote and as high as 29.2 per cent in the regional elections in Provence-Alpes-Côte d'Azur of March 1998. But its electoral progress was checked for a time by a serious split in the party in December 1999 between the President, Jean-Marie Le Pen and Bruno Mégret, who had come from the Gaullists, and had risen to the rank of 'delegate-general', number two in the party. Rivalry between the two leaders led to the secession of Mégret to form the *Front national-Mouvement National Républicain* (later *MNR*). This came at a time when the FN was posing a serious threat to the right-wing parties in France. Le Pen and Mégret both stood at the 2002 Presidential elections, the latter as National Republican. Le Pen obtained 16.95 per cent (4.8 million votes) and Mégret 2.35 per cent (0.67 million votes) in the first round (21 April), making a total for the extreme nationalist right of almost 20 per cent. Le Pen's share was sufficient to propel him into the 2nd round, as he beat Prime Minister Jospin by a little under one per cent. This sensational result shook France, and caused demonstrations against the FN in several cities. But, although it was largely unanticipated, it was in part a by-product of the *cohabition* (working in tandem) of the Gaullist President Chirac (whose share of the vote was just marginally above Le Pen's at 19.7 per cent – 5.6 million) and the Socialist Jospin, an unpopular arrangement leaving voters with the feeling that there was no difference between these normally opposed parties. Le Pen's vote went up marginally (by under 2 per cent), but he was not the only non-mainstream candidate to do well. The Left was particularly split into different parties, and the high (for France) abstention rate (28 per cent) indicated that the Left was reluctant to vote for Jospin, who received 4.6 million votes, or 16.1 per cent. The two mainstream candidates (Chirac and Jospin) between them got only 36 per cent of the vote. The mainstream Right (including the UDF candidate, François Bayrou and the Liberal Democrat Alain Madelin) declined by 4.5 million votes, and the mainstream Left (Socialists and Communists) by 4.1 million votes. Thus the election was a rejection of De Gaulle's hope that France would achieve a two-party system on the lines of that once prevailing in Britain. But that system is also under strain in Britain, as the main parties converge in policy, something that also happened in France. Thus 'consensus' politics may exist at elite level, but not among the voters in general. Nevertheless, in the second round of the 2002 Presidential election (5 May) all the anti-Le Pen votes consolidated behind Chirac, who won 82 per cent of the vote. This was clearly an artificial result, since Chirac had obtained only 20 per cent of the vote at the first round. He was supported by nearly all the Trotskyites, Communists, Socialists, Liberals and Conservatives, most of whom actually detested Chirac's politics, but not as much as they detested Le Pen's.

The issues in the campaign helped to highlight Le Pen's policies. These were predominantly law and order ('security' in French terms) and immigration, both of which Le Pen was eminently able to exploit. There were clear signs of nationalism in Le Pen's appeal, which some described as fascism, although it should more accurately be described as nationalism. This is because the anti-democratic, authoritarian aspects of fascism were absent in Le Pen's programme, although his notion of democracy was direct democracy through the use of referendums, rather than parliamentary democracy ('a referendum republic'). What linked the FN to right-wing parties (but not always the extreme Right) throughout Europe was the anti-EU, anti-immigration and anti-globalisation feeling, linked to the pride in nation and the aspiration to preserve national sovereignty. This brought Le Pen quite close to the Gaullists and the Conservatives in Britain. Perhaps curiously, some other extreme Right, nationalist and anti-immigrant politicians in the rest of Europe did not welcome Le Pen's success in 2002 (e.g. Gianfranco Fini of the National Alliance in Italy, Christoph Blocher of the Swiss People's Party in Switzerland, Pim Fortuyn (Fortyun List) in the Netherlands and Alex Salmond of the Scottish National Party). However, others did, for example, Jörg Haider of the Austrian Freedom Party and Filip Dewinter of the Vlaams Blok (Belgium).[15] Le Pen's French nationalism brought him into opposition with sub-state nationalism in Corsica, his native Brittany and elsewhere in Europe. He had fought in the French Army in Indo-China and Algeria, which made him a strong imperialist in opposition to colonial nationalism.

What were the other bases of the Front's appeal? Le Pen advocated the ending of immigration and the restriction of the right of asylum. He wanted the reestablishment of frontier controls, economic protectionism and the 'reaffirmation' of a national preference in the Constitution. He sought the repatriation of France's three million immigrants of north African descent (the total number of immigrants is 4.3 million, but around 570 000 of these are from Portugal, which does not appear to worry Le Pen. In 2002 he appeared to qualify this by relying on the 'good will' of the immigrants, and some financial aid). Other nationalist features of his policies were preferential treatment for French citizens, as opposed to immigrants without citizenship in employment, social security and housing as well as in fiscal matters; the protection of French culture, more spending on national defence, referendums on the renunciation of the EU's Maastricht, Amsterdam and Schengen treaties; the return of the franc; the abolition of income tax. More sinister is Le Pen's anti-Semitism, and his statement that the Nazi gas chambers were 'a detail in history'. For this he was fined twice under anti-racism laws, in 1987 and 1997. Anti-Semitism is on the rise in Europe generally, and can be related to Israel's generally unpopular policies in Palestine. But anti-Muslim feeling, already strong because of rising immigration and problems of integrating immigrants into French culture also increased after the terrorism in New York and elsewhere in 2001. So both Jews and Muslims were the objects of attacks for reasons of external politics, but consistent with feelings of social and ethnic nationalism.

The electoral history of the FN and Le Pen shows a steady rise from obscure beginnings in 1972. Le Pen broke through in 1988 to obtain 14.4 per cent at the first round of the Presidential elections, and 15 per cent in 1995, with fourth place (his rise to second place in 2002 with 16.9 per cent is not so impressive in purely statistical terms) but his rank in second place was traumatic for the French establishment. The Front won 12.5 per cent of the vote in the first round of the National Assembly elections in 1993, but no seats at that round or in the second round. Under proportional representation in operation at previous elections, the Front won 10 of the 81 seats in the European Parliament elections in 1984, and 35 National Assembly seats in 1986. But under the second ballot system later introduced for the National Assembly, the Front lost all but one of its seats in 1988, and won no seats in 1993. In local elections in June 1995 Front mayoral candidates won in three municipalities in the south, including Toulon (population 437 000), and went to the second round in 105 of the largest towns. In Nice, a former Front member was elected mayor. However, the Front's vote in France as a whole was only 4.3 per cent, and while it won 1249 seats (a threefold increase), the ruling Coalition had 312 678 seats, and the Opposition

192 197 seats. These figures put the Front's electoral performance into perspective, although it is also true that in 14 towns with populations over 30 000, the Front took more than 30 per cent of the vote, rising to 43 per cent in Vitrolles, a suburb of Marseilles and 44 per cent in Noyon, a small north-eastern town. But the operation of the electoral system and the hostile actions of the other parties conspired to defeat most Front candidates at the second round. The major parties often withdrew their candidates at that round if it seemed that Front candidates would win. Thus the Front's Vitrolles mayoral candidate was defeated at the second round despite coming top in the first round.[16]

In the 1992 regional elections the Front secured 239 councillors, an increase of 100, and 273 in 1998. In the 1992 departmental elections, which run to two rounds, the rule that 10 per cent of the vote has to be obtained in the first round in order to proceed to the second round of elections eliminated 7 out of 10 Front candidates. In the March 1998 local elections, the FN won 7.4 per cent of the vote in metropolitan France, but won three councils and retained five. This again demonstrates that electoral systems and party strategies can severely affect the fortunes of small nationalist parties such as the FN. However, not many countries operate such a complex set of electoral laws as France, many of which are deliberately designed to help or hinder particular parties.

The 1999 split in the FN quickly affected its electoral fortunes adversely. In the June 1999 European Parliament elections Le Pen's party was reduced to 5.7 per cent and 5 seats (previously 11). The Mégret faction won 3.5 per cent and no seats.[17] In the 2002 Presidential elections, Le Pen's vote in the first round was 17 per cent. When the two factions of the original NF are added together, they come to 19.4 per cent. But Mégret had clearly shown his ability to gather in the vast majority of Front voters to his candidature. Mégret advised his supporters to vote for Le Pen in the second round.

Although the FN vote is based largely on hostility to immigrants, paradoxically some of it comes from a type of immigrant, the '*pieds-noirs*'. These are the French settlers in Algeria who were forced to return to France when Algeria became independent in 1962. Most settled in southern France and Corsica, and bore a grudge against De Gaulle for 'selling them out'. They have sought a right-wing party which was anti-Gaullist, and the Front fits the bill, especially as it shares an antipathy to Muslims, whether in France or Algeria. The main part of the Front vote is a protest vote on special issues such as immigration, law and order, and more generally on a perceived loss of national identity. As we have seen, its vote is strongest in the Mediterranean area and Alsace and in some suburbs of Paris and Lyons, and has been steadily rising in the last 10 years. The explanation for this seems to be a combination of social despair (formerly expressed through Communist voting), anti-immigrant attitudes (which have increased as immigration has increased) and opposition to European integration. However, the last reason is sometimes ambiguous for some areas of FN strength. Alsace was the French region most in favour of the Maastricht Treaty in the Referendum of September 1992, with 65.5 per cent voting Yes, but it also returned the third highest FN vote in any region (17.2 per cent) in the Regional Elections in March of the same year.[18]

Corsica and Brittany

Subnational nationalism which seeks to differentiate itself from France and French nationalism is found in Corsica, Brittany, the Basque Country and Occitania. Only the first is strong today in electoral terms, but the others remain active in the cultural sphere, and there is the threat of terrorism from the Basques, especially in conjunction with the Basques in Spain, whose irredentism is a worry to the French state. There are strong security measures in the Basque areas of France to prevent terrorism from spreading across the border. There are Catalans in France as well as in Spain, but although there is a French Catalan nationalist party, *Unitat Catalunya*, which is a member of the European Free Alliance of regionalist parties aiming at representation in the European Parliament,[19] it is very weak, and there is little sign of Catalan irredentism in Spain.

Corsican nationalism is divided today into two main strands, militant and moderate, rather like Irish nationalism in Northern Ireland and, as we shall see, similar to other nationalisms such as the Basque in Spain and the Flemish in Belgium. In Corsica, to complicate matters further, the militants are themselves divided in two. The paramilitary *Front de Libération Nationale de la Corse* (FNLC) is now split into the '*canal habituel*' (moderate) *and* the '*historique*' (radical). The corresponding political wings are the MPA (*Mouvement pour l'autodétermination*) (MPA) and the Cuncolta (*A Cuncolta Naziunalista*) (AC), which was part of a wider grouping called *Corsica nazione* (CN) formed in 1991 to contest the 1992 regional elections. This 'list' also included *Accolta Naziunale Corsa* (ANC), formed in 1989 as a breakaway from the Cuncolta. The ANC opposes making armed struggle a priority. In the 1992 list was the moderate 'autonomist' *Unione di u Populu Corsu* (UPC) led by Max Simeoni, and the Greens (*I Verdi corsi*). In all, nine seats were won by the list, but by 1993 all these parties were at each other's throats. The two

ANC members broke away, as did the three UPC members, leaving the CN group with only four members made up of three AC and one Green. The AC was now more extreme in its nationalism, and looked to a rupture with France with renewed paramilitary activity.

Corsica was drifting further into civil unrest and lawlessness. In August 1993 the *FLNC-Canal Historique* claimed responsibility for the assassination of a rival nationalist, and in February 1994 it formally called off its two-year truce. In May 1994, Edmond Simeoni (brother of Max), President of the *Corsica Nazione* coalition, and a Corsican Assembly member, resigned his positions and left politics altogether, on the grounds that the Cuncolta was giving 'hegemony' to the military wing over the political wing of the party. This he felt was leading to a drift into uncontrolled terrorism. He believed that the nationalist movement in general was in crisis since the *loi Joxe* had come into force, splitting it more sharply into constitutionalists and terrorists.[20] This was confirmed when on 18 July 1994, a founder of the nationalist movement and Corsican Assembly member, Pierre Poggioli (ANC), was the victim of an assassination attempt, and in February 1995, 66 properties were destroyed by bombs in the extreme south of the island. This campaign continued throughout 1995, leading to a considerable falling-off (down a third) of the tourist trade in the summer.

The main split in Corsican nationalism, apart from whether to use armed struggle or to adopt electoral means, is about its ultimate aims. The moderate 'autonomists' of the UPC led by Max Simeoni want to work within the devolution system, while the extremists wish to break with metropolitan France altogether. This would mean either giving Corsica total independence, or the status of an Overseas Territory such as New Caledonia, which is proposed by *A Cuncolta Naziunalista*.[21] An Overseas Territory is still technically part of the French Republic, but not of metropolitan France, and it would still have seats in the National Assembly.

The main impact of Corsican nationalism comes from its violence, but it has also made headway in electoral terms. The CN list obtained 13.7 per cent of the vote in the first round of the 1992 Corsican Assembly elections. MPA received 7.5 per cent. At the second round, the combined nationalist vote was 25 per cent. However, the result of the election in terms of seats gave only nine seats out of 51 to the *Corsica nazione* list, and four to MPA. As we have seen, the former soon broke up, leaving four in the group. The strongest electoral force in Corsica is the right-wing coalition of RPR and UDF, which got most votes and seats (27/51) in the Corsican Assembly in 1992, and controlled the two local

Table 3.4 The nationalist and autonomist vote in the elections (1993) to the National Assembly (in %)

Regions	MPA %	CN %	ANC %	Total nat./aut. %
Ajaccio	11.4	10.9	3.9	26.2
Sartène	7.0	10.4	3.8	21.2
Bastia	2.8	14.4	17.2	
Corte, Calvi	3.8	16.2	20.0	

government departments of *Haute-Corse* and *Corse-du-Sud*.[22] As for elections to the National Assembly, in 1993 the nationalist and autonomist vote at the first round was as shown in Table 3.4.[23]

This shows a fairly even spread of nationalist/autonomist support in the different parts of Corsica.

In the 1997 National Assembly elections, no nationalists or devolutionists stood, indicating a hardening of their position with regard to participation in French elections. 'Territorial' elections (i.e. for the Corsican Assembly), however, attracted their participation, and in March 1999 they achieved 23.4 per cent in the first round (see below).

Curiously, the main electoral success for the nationalists outside the Corsican Assembly and local government was the election of the UPC/CN leader, Max Simeoni, to the European Parliament in 1989, in a list of candidates grandly titled *Liste Régionaliste et Fédéraliste-Régions et Peoples Solidaires* (Regionalist and Federalist List – Regions and Peoples in Solidarity), which was itself part of the Greens' List. (It should be explained that elections to the European Parliament in France, as in some other countries is on the party list system, which requires small parties to combine with other to have any chance of election. The list is allocated seats according to the share of votes in France as a whole, and Simeoni was placed second in the Greens' list, which won nine seats. Paradoxically, the list came only third in Corsica itself, with the UDF-RPR Right Wing-Gaullist list top. The 1989 list arrangement broke down in 1994, and Simeoni lost his seat).

The next elections to the Corsican Assembly, on 17 and 24 March 1998 showed the electoral weakness of the nationalists. The context was the assassination of the Prefect Claude Erignac on 6 February, which reflected badly on the nationalists. Six lists of nationalists were put forward but only the Cuncolta list passed the 5 per cent threshold, with 5.2 per cent. The autonomists led by Edward Simeoni failed to qualify by 40 votes, with 4.96 per cent of the vote. Of the 51 seats, the nationalists won only five under the banner of A Cuncolta, the legal wing of the FLNC-canal historique, including the leader, Jean-Guy Talamoni. They obtained 9.9 per cent of the vote in the second round. In the first round the nationalists' six lists received 17.3 per cent of the vote (cf. 21.1 per cent in the first round in 1992). The majority of the voters for the eliminated lists preferred to cast their votes for non-nationalists in the second round, and the nationalist vote dropped by 15 per cent compared to 1992 when it won 24.8 per cent.[24] So a combination of adverse electoral rules and splits among the nationalists reduced the nationalist vote dramatically in 1998. The same was even more true of the local (departmental and cantonal) elections held at the same time, which the nationalists did not even contest (they object to dividing the island into departments). By comparison, the right-wing list obtained 37 per cent of the vote, and the Socialist/Communist list 33.2 per cent. The right-wing President of France, Jacques Chirac seems to have attracted support from the Cuncolta leader François Santoni. This may account for his assassination in August 2001.[25]

On 7 and 14 March 1999, further elections were held to the Corsican Assembly. Five Nationalist lists (including devolutionist] were put up, and in the 1st round achieved a record 23.4 per cent of the vote. The most successful list was that of CN, formed in 1998 out of Cuncolta and led by Jean-Guy Talamoni. This achieved 10.4 per cent of the vote and was the only list to exceed the 5 per cent threshold to proceed to the 2nd round. At that round, the list achieved 16.8 per cent (the second largest list in Corsica), with eight elected out of 51 Assembly members. The nationalists had only one list at this round, compared to the Left (two lists) and the Right (three lists). This shows that many of the 1st round 'nationalist' voters refused to vote for the CN list. Talamoni represents the more moderate nationalists who have been involved in negotiations with Paris over stronger devolution. Unfortunately, Talamoni's view that the elected representatives alone should speak for Corsica is rejected by the nationalists engaged in violence. The French Government too was split, with the Interior Minister Jean-Pierre Chevènement (Citizens' Movement), resigning in 2000 over the Government's devolution proposals, and standing against Jospin in the Presidential elections in April 2002 (he won 5.3 per cent of the vote).

Another party was formed out of *A Cuncolta Indipendenza*, the political arm of the illegal Front for the National Liberation of Corsica – Historic Wing (*FLNC-CH*) and two other organisations in May 2001, Independence (*Indipendenza*). This, however said it would support Corsican Nation in the next Corsican elections, in opposing the Government's autonomy plans.

The list is completed by National Presence (*Presenza Nazionale*), also opposed to the autonomy plans.

Election results are only part of the story of Corsican nationalism. There is a tradition of direct action in Corsican politics which may derive from old-style banditry and clan warfare, but is now a confusing mixture of anti-French militancy and rivalries amongst the nationalist themselves. Bombings are frequent, especially of wine-growing establishments, shops and garages run by non-Corsicans, and in summer 1995 there was an outbreak of killings of nationalists by other nationalists, and by state authorities. Then in the late 1990s and early 2000s assassinations of French government officials and nationalists hit the headlines. It is never quite clear which of these acts are motivated by nationalism and which by business or political rivalry, although the two are related. There is a feeling among native-born Corsicans (around 80 per cent of whom speak Corsican) that too many enterprises are run by French-speaking *pieds-noirs* from Algeria or immigrants from continental France. Then there is a continual disputation with Paris over the cost of transport, prices, taxes and state expenditures in the island. This is fairly typical of islands everywhere, but not all islands assert nationhood and nationalism. Corsica is such an island, and is recognised in law as 'special'. Yet the strength of its nationalism is difficult to assess. In electoral terms its successes are confined to the island Assembly and local government – there are no Nationalist Deputies in the French National Assembly to worry the Government, unlike the nationalists in the British and Spanish Parliaments, and in Corsica itself the nationalists are in violent opposition to one another. While there are certainly a strong nationalist demand for further autonomy, even independence, there is little evidence that a majority of the population of Corsica wishes to break away from France. Most seem to be satisfied with devolution, and extracting the maximum economic aid from Paris. In an opinion poll in December 1996, at the height of nationalist violence, 47 per cent declared that they had no sympathy with the 'autonomists', against 25 per cent who had 'a little' sympathy, 10 per cent 'a fair amount' ('*assez*') and 7 per cent 'a lot'. At the same time, although 50 per cent approved of the firmness shown towards the 'indépendantistes', 77 per cent of these felt that the government had not adopted a good solution for dealing with the problems of Corsica.[26] So even among the loyalists there is discontent with Paris. Corsica is a society divided by language and history, with the Corsican-born hostile to incomers. The political culture is a violent one, with frequent bombings and other illegal actions. Even moderate nationalist leaders such as Dr Edmond Simeoni (brother of

Max) have been imprisoned, as have those guilty of *attentats* (bombings and assassination attempts). Their status as 'martyrs' is cultivated by the nationalist organisations, but the net result is to keep political power in the hands of the 'clans' who are today part of the right-wing coalition which runs the island along with the state authorities. So there is as much to bind Corsica to France as there is to divide it, even if France is finding it increasingly difficult to maintain law and order there.

Brittany is now less nationalist in political terms than Corsica, although in the 1960s and 1970s it was the other way around. At that time the *Union Démocratique Bretonne/Unvaniezh Demokratel Breizh* (UDB/ Breton Democratic Union) (1964) had electoral successes at local government level. In 1977, 33 candidates were elected, but by the 1994 local elections none succeeded, despite the fact that in Morbihan the UDB put up joint candidates with the Greens in 11 cantons. The UDB is a member of the Democratic Party of the Peoples of Europe – European Free Alliance. There is also the Party for the Organisation of a Free Brittany (POBL), which seeks self-rule and independence for Brittany. This remains electorally dormant. In the 1992 regional elections there were no nationalists elected and the total 'regionalist' vote was only 2.6 per cent. However, the Ecological Generation and Green lists (12 seats in a Council of 83) contain members favourable to further devolution. In the 1998 local elections, no Breton nationalists stood. The Socialists control two of the four departments in Brittany, with the Right predominant in the other two. The largest party grouping in the Breton Regional Council is the Right, with 41 seats in 1994 and 38 in 1998, with the Socialists next (19 seats in 1994). Needless to say, there are no nationalist Deputies in the National Assembly from Brittany.

Breton nationalism was historically a right-wing movement, but today its sympathies are more with the Left and the Greens. This may be related to the regional reforms introduced by the Socialists in 1982, although these by no means satisfied the nationalists. For one thing, the region of Brittany does not correspond to the historic Brittany but is the arbitrary creation of the French state, with some parts of Brittany missing. Then there is the general complaint about the lack of real autonomy and the continued dominance of the French language and culture. Brittany is even more penetrated by incomers than Corsica, and its language and culture is comparatively weaker. There has been a Breton cultural revival at all levels of education and society, but the impression is of a largely folk-orientated cultural nationalism with no strong political dimension. As in Corsica there is a paramilitary organisation, the

Front de Libération de la Bretagne (FLB), which from the late 1960s engaged in bombings and so on, but this is now largely inactive.

Other nationalisms

There is little to say about the politics of Norman, Occitan, Basque, Savoyard and Catalan nationalism in France.[27] These nationalisms manifest themselves mainly in cultural organisations and regional pressure groups rather than in parties or elected representatives at the local, regional or national level, although they also get involved in economic issues and strikes. Occitan nationalism is manifested in nationalist newspapers, in the promotion of the Occitan language (which is tested in the Baccalaureate) by the *Institut d'études occitanes*, and in support for local demonstrations and strikes.[28] As in Brittany, there are no nationalists elected to local office or to the Regional Council (which is in any case not based on Occitania as a whole), or to the National Assembly, although there are a few candidates at local and regional elections.

As for the Basques in France, there has been some nationalist activity. Some of this is ETA-related terrorist activity which has spilled over from the Basque Lands in Spain. Indeed, ETA uses the French Basque country as its base for activities in Spain, and this has led the French authorities to exile Basque nationalists to other parts of France. The Basque population in France (*c.*100 000) is found in the Pyrénées-Atlantiques department, of which it takes up about a third of the territory. This compares with around 2.5 million Basques in Spain. In the 1994 local elections there were only three nationalist candidates in the French Basque country, but one was nearly elected. In the 1998 elections, two nationalists stood and then withdrew. The French Basques seem more content with the French state than the Basques in Spain are with Madrid. Even so, in the last 10 years a Basque nationalist movement has developed in France and there are nationalist hopes that in a federal EU based on a 'Europe of the nations and regions' the Basques of France and Spain would be combined in one pan-Basque state/region.[29] There are faint echoes of this in Catalonia too, where in such a European Federation French Catalans might be combined with those in Spain.[30] However, there is not much sign that either the French or the Spanish Catalans are prepared to do anything to achieve that. There is a pervasive dual national identity in both parts of Catalonia, with the French and Catalan identities coexisting harmoniously in Northern Catalonia.

An anthropological study by Oonagh O'Brien of a small town there in the 1980s found that French state employees (*fonctionnaires*) were labelled Catalan nationalists (*Catalanistes*), 'which is on the whole a pejorative title suggestive of a lack of the balance in ethnic identity which is so valued in the community'.[31] The *fonctionnaires* were apparently stressing their Catalan identity to compensate for their job-related loyalty to the French state, whereas local Catalans saw no tension between their French and Catalan identities. Nevertheless, according to O'Brien, 'French Catalans feel a need to express their French identity but feel out of place at the core where a sizeable number of them go to work. They are often called Spanish and their accent and manner of speaking are a cause for jokes.'[32] So they have 'Marginal French Identity' whereas Catalans in Spain are more secure and do not have a 'Marginal Spanish Identity'. Nevertheless, there are some Spanish Catalan immigrants in Northern Catalonia. The contrast between Spanish and French Catalans is reflected in the different politics of the two groups. Spanish Catalans show strong Catalan nationalism and nationalists control the Government of Catalonia, while French Catalan nationalism seems to be confined to language, culture and pressure politics.

Finally, in German-speaking Alsace there were eight regionalist or autonomist candidates in the 1994 local elections, but none did at all well. They did not stand in 1998; two regional parties still exist (Alsace-Lorraine National Forum and Union of the Alsatian People). The FN did better, with a councillor elected in 1998 in Haut-Rhin. In the 1993 National Assembly elections the FN came second in three seats. In the 2002 Presidential elections (first round), Le Pen came top in Bas-Rhin with 23.4 per cent, and in Haut-Rhin with 23.5 per cent.

Conclusion

France is a multinational state, but its Constitution recognises only one 'people', the French. This is despite the fact that there are other historic nations in the French Republic: the Corsicans, Bretons, Catalans, Occitans and Basques, as well as 4.3 million immigrants, mainly from Portugal and North Africa, as well as old-established ethnic Germans in Alsace and Lorraine. The main nationalism in France today is French nationalism, which is expressed in politics mainly by Gaullism and the FN, but spilling over into all the parties. While the 'Revolutionary' tradition of nationalism was inclusive of all ethnic groups, and was indeed international in its aims, today ethnic nationalism is as important in France. It has been on the increase since the 1980s, because of the combination of economic problems, increased immigration and the threat to French sovereignty from the EU. This ethnic nationalism seeks to exclude from French citizenship or even residence in France those considered to be not French in colour, culture and religion. While there are some historic antecedents for ethnic nationalism in France, notably the anti-Semitism at the time of the Dreyfus Case (1898) and during the 1930s, the rise of the FN of Jean-Marie Le Pen in the 1980s, continuing into the 1990s has forced the mainstream parties to change their policies towards exclusive, ethnic nationalism. This has meant that the limited electoral successes of the FN tell only part of the story of this kind of French nationalism, since it is to be found in the other parties as well, and more generally in the rising nationalism or racism in French public opinion. There is little sign that this is diminishing, and the Presidential and local elections show that the Front itself is making some advances.

Ethnic nationalism based on French nationality is not the only ethnic nationalism in the French Republic, for there are nationalisms which oppose the French state. However, these sub-state nationalisms with one exception are not as much of a challenge to the French state as the equivalents are to some other western European states, notably Britain, Spain and Belgium. Only Corsica today is a serious problem to the state, and that relates to law and order more than to nationalist voting and support for independence. Even their French national identity and culture are quite strong, despite 'Italianisation', and the nationalist parties are weaker than the French parties. Corsica is heavily dependent on the French state economically, and Paris has been quite accommodating since the 1980s to Corsican demands for home rule and economic subsidies. Nevertheless, Corsica is as nationalist in general as Scotland, if the votes for nationalist parties in the Corsican Assembly elections are a guide. But there the similarity ends, for Corsican nationalism is not yet clearly secessionist, and its violent expression and intra-nationalist feuding is not found in Scotland. As Northern Ireland and the Basque Country, Corsica demonstrates the violence more than votes challenges the authority of the state, and forces it into making concessions.

The other historic nations in France such as the Bretons, the Basques and the Catalans offer in contrast a very weak challenge to the state, and indeed they seem reconciled to it. Most people in these nations profess a French identity as well as a Breton and other identity, and voting for French parties is now almost universal. The difference between these nations and Corsica is in part to be explained by the fact that Corsica is an island with special linguistic, educational and economic problems and increasing links with Italy, and has lately been 'settled' by incomers from 'continental' France and Algeria whose presence is not welcomed. But there is a dominant native Corsican political elite, made up of traditional 'clans' and modern nationalists, who run Corsica through the French state and the Corsican regional government, which is itself technically a part of the French state. Nearly all Corsican politicians are nationalists of a kind, even if they run under the banner of the French parties. The explicitly nationalist politicians are split into warring factions and have been unable to successfully challenge those loyal to the French state. As of now, the balance seems to be in favour of the French state continuing to command majority support in Corsica for the devolution settlement, but the relationship between Paris and Corsica is strained, and the representatives of Paris in the 'Isle of Beauty' are faced with continual strikes, bombings and assassinations, which have escalated in recent years. What is difficult for French governments and for observers of Corsican nationalism to understand is what motivates this nationalism and what would satisfy it. It seems that the conflict is as much within Corsica as between Corsica and France, but the solution may be further recognition of Corsica's nationhood. That is because the elements of 'difference' based on ethnicity, and thus nationalism, grow ever stronger with the passage of time.

4
Spain/*España* and Portugal

Historical context

The Iberian Peninsula contains two of the oldest states in Europe. Spain dates from 1492, when unification was completed under Ferdinand of Aragon and Isabella of Castile. Their marriage in 1469 had already united their respective kingdoms, and in 1492 Granada was captured from the Moors, which completed the unity of Spain. However, in 1704 Gibraltar was lost to England, and became a British colony after the Union of 1707 with Scotland. Despite attempts to retake it, it is still British, which is a source of dispute between Spain and Britain to this day. So here is an irredentist claim involving two members of the European Union (EU), a Union supposedly based on respect for each member's territory. In fact, Britain's control over Gibraltar meant little in 2002 in comparison with the unblocking of the Spanish veto over British proposals in the EU, which was being used to blackmail Britain over Gibraltar.[1]

There is what might be called anti-colonial nationalism directed against Spain in the territories overseas of the Canary Islands (conquered between 1483 and 1496), and a dispute with Morocco over the Spanish possessions in North Africa, the enclaves of Ceuta (captured by the Portuguese in 1415 and transferred to Spain in 1580) and Mellila (captured 1496). Both of these are administered as autonomous communities of Spain (under direct Spanish administration are the volcanic islands of Islas Chafarinas and Peñon de Alhucemas and Peñon de Vélez de la Gomera, a garrison location). These are 'Places of Sovereignty in North Africa'. In 1990 a political movement was formed in Ceuta (Initiative for Ceuta/*Iniciativa por Ceuta*) to represent the Muslims in opposition to the Spanish-based parties. In Mellila, the mayor in 1993 declared that the city was an autonomous community within Spain. These two developments led Spain in 1995 to make Ceuta and Mellila 'autonomous communities' in line with the 17 such communities in mainland Spain. Morocco attacked this, and considered that Spain should return these territories to Morocco, in line with the forthcoming reversion of Hong Kong and Macao (Portuguese) to China.

Portugal is older than Spain, and dates from the twelfth century. It remained independent from the Moors, but succumbed to annexation by Spain in 1580. This was reversed in 1668 after a long war of independence. Both Spain and Portugal owe their existence to a mixture of dynastic expansionism and language differences. It could be argued that they are 'nation-states', but Spain at least is a multilingual state whose exclusive nationhood is challenged by several nations within it, notably the Basques, the Catalans and the Galicians. To complicate matters further, the Basques and Catalans each straddle two states, Spain and France, and their nationalism, as we have seen, affects France as well as Spain. Galician nationalism is confined to Spain, although the Galician language (*Galego*) has a basis in both Castilian Spanish and Portuguese. Galician linguistic nationalists today wish to cultivate the Portuguese features and minimise the Castilian ones.[2] Portugal however has shown no irredentism with regard to Galicia. Portugal's overseas territories of the Azores (taken in 1439) and Madeira (also colonised in the fifteenth century), display some anti-colonial nationalism, but this has been largely satisfied by the granting of autonomy in 1980. In 1975 the Azorean Liberation Front (FLA) was formed which sought to break from Portugal, as did the Madeira Archipelago Liberation Front (FLAM), which established a provisional government. Portugal, now freed from military dictatorship, responded quickly by granting both the Azores and Madeira regional self-government. The Portuguese Constitution of 1976 and electoral laws practically prohibit nationalist/regional parties (see Article 51(4), below, p. 87). This makes it impossible to test the strength of nationalism and regionalism in Portuguese elections.

These Spanish and Portuguese overseas regions are officially considered part of the state, and not colonies. As in France, such areas are represented in the metropolitan Parliament. However, they have at times displayed anti-colonial nationalism or separatism. In Spain, the Canary Islands have a separatist movement, the *Congreso Nacional de Canarias*/Canaries National Congress, founded in 1986 to campaign for the independence of the Canaries. The Congress also opposes membership of the EU, and would prefer the Canaries to join the Organisation of African Unity (OAU). The OAU supports this aspiration, and would rename the Canaries 'the Guanch Republic' after the indigenous islanders, who are a branch of the African Berbers. This kind of nationalism is not, however, an important political force, since the economic benefits of the links with Spain and the EU, coupled with the extensive European settlement, have weakened the African dimension of Canarian identity. The centrist non-separatist 'Canarian Coalition' (*Coalicion Canaria*) heads the islands' government and its candidate was elected to the European Parliament in 1989 and 1994. In the 1999 European Parliament elections the Canarian Coalition MEP was re-elected and joined the Group of the European Liberal, Democrat and Reform Party.

In Portugal, the Azores has the FLA, founded 1975, and the Madeira Islands the FLAM, also founded 1975. These demand independence from Portugal, with the possible formation of a federation to include the Canary, Azores and Madeira islands. For a time these liberation movements represented a threat to the Portuguese and Spanish states, but the speedy introduction of autonomy in 1976 has greatly reduced the separatist momentum. So island separatism has been contained in Spain and Portugal, unlike in France (Corsica).

The Spanish mainland is different. There, nationalism – official, social and ethnic – dominates politics, and there is a violent movement for secession (*ETA/Euzkadi ta Azkatasuna*: Basque Homeland and Liberty) in the Basque country. Since the death of General Franco in 1975 official Spanish nationalism has lost its hegemonic power. There is no Spanish nationalism equivalent in strength to French nationalism in its Gaullist and National Front (NF) varieties. That is because the Spanish state has been weaker than the French state for at least two centuries, yet at the same time Spain has not suffered in the twentieth century the trauma of defeat in war, or immigration on a large scale, yet it did have a civil war in the 1930s, in which nationalism was as important a division as fascism and republicanism.

Although an attempt had been made in the nineteenth century to imitate the Napoleonic nation-building strategy in Spain, this was half-hearted, and left the historic national and regional divisions much stronger than their counterparts in France. A unifying political nationalism was largely lacking in the construction of the Spanish state, and Spain was out of line with other western European states in the development of national consciousness.[3] This left the sub-state nationalisms in a potentially strong position when they were faced with a latter-day attempt to make a centralised state based on official nationalism, not along the lines of the French democratic and bureaucratic nation-state, but in the form of first the dictatorship of General Primo de Rivera (1923–30), then the fascism of General Francisco Franco (1937–75). In order to establish his fascist regime, Franco had to wage a civil war against both republicans and Basque and Catalan nationalists. So his destruction of democracy was accompanied by the repression of non-Spanish nationalism and even cultural diversity in the form of non-Castilian languages.

Thus nation-building in Spain might have led to a nation-state had not successive periods of state repression, ultimately unsuccessful, been experienced by the historic nations. Especially the Catalans and Basques. Such repression was directed at their languages and their autonomy in laws and government which had come down from the past. This, coupled with economic problems relating to the decline of the Spanish Empire, which had an impact especially on the Basques and Catalonia, inspired a stronger social and ethnic nationalism in opposition to the official nationalism of Madrid, which no longer offered the benefits of Empire, and seemed parasitic on the more modern and prosperous Basque and Catalan nations.

In the post-1975 period too, economic changes stimulated Basque and Catalan nationalism. The EU has replaced the Spanish Empire as the focus of non-Spanish nationalisms, and the still relatively prosperous economics of Catalonia and the Basque Country, which attract immigration from other parts of Spain, gave a new confidence to their nationalisms.

Constitutions

Spain

The Spanish state since the death of Franco moved quickly to decentralisation, with the establishment of 'autonomous communities' from 1979 to 1983, now 17 on the mainland and two in North Africa. These also have special representation in the Senate, with 48 members chosen by the autonomous legislatures, weighted by population. The islands and North African territories are also guaranteed Senate seats. So the Spanish Constitution recognises the distinctiveness of the historic nations, and has given them (and the other non-national regions) a degree of home rule.

The main features of the Spanish Constitution[4] which impinge on nationalism are

Article 2 (National Unity, Regional Autonomy)
The Constitution is based on the indissoluble unity of the Spanish nation, the common and indivisible homeland of all Spaniards and

recognises and guarantees the right to autonomy of the nationalities and regions which make it up and the solidarity among all of them.

Article 3 (Official Language)
(1) Castilian is the official Spanish language of the state. All Spaniards have the duty to know it and the right to use it.
(2) The other languages of Spain will also be official in the respective autonomous communities, in accordance with their Statutes.
(3) The richness of the linguistic modalities of Spain is a cultural patrimony which will be the object of special respect and protection.

Article 4 (Flag)
(2) Recognition of flags and ensigns of the autonomous communities is admissible by law. These will be used beside the flag of Spain on their public buildings and in their official acts.[5]

Article 145 (Restricted Cooperation)
(1) In no case shall the federation of Autonomous Communities be permitted.

Article 149 (State Competences) [i.e. reserved powers to Spain]
(32) Authorisation for the convocation of popular consultations via referendum.

The relevant parts of the Constitution for nationalism are the restrictions on nationalist parties and Autonomous Communities, some of which are run by nationalist parties. The 'indissoluble' nature of the Spanish state is asserted, and federalism is ruled out. If any autonomous government tries to use a referendum to test opinion on independence or federalism this would be ruled unconstitutional. The Basque government is particularly concerned about that restriction.

In July 1999, the Constitutional Court forced the Spanish government of José Maria Aznar to free 22 members of the National Committee of *Herri Batasuna* (HB) (United People), who had been imprisoned for at least seven years in 1997 for supporting terrorism by featuring members of ETA in a party political broadcast in 1996. In May 2002, the Supreme Court ruled that HB's leader, Arnaldo Ortegi, had not broken the law by shouting 'Long live the Basque Homeland and Liberty', although this was clearly a reference to the banned ETA. Nevertheless, legislation was passed in June 2002 making it possible to ban HB, despite the protests of three Bishops in the Basque County (Bilbao, Vitoria/Gastheiz and San Sebastian/Donostia). This law bans the promotion of 'hatred, violence and civil confrontation' or a challenge to existing Spanish institutions, both of which HB could be said to be guilty of. On 26 August 2002, the Spanish Parliament passed a motion asking the government to outlaw the party, and stop its state aid. A magistrate went ahead to suspend the party's activities by freezing its bank accounts and forbidding it to demonstrate. More bombings immediately ensued. The moderate nationalists of the governing Basque Nationalist Party (PNV) in the Basque Country did not support the ban (neither did the moderate Catalan Nationalists of the Convergence and Union (*CiU*), but they were obliged to uphold the law. The Spanish government did not take responsibility for the ban, which was initiated in and sanctioned by a court. Either way, banning HB is an extreme measure likely to lead to further violence. The British Government never banned Sinn Féin, despite its links with the IRA.

Despite this hard-line attitude towards nationalists on the part of Spanish Governments, the Constitution allows for autonomy through devolution, with special powers for the 'nationalities' in Spain. What this means is that the Basque Country, Catalonia and Galicia have more devolution than other regions, and use their own languages as official languages, along with Spanish. The Constitution also permits national/regional flags, with the proviso that the Spanish flag be flown alongside these. All these areas are subject to dispute and tension between Madrid and the 'nationalities', and it cannot be said that the Constitution has produced a stable system of government. All the time, the nationalists are pushing for more devolution, federalism and even independence.

But the nationalists are also integrated into the Spanish Parliament, and have used their votes to prop up minority Spanish Governments. This has preserved the state in a democratic, quasi-federal and multinational form.

Portugal (1976)

Article 5 (Territory)
(1) Portugal comprises the territory defined by history on the European continent and the archipelagos of the Azores and Madeira.
(3) The State may not, except for frontier rectifications, alienate any part of the Portuguese territory or of the sovereign rights it exercises over it.

Article 6 (Unitary State)
(1) The State is a unitary one organised to respect the principles of the autonomy of local authorities and democratic decentralisation of the administration.

(2) The archipelagos of the Azores and Madeira constitute autonomous regions with their own political administrative statutes and self-governing organs.

Article 11 (National symbols)
(1) The National Flag is the symbol of the sovereignty of the Republic, the independence, unity and the undivided nature of Portugal...

Article 51 (Political Associations and Parties)
(4) No party may be established whose name or displayed aims indicate a regional nature or field of action.

(Note especially this ban on regional and nationalist parties, which affects in particular the Azores and Madeira. However, Madeira displays its own flag, despite Article 11.)

Electoral nationalism

Spain

There were Catalan and Basque nationalist parties before the First World War,[6] and these had some successes in local elections. What concerns us here is their position since the death of Franco in 1975. The democratisation of Spain was a regime change with profound consequences for nationalism, for not only did it release the repressed nationalisms of Catalonia and the Basque country, but it inspired Galician nationalism and Andalusian Canarian, Balearic and Navarran regionalisms (perhaps nationalisms) as well. This can be seen in the most recent Spanish elections (March 2000) for the Congress of Deputies (lower house of the Spanish Parliament: 350 Deputies) as in Table 4.1 and the Regional elections (see Table 4.2).

Thus nationalists and regionalists won 33 seats and 11.2 per cent of the Spanish vote (of course their share of the vote in their own nations/regions was much higher).

There are secessionists in some of the autonomous communities who are not satisfied with autonomy and press for a nation-state. These do not make deals with Madrid, which conducts a sometimes covert and violent struggle against them. The most notable are the Basque nationalists of *Euskal Herritarrok (EH)* (We Basques), the successor in 1998 to HB, whose leadership was imprisoned in 1997 for collaborating with 'an armed band', ETA, the 'terrorist' organisation. HB had two members of the Congress and one in the Senate in the 1993 Spanish elections. It retained its Congress seats in the 1996 Spanish elections with 12.7 per cent of the Basque vote. In the regional election of October 1994 it obtained

Table 4.1   Regionalisms in Spanish elections (March 2000)

Party	Seats	% of votes
Catalonia		
Convergence and Union (*CiU*)	15	4.2
Republican Left of Catalonia (*ERC*)	1	0.8
Initiative for Catalonia-Greens	1	0.5
Basque Country		
Basque Nationalist Party (*PNV*)	7	1.5
Basque Solidarity (*EA*)	1	0.9
Galicia		
Galician Nationalist Bloc (*BNG*)	3	1.3
Andalusia		
Andulusian Party (*PA*)	1	0.9
Canary Islands		
Canarian Coalition	4	1.1
Balearic Islands		
Nationalists/regionalists not represented in Spanish Parliament, but are elected to Regional Assembly (see below, p. 93).		

16.3 per cent of the vote and 11 out of 75 seats. In the European Parliament elections of 1999, HB got nearly 20 per cent of the vote in the Basque Country (1.5 per cent of the Spanish vote), and regained a seat in the European Parliament. HB transformed itself into EH in 1998 and increased the number of seats to 14 in the Basque elections of October 1998. It then joined the PNV and EA in a minority regional government. ETA called off its 14-month cease-fire in December 1999, and EH suffered at the polls, winning no seats in the March 2000 Spanish elections, and only seven seats with 10 per cent of the vote in the Basque regional elections of May 2001. It then left the regional coalition government.

None of the extreme nationalist parties has achieved anything near a majority of votes in their nations and, perhaps as a result, there is some nationalist terrorism, mainly in the Basque Country. Moderate (non-secessionist) nationalists in Catalonia and the Basque Country get more votes and form the governments of their nations, sometimes in coalition with Spanish parties. They also participate fully in Spanish politics, through their representatives in the Spanish Parliament. The main Catalan nationalist party, (*Convergència i Unió/CiU*) supported the minority Socialist Government from 1993 to 1995 with its 17 seats. This integrated the moderate nationalists into the state, although they constantly engage in negotiations for more autonomy, which arouses some resentment at the centre and in some other communities. The future of

Spain depends on the give-and-take between the state and these moderate nationalists. If the state were to revert to centralisation and repression, the secessionists would probably get the upper hand in their nations if democratic elections were allowed, and Spain might then break up. But so far, the state has given timely concessions and more autonomy.

There has been a current of anti-state nationalism for over 100 years which has been stronger than any found in France, and equivalent to Irish nationalism in Britain. There were Catalan and Basque nationalist parties before the First World War, and these had some successes in local elections. Autonomy was granted to Catalonia in 1913 but was cancelled by General Primo de Rivera in 1923. It was revived under the Second Republic in 1932, and the Basques got home rule in 1936. Galicia was also promised autonomy at this time, but once again dictatorship intervened, this time after General Franco precipitated a Civil War. His victory meant the cancellation of all forms of autonomy and even linguistic diversity.

After the death of Franco in 1975, the present era of democracy and autonomy began, and the full range of nationalisms manifested itself. The most secessionist and violent is Basque nationalism, which has an ethnic and terrorist dimension, alongside a moderate, social and constitutional nationalism which is autonomist in its aims. There is the added complication of an irredentist claim to Navarre, which the more extreme nationalists claim is Basque territory, but which is recognised by the Spanish state as a separate autonomous region, with its own parliament and government. Basque nationalists contest elections in Navarre, and in the 1991 regional elections won nine out of the 50 seats in the Navarre Parliament, with 17.8 per cent of the vote, distributed between the secessionist *Herri Batasuna*/HB with 11.2 per cent and six seats, the more moderate EA (Basque Solidarity) (5.5 per cent and three seats) and the mainstream PNV, which won 1.1 per cent and no seats. In the regional elections in June 1999 EH won eight seats and EA three seats. Navarre has a strong nationalism or regionalism of its own, with a history of a separate kingdom until 1514 and a separate legislature, customs and coinage until 1841. It is not surprising that most Navarrese reject the claims of the Basques, who are a militant minority in their midst. The paramilitary ETA is active in Navarre. While there are no Navarre nationalist parties, the main Spanish parties operate in alliance with similar Navarre parties in Spanish and regional elections. In the 1995 local elections, the *Unión del Pueblo Navarro*/UPN(Navarrese People's Union) came top with 26.7 per cent of the vote and 291 seats. This party is allied to the (Spanish) Popular Party. In the 1999 regional elections it won 22 seats, the Socialist Party of Navarre 11 seats and the Convergence of Navarran Democrats three seats (see Tables 4.1 and 4.2 for the most recent Spanish and regional elections). Thus Navarre, while expressing its regional/national identity in Navarran parties, is integrated with Spain, and the Basque claim to it won only 11 seats out of 47 in the Regional Assembly in 1999.

In the Basque Country (i.e. the Autonomous Community recognised by the state, not that claimed by Basque nationalists), the complexities of political nationalism are fully revealed. The PNV is one of the oldest nationalist parties in Europe (founded in 1895) and played a significant part in the Civil War (1936–39) in opposition to Franco. It is however quite conservative and Catholic, although liberal democratic and anti-centralist. As a result of intraparty disputes relating to the devolution of power to the provinces within the Basque country and ideological differences in the party, in 1986 the EA split off to form a more secular and social democratic nationalist party. It obtained 15.9 per cent of the vote and 13 seats in the 1986 Basque parliamentary elections. The diminution of the PNV vote (it fell from 42.7 per cent and 32 seats in 1984 to 23.7 per cent and 17 seats in 1986) threatened the party's position as the governing party, which it had held since 1984. It now entered into a coalition with the Basque Socialist Party, which is affiliated to the Spanish Socialist Party. The PNV was not at all inclined to ally with HB, although it is a nationalist party (HB obtained 17.5 per cent of the vote and 13 seats in 1986), for its links with terrorism and Marxism offended the constitutionalism and conservatism of the PNV. Subsequent Basque parliamentary elections in 1990 and 1994 maintained these positions, with Spanish parliamentary elections in 1989 and 1993 shifting votes somewhat away from the nationalists to the Spanish parties. Nevertheless, the PNV won five seats in both houses of the Spanish Parliament in 1993. It also headed a regional list for the European Parliament in 1994, which obtained 2.7 per cent of the Spanish vote and two seats, and formed part of the European People's Party group of 157 MEPs and 23 parties, including in Spain the Popular Party (PP) and CiU, and in Britain the Conservative Party and the Ulster Unionists. Clearly, there was nothing particularly nationalist about this group, rather a 'marriage of convenience' for European Parliament purposes. But even in the Basque and Spanish Parliaments political advantage weighed as much as nationalist solidarity for the nationalist parties.

In the 1996 Spanish elections, the PNV retained its five Congress seats, with 25.9 per cent of the Basque vote (up 0.3 per cent on 1993), but lost one of its Senate seats (down to four). HB stayed at two Congress seats, but its share of the vote was down to 12.7 per cent from 15.5 per cent. EA retained one Congress seat and its share of the vote also slipped to 8.5 per cent from 10.4 per cent. The Basque nationalist parties together won eight Congress seats out of 19 in the Basque Lands, with 47.1 per cent of the vote (down from 51.5 per cent in 1993). These election results show that nationalism is relatively strong in the Basque country, but the nationalist vote is split between three parties. There is the added complication that voters vote differently in different types of election. In the Spanish elections, there are more votes for Spanish parties, while in regional and local elections the nationalists do better.

Support in elections is vital to the success of nationalist parties, and we have seen that in Catalonia and the Basque countries such parties have been the most successful, and actually form the governments in their 'communities', in the case of the Basques at times with the support of the Socialists. The nationalist parties have also used their seats in the Spanish Parliament to obtain concessions from the Spanish government.

Another electoral weapon is the referendum, often used when constitutional matters have to be decided. Nationalists can claim a mandate from the nation if they win a referendum on independence or some strengthening of autonomy. Many of the new states established in Europe in the 1990s owe their legitimacy to a referendum, although the Czechs and Slovaks separated without holding one. In Spain, referendums were held in each region to legitimise the Autonomy Statutes passed by the Spanish parliament in the late 1970s and early 1980s. Starting with Catalonia and the Basque Country in 1979, referendums gave approval by 1983 to all 17 autonomy statutes, and there was even a provision that a subsequent referendum could be held in a region to upgrade its constitution to the level of autonomy given to the favoured 'historic' regions of Catalonia, the Basque Country and Galicia. Andalucía achieved this, and Valencia, the Canary Islands and Navarra gained an intermediate status between maximum and minimum autonomy.

It is interesting that the nationalists have not tried to use a referendum to gain a mandate for independence. Indeed, in Galicia even the Autonomy Statute got a lukewarm reception, with 71 per cent of the electorate abstaining, and only 73 per cent voting in favour.[7] In fact, the big nationalist parties, the CiU in Catalonia and the PNV in the Basque Country, are not pressing for independence anyway, and their aims are to negotiate with Madrid for stronger autonomy. They are aware that the support for independence in their nations is relatively low, even if it is rising. Surveys in the Basque Country show support for independence as 11 per cent in 1976, 30 per cent in 1979 and

31 per cent in 1987.[8] In Catalonia, it appears that the trend is the other way, with support for independence at 15 per cent in 1979 and 8 per cent in 1987.[9] However, caution should be exercised in using survey responses as evidence for referendum voting. It might be that in a referendum support for independence would be higher, if the political circumstances were favourable. Thus a period of tension between Madrid and the nations, or the discrediting of the central government, would likely increase the support for independence.

As can be seen from Table 4.2, nationalist and regional parties play a significant part in Spanish elections, and are dominant in the regions of the Basque Country, Catalonia and the Canary Islands. However, each of these parties is different in its aims, with some playing an 'autonomist' card, while others seek secession from Spain.

The Basque parties range from the moderate PNV which dominates the regional government, albeit with a minority of votes and seats, to the anti-Spanish nationalist EH and EA. The EH succeeded HB which was linked to the terrorist group Basque Nation and Liberty (ETA). The existence of terrorist activity makes Basque nationalism unique in Spain,

Table 4.2   Spanish, Catalan, Basque, Galician, Navarran, Canarian and Balearic elections[10]

Party	% of vote	Seats
Spanish election: Congress of Deputies (12 March 2000)[11]		
Popular Party	44.6	183
Spanish Socialist Workers Party	34.1	125
Convergence and Union (Catalan nat.)	4.2	15
United Left	5.5	8
Basque Nationalist Party	1.5	7
Canarian Coalition	1.1	4
Galician Nationalist Bloc	1.3	3
Andalusian Party	0.9	1
Republican Left of Catalonia	0.8	1
Initiative for Catalonia/Greens	0.5	1
Basque Solidarity	0.4	1
Aragonese Union	0.3	1
Catalan regional election (17 October 1999)		
Convergence and Union	37.5	56
Party of Socialists of Catalonia	38.0	52
Popular Party	9.5	13
Republican Left of Catalonia	8.7	11
Initiative for Catalonia/Greens	2.5	3
Basque regional election (13 May 2001)		
Basque Nationalist Party/Basque Solidarity	42.7	33

Table 4.2 (Continued)

Party	% of vote	Seats
Popular Party	23.0	19
Spanish Socialist Party	17.8	13
We Basques (EH)	10.1	7
United Left	5.5	3
Galician regional election (21 October 2001)		
Popular Party	51.6	41
Galician Nationalist Bloc	22.6	17
Party of Galician Socialists	21.8	17
Others	4.0	–
Navarran regional election (13 June 1999)		
Union of the Navarrese people	41.4	22
Socialist Party of Navarre	20.3	11
We Basques	15.6	8
Convergence of Navarran Democrats	6.9	3
United Left	6.9	3
Basque Solidarity/Basque Nationalist Party	5.4	3
Canarian regional election (13 June 1999)		
Canarian Coalition	37.0	25
Spanish Socialist Party	23.9	19
Popular Party	27.1	14
Canarian United Left	2.9	–
Hierro Independent Grouping	0.3	2
Balearic Islands regional election (13 June 1999)		
Popular Party	43.9	28
Spanish Socialist Party	22.0	13
Nationalists of the Islands	11.7	5
Mallorquinian Union (regionalist)	7.3	3
United Left-Greens of the Balearic Islands	5.4	3
Others	7.2	7

and a constant threat to law and order, both in the Basque country and in (mainly) Madrid. The PNV has been criticised by Madrid for being 'soft' on ETA and the EH (with which it formed a coalition in 1998), and the main difficulty is whether negotiations should be held with the extremists and concessions made about the location of terrorist prisoners. The PNV has been in office since 1980, when it won 37.6 per cent of the vote and 25/60 seats in the Basque parliament. This rose to 42 per cent and 32/75 seats in 1984, but fell to 22 seat in 1994, but continued in government in coalition with the Basque Socialists and Basque Left (*PSE–EE*). This coalition collapsed and the PNV won only 21 seats in October 1998 after ETA terrorism had been at its height (although a cease-fire was declared in September). It nevertheless continued in government, now in coalition with EA and EH. The combined PNV–EA list won 43 per cent and 33 seats in 2001. The Basque country is unique in Spain in the form of devolution it possesses (for example, it raises all taxes), its distinctive language and history. But above all, the violence and anti-Spanish tone of its nationalism mark it off from the other nations and regions in Spain.

The Catalan nationalists are also split into several parties, with the moderates led by the CiU, which has been in government since 1980 (28 per cent of vote and 43/135 seats), at that time in coalition with the Union of the Democratic Centre. The CiU leader Jordí Pujol was elected Prime Minister of the Catalan Government (*Generalitat*) and has remained in that position. In 1984 the CiU rose to 46.8 per cent of the vote and 72 seats and stayed at that level until 1999 when it slipped to 37.7 per cent and 56 seats. It was still the largest party, but the Socialists had marginally more votes, at 37.9 per cent. The CiU's strong showing in the Spanish Congress (17 in 1993, 16 in 1996 and 15 in 2000) allowed it to hold the balance of power in the Parliament where the Conservative Popular Party was the minority government. Despite its anti-regionalist stance, the Popular Party was forced to concede higher tax powers to the regions in order to get the support of the nationalist/regionalist parties.

The other nationalist party in Catalonia is the Republican Left of Catalonia (*ERC*), which dates back to 1931, and is more separatist than the CiU, especially after 1991 when it merged with Free Land (*Terre Llure*), which believes in independence. In 1980 ERC obtained 9 per cent of the vote and 14/135 seats in the regional parliament, but this fell to 11 in 1992, rose to 13 in 1995 and fell to 12 (8.7 per cent of vote) in 1999. It has had one seat in the Spanish Congress since 1979, and a seat in the European Parliament (1987–94).

The Party of Socialists of Catalonia (PSC) is affiliated to the Spanish Socialist Workers' Party, but differs from it in seeking a federal system for Spain, rather than the present devolution system. As we have seen it came first in votes in the 1999 Catalan elections with 37.9 per cent of the votes, but second with 52 seats. It is important to realise that apart from the conservative Popular Party (9.5 per cent and 13 seats in the Catalan elections of 1999), all the parties operating in Catalonia are Catalan parties in name, and often in substance. Nevertheless, in Spanish elections the PP does much better than in Catalan elections (18.0 per cent in 1996 and 22.8 per cent in 2000).

Catalan nationalism is split, like Basque nationalism into autonomists (devolutionists) and separatists, but the proportions supporting each tendency are different. Roughly 10 per cent of voters backed the party of total independence in Catalonia, and 38 per cent the federalist Catalan Socialist Party. Convergence and Union is difficult to place on the regionalist–nationalist spectrum, but statements by Pujol place the party towards the independentist side. There is however, no equivalent to ETA, HB, EH or EA in Catalonia, for the Catalan nationalists do not indulge in terrorism as do the Basque extremists. The electoral support for parties backing independence in the Basque country is about 27 per cent (the combined votes of HB and EA in the 1994 Basque elections; in 2000 the EA combined with the PNV). However, votes for separatist parties cannot be taken as an endorsement of secession in Spain or elsewhere.[12]

Portugal

In Portugal, nationalism manifests itself on the mainland in the historic opposition to threats of takeover by Spain, although today these have disappeared, especially since the death of General Franco and accession of both Spain and Portugal to the European Community in 1986. Mainland Portugal is highly integrated as a nation, and even proposals for regionalisation were defeated by referendum in 1998. This makes Portugal a more centralised state than Spain.

Portugal's overseas territories are another matter. Madeira and the Azores both had Liberation Fronts from 1975 which sought independence from Portugal. However, with the establishment of autonomous regions in 1976, these had an insignificant presence in Portuguese politics. It is not possible under the Portuguese Constitution to stand for separatist or regionalist parties, but there is no evidence of a reaction against this ban. At the regional elections held on 15 October 2000, the Socialists came top in the Azores with 49.2 per cent of the vote and 30/52 seats. In Madeira, the Social Democrats were top with 55.9 per cent of the vote and 43/61 seats.

All the other overseas territories of the Portuguese Empire have now been given independence.

Conclusion

What are the predictors for nationalism and secession in Spain and Portugal? Spain is a multinational state, but its recognition of this fact is inconsistent. While it has reconstructed itself along regional lines, it does not really recognise that there are nations in the state other than Spanish. This is similar to the 'indivisible' French republic. What this means is that there are both status and practical disputes which are unresolved. Basques, Catalans and Galicians may be granted 'historic' status as special regions, but they are not nations in the view of Madrid. This leads to an inferiority complex in these nations. A practical example of this derogation of status is that Spain refuses to appoint members of the Catalan or Basque governments to its delegation to the EU, unlike the practice in Germany, Belgium and Britain. Madrid is very jealous of its own status in the state, but this attitude leads to a continuous outpouring of nationalist demands in the 'historic' regions.

The violence of extreme Basque nationalism, and the counter-measures by Madrid put Spain at the top of the list of unstable democracies in Europe. As long as law and order is precarious, and the state itself is drawn to illegal activities (death squads and so on), the cycle of violence continues. Possible solutions are often avoided by the state, for example, the transfer of ETA prisoners to the Basque Country, and talks with 'terrorists'. There seems to be more intransigence in Spain than even in France with regard to Corsica and certainly compared to Britain in Northern Ireland. The very strong electoral position of nationalist parties in Catalonia and the Basque country, and their continuous governing position in their devolved governments is unusual in Europe. It puts at least two parts of Spain in an ambiguous position with regard to their loyalty to the state. The PNV and the CiU are both nationalist parties which do not rule out eventual independence from Spain, and couch their devolutionist demands in maximalist terms. Their relationship with out-and-out nationalists is also ambiguous. They decry any violence, but cannot contradict the logic of the aim to withdraw from Spain. Moreover, they will govern with and talk to these nationalists, as long as their connection with terrorism is not patent. In sum, the prospects for stronger nationalism at the sub-state level in Spain are very good, especially as these nationalists are in the wealthiest, most developed and most 'European' parts of the country. Whether Spain is ripe for break-up depends on whether Madrid can grant the status and practical demands of the moderate nationalists, and whether these in turn can contain the terrorists or more extreme nationalists in their midst. The chances are that the influence of the EU will help to moderate these, as without EU membership the prospects for the Basque country and Catalonia would be poor.

Similarly, Portugal gains a great deal from EU membership in economic terms, as do the aspiring 'nations' Madeira and the Azores. Independence from Portugal is off the agenda at the moment in the islands, partly because of the Constitution of 1976, which granted a special form of devolution to the islands, but also because the

Constitution forbids nationalist or regionalist parties. The strong economic ties which the islands have to Portugal and the EU through tourism and economic aid effectively limit aspirations for independence. But island possessions remain problematic for all European states, and special ethnic, linguistic and political characteristics adhere to all of these. Circumstances can change, and the example of states such as Malta show that these may be viable as independent states.

5
Italy/*Italia*

Historical context

Italy owes its origins in modern times to a nationalist movement known as the *Risorgimento* (1849–71). This had the aim of reviving the classical concept of *Italia*, a single political entity stretching from Lombardy in the north to Sicily in the south. Before Italian unification, Italy in the early nineteenth century consisted of many political units:

1. The Kingdom of Sardinia (House of Savoy) (included Piedmont, Genoa after 1815, Sardinia and before 1860, Savoy and Nice). Sardinia itself only came under the House of Savoy in 1720, when it was exchanged with Austria for Sicily. At that point the Duke of Savoy started to call himself the King of Sardinia. Sardinia proper is distinct from the rest of Italy by language, but Sardinian is closely related to Italian, the official language. Corsica belonged to Genoa before 1768, when it was sold to France. Corsican is an Italianate language, but there is no move to reunite with Italy. Genoa itself was taken by Sardinia in 1815. The Kingdom of Sardinia was transformed into the Kingdom of Italy in 1860. The Principality of Monaco, which has been independently ruled by the Grimaldi family since 1297, came under the protection of Sardinia in 1815. It felt threatened by Italian unification, and was able to secure the protection of France in 1861, which is still in practical effect. There appears to be no claim by Italy to Monaco today. Monaco is not a member of the United Nations (UN) or the European Union (EU), but is in several intergovernmental organisations including the OSCE (Organization for Security and Cooperation in Europe). Another part of the old Kingdom of Sardinia which became part of Italy is the largely

French-speaking Val d'Aosta/Vallée d'Aoste. This is an autonomous region (1948) of Italy and is officially bilingual. All street signs are in both Italian and French. There is a strong Aostan nationalism, represented by the Valdostan Union (*Union Valdôtaine/Unione Valdostana*). This seeks a cantonal system along Swiss lines, a total and permanent free zone, Valdostan control over water, mines and the sub-soil and an international guarantee of the rights of the Valdostan people.[1] So far, it has achieved special autonomy and is in control of the government of its region.

2. The Austrian (Hapsburg) Empire included the County of Tyrol, the Bishopric of Trent (Trentino), Lombardy and Venetia, which stretched down the Adriatic coast as far as Ragusa (Dubrovnik), now in Croatia, and Cattaro (Kotor), now in Montenegro. It also acquired the Duchies of Parma, Modena, Lucca and the Grand Duchy of Tuscany. The last two were united in 1847. Lombardy was acquired by Sardinia in 1859, the Marches, Umbria, Parma, Modena and Tuscany declared by plebiscite for union with Sardinia (Italy) in 1860. The Tuscan language was adopted as classical Italian in the united Italy. Venezia was gained from Austria in 1866. Today, the Venetian Republic League/Venetians for Europe seeks the restoration of the Republic of Venice, and has six representatives on the Veneto regional council. Much of the former Hapsburg territory is claimed by the Northern League (*Lega Nord*) as 'Padania', a separate nation from Italy as now constituted. The South Tyrol has strong nationalism, with two nationalist parties (South Tyrol People's Party/*Südtiroler Volkspartei, SVP* and Union for the South Tyrol/*Union für Südtirol, UfS*). The For Trieste party (*Per Trieste*) seeks a special status for Trieste within the region of Friuli-Venezia Giulia, and a repeal of the 1975 Osimo Treaty with Yugoslavia.

3. San Marino an independent state which joined the UN in 1992, but closely linked to Italy in language and currency. It is not a member of the EU.

4. The Papal States (Romagna, the Marches, Umbria and The Patrimony (Rome)). After plebiscites, Sardinia (Italy) acquired the first three in 1860. It took Rome by force in 1870. The Vatican City in Rome remains an independent state, but is not a member of the UN or EU. It is, however, a member of the OSCE and Intelsat (International Telecommunications Satellite Organization).

5. The Kingdom of the Two Sicilies (Naples and Sicily). Within this Kingdom were two ecclesiastical enclaves, Pontecorvo and Benevento, which had joined the Papal States but which joined Italy in 1860.

In the context of contemporary nationalism, some of the complex historical divisions of Italy continue to have resonance, in particular that between the provinces of the north and those in the south. The concept of the nation of Italy is contested by the Northern League, which asserts that there is a separate nation called Padania (lands of the Po River), a vague stretch of land in the north of Italy, which according to the League includes, apart from the core of Lombardy, Emilia-Romagna, Liguria, Piedmont, Venice and Tuscany. The further north of Italy, Trentino-Alto Adige and Valle d'Aosta, are not usually claimed for Padania, and are in part not ethnically Italian. Sometimes the League has demanded total independence for Padania, and has used a Padania flag rather than an Italian flag. At other times, and more recently, the League has sought a federal system for Italy, with Padania as one of the federal states. In the Italian Government of Silvio Berlusconi, himself a kind of Italian nationalist (his party is *Forza Italia*, which means Go Italy!), appointed after the election of 13 May 2001, three Northern League Deputies became Ministers, including the League's leader (Federal Secretary), Umberto Bossi, who became Minister without Portfolio for Institutional Reform and Devolution. This was a reward for the League's support as part of Berlusconi's alliance (House of Freedom) for the election.

Berlusconi appointed four Deputies from the National Alliance party (*Alleanza Nazionale*) to his Government, as that party had also joined his electoral alliance. The National Alliance is heir to Mussolini's Fascist Party, and so represents an extreme form of Italian nationalism, which in theory is totally opposed to the Northern League's anti-Italian nationalism. The contradictions in Berlusconi's Council of Ministers mirrored the contradictions in the nature of Italy itself.

As we have seen, the boundaries of Italy today are the result of various international settlements, and this has implications for nationalism. France's annexation of Savoy in 1860 is contested by the Savoy League, which wants to restore Savoy as an independent state. This is despite the fact that the Kingdom of Italy was proclaimed by the King of Piedmont, which historically included Savoy. Savoy, however, is French-speaking, and its independence or even union with France could be justified on linguistic grounds. Conversely, Nice (also given to France in 1860) has still an Italian-speaking minority.

More controversial in history was what was called *Italia Irredenta*, parts of other countries claimed by the nationalist Italian Irredentists. Before 1914, these included the southern Tyrol, Trieste, Görz (Gorizia), Istria (including Fiume, now Rijeka in Croatia) and Dalmatia (now part of

Croatia), which were part of the Austrian Empire. The defeat of Austria-Hungary in the First World War led to the dismemberment of the Hapsburg Empire. Italy gained the South Tyrol and Trieste, but not Fiume, Istria or Dalmatia, which went to the new state, the Triune Kingdom of Serbs, Croats and Slovenes (Yugoslavia after 1929). There were thus actual or potential disputes about Italy's boundaries with Austria and Yugoslavia, which in some form or other continue to this day. In particular, Austria has an interest in protecting the German-speaking inhabitants of what it calls the Südtirol (Italian: Alto Adige), especially with regard to the use of the German language use and the special form of devolution which was introduced there in 1968. The South Tyrol People's Party was founded in 1945 to seek self-determination for the South Tyrol, and soon had 50 000 members. A petition with 155 000 signatures was presented to the Austrian Chancellor in 1946 seeking the return of South Tyrol to Austria. While Austria was sympathetic to this demand, the four Great Powers rejected it, along with small frontier revisions. Nevertheless, the peace settlement in 1946 included joint protection of the linguistic and economic interests of the region by Austria and Italy. However, in 1948 the South Tyrol was included in the Trentino-Alto Adige Region, which meant Italian domination, and Italianising policies. This aroused the opposition of the Austrian Government which by 1956 was requesting negotiations, particularly a new region of South Tyrol. Demonstrations followed, and in 1959 the question was raised in the UN by the Austrian Foreign Minister. In October 1960 the UN General Assembly unanimously approved a resolution requesting negotiations between Austria and Italy, but these had no result. The Government of Italy now made arrests and was accused of torture by the SVP. In 1964 an Austrian Commission negotiated with the SVP and Italy, and by 1969 a new settlement was agreed which in 1972 gave autonomy to the South Tyrol in a Provincial Government and Assembly. This autonomy gradually grew in scope and allowed the SVP to run the government. It also led to the South Tyrol sending its representative to the EU Committee of the Regions. Thus the Tyrol problem has been largely resolved with political and economic cooperation between Austria (North Tyrol) and Italy (South Tyrol), strengthened by cross-border (Tyrol) programmes financed by the EU.

Of the other border regions populated by Italians – Savoy, the Romansch part of Switzerland and the coastal parts of Slovenia and Croatia, only the last is a political problem at the present time. In Croatia, Fiume (Rijeka) had been seized by the Italian nationalist d'Annunzio in 1919 and was recognised as Italian in 1924. But with the defeat of the Fascists in the Second World War, Fiume was awarded to Yugoslavia. Today, Croatia is the successor there to Yugoslavia. Both Croatia and Slovenia have resisted Italy's claims to compensation for Italians whose property in Istria had been appropriated after 1945, when boundary changes favoured Yugoslavia. The Italian Government under Berlusconi in 1994 said it would block Slovenia's application for EU membership if its claims were not satisfied. However, the succeeding government lifted the veto in 1995, and Slovenia signed an association agreement with the EU in 1996. In 1998 Slovenia compensated 21 000 ethnic Italians for property abandoned by them when they fled to Italy at the end of the Second World War. Croatia is also an EU hopeful, but its status as an applicant is much lower than Slovenia's. Meanwhile, there are three parties in Croatia representing Dalmatia and Istria, and one (Dalmatian Action) was engaged in terrorism in 1993. These parties do not seek union with Italy, but greater independence for Dalmatia and Istria. None of them has gained seats in the 1995 or 2000 elections.

Constitution (1948)[2]

Article 5 (Local Autonomy)
The Republic, one and indivisible, recognises and promotes local autonomy...
[The Italian Constitution gives Italy a system of devolution with 20 regions, but only a few have ethnic or national characteristics. According to the Northern League for the Independence of Padania, Padania consist of 11 of these regions, but some of these have non-Italian ethnic populations, namely Valle d'Aosta (French) and Trentino-Alto Adige/Südtirol (German and Ladin). Special forms of devolution are given to these, and also to Friuli Venezia Giulia, Sardinia and Sicily. See Article 116.].

Article 6 (Linguistic Minorities)
The Republic shall safeguard linguistic minorities by means of special provisions.
[This has given German and Ladin official status in the South Tyrol, along with Italian, and French in the Vallée d'Aoste/Valle d'Aosta.]

Article 116 (Special Forms of Autonomy)
(1) Friuli Venezia Giulia, Sardegna (Sardinia), Sicilia (Sicily), Trentino-Alto Adige/Südtirol and Valle d'Aosta/Vallée d'Aoste enjoy particular forms and conditions of autonomy, according to their special Statutes adopted by constitutional law...

(3) Upon the initiative of the Region concerned, having consulted the local administrations, State law may assign further particular forms and conditions of autonomy to other Regions ...

Article 117 (State and Regional Legislative Power)
(8) ... Within its field of competence, the Region may establish agreements with foreign states and understandings with territorial entities that belong to a foreign state, in the cases and forms provided for by State law.
[This has allowed the South Tyrol to liaise with the North Tyrol, part of Austria. The EU encourages such cross-border arrangements, and this has helped to soften the nationalism of the German-speaking South Tyrol, which looks to German-speaking Austria for support.]

While the flag of the Republic is the Italian Tricolour (Article 12), there is no ban on regional flags, which are particularly prominent in 'Padania'. Yet the substance of Italian devolution falls short of devolution in Spain and Britain, and well short of federalism as practiced in Belgium, Germany, Switzerland and Austria, and it is debatable whether Italy considers itself a multinational or a one-nation state. It is constitutionally more multinational than France, but not as much as Spain, Britain or Belgium. Switzerland is ethnically diverse, but is organised along cantonal not national lines. Yet these cantons are divided along linguistic and religious lines.

Electoral nationalism

There are numerous regional parties[3] in Italy, but only a few claim to represent nations, and only four, the Northern League, the South Tyrol People's Party, the Valdostan Union and the Sardinian Action Party have made a strong impact electorally. It is more difficult to place Italian parties within the category of nationalist, but the National Alliance is the descendant of the Italian Social Movement (1946), founded as the successor to the illegal Fascist Party of Mussolini (see Table 5.4).

The Northern League is a federation of parties or Leagues in Lombardy, Emilio-Romagna, Liguria, Piedmont, Tuscany and Venice. It started as the Lombardy League in 1979, which harks back to the twelfth-century federation of northern Italian cities. In fact the Lombardy League sought a federation for the whole of Italy, but this switched to independence for 'Padania', the lands north of the River Po. This would give Padania the right to restrict immigration from the south of Italy, which the League considered detrimental to the north. By the

Table 5.1   Northern League for the independence of Padania (*Lega Nord*)

Year		% of vote	Seats
Chamber of Deputies (Italian Parliament: Lower House, 630 members)			
1992		8.7	55
1994		8.4	(118)[4]
1996		10.1	59
2001		3.9	30[5]
European Parliament (Italy: 87 MEPs)			
1994		6.6	6
1999		4.5	4
Best city mayoral, regional and provincial results			
1993	Mayoral: Milan	40.0	
1995	Regional: Lombardy	17.7	12
	Veneto	16.9	9
2000	Regional: Lombardy	15.5	10
	Veneto	12.0	6
1997	Province: Como	33.0	18
2002	–	17.5	6
1997	Province: Vicenza	41.3	22
2002	–	16.0	6
1997	Province: Varese	38.0	22
2002	–	18.3	7

Note: the Presidents of the Provinces of Como, Vicenza and Varese in 2002 were elected by an alliance including the Northern League, Forza Italia, the National Alliance and the UDC.

late 1990s, however, the League had reverted to support for federalism, and in effect was prepared to work within the devolutionary institutions of Italy, at least for the time being. Whether the League can be called nationalist, racist or just regionalist is debatable. At times all features are present. Its electoral breakthrough came in 1992, when it won 8.7 per cent of the Italian vote and 55 seats in the Chamber of Deputies (see Table 5.1). In Milan, the League won 40 per cent of the vote in the mayoral election of June 1993, and joined the Italian Government after winning 8.4 per cent of the Italian vote as part of the right-wing Freedom Alliance headed by Silvio Berlusconi. In the European elections of June 1994, the League won six seats with a 6.6 per cent share of the vote. The League leader, Umberto Bossi, is a flamboyant character given to public displays proclaiming the Republic of Padania convening a Parliament in Mantua in May 1996 and proclaiming 'the Republic of Padania' in September 1996, and setting up a 'national guard' to protect the interests of Padania. This led to a police raid of the League HQ in Milan, as this appeared unconstitutional. Worse was to come. Bossi was sentenced to a year in prison with a hefty fine in January 1998 for criminal acts at a League rally in 1995.

Meanwhile, Bossi had become uneasy with the League's collaboration with Berlusconi, and the League soon left the coalition, and increased its vote in the 1996 election to 10.1 per cent and 59 seats. This made the League the most successful party in northern Italy. By 1997, Bossi was apparently moderating his policies, and was losing support at the polls in the local elections.[6] But in November 1997 a 'constituent assembly of the Republic of Padania' was convened in the presence of guest nationalist from Russia, Vladimir Zhirinovsky (Liberal Democratic Party).

In the June 1999 European elections the League fell to 4.6 per cent of the vote, and to four seats from six. These MEPs are not part of any party group. Then in 2000 Bossi and Berlusconi curiously came together again in the electoral alliance known as the House of Freedom. In the ensuing parliamentary election in May 2001 the League was part of the House of Freedom's victory (3.9 per cent out of the House's total of 45.4 per cent). Now it had 30 members in the Chamber and 17 in the Senate, and was given three ministers in the new Berlusconi Government.

Table 5.2 South Tyrol People's Party (*SVP*)

Year	% of vote	Seats
Chamber of Deputies		
From 1948 has elected 3 Deputies, in 2001 with 0.5 per cent of the Italian vote.		
European Parliament		
One MEP elected since 1979.		
Regional, provincial and mayoral elections		
Trentino Alto-Adige (Südtirol)		
Region/(Electoral College of Bozen)		
1948	30.2/67.6	13
1993	26.0/52.0	19
1998	29.2/56.6	21
Province of South Tyrol		
1998	56.6	21/35

The Provincial Assembly had a Green Alternative Fraction President and the SVP occupied the positions of Vice-President and the three other members of the Presidency. In 2000 there were 25 German-speaking, nine Italian-speaking, and one Ladin-speaking deputy.

Table 5.3 Valdostan Union (*UV*)

Year	% of vote	Seats
Chamber of Deputies		
2001	35.0 (Valdostan)	1 (also 1 seat in the Senate)
Regional assembly		
1998	40.1	17/35

Table 5.4 National Alliance (*AN*)

Year	% of vote	Seats
Chamber of Deputies		
1948		6
1953–72		Won between 24 and 29 members.
1972		In alliance with Italian Democratic Party of Monarchical Unity, and list won 56 seats.
1976–83		Parties merged to become MSI-DN. Won 35 seats. After split, MSI-DN won 30 seats in 1979.
1983	6.8	42
1987	5.9	35
1992	5.4	34
1994	13.5 of PR vote in Freedom Alliance List (*Pollo*).	
1996	15.7	91
2001	12.0[7]	99 (24 in Senate)

Note: The National Alliance was given four seats in Berlusconi's Council of Ministers.

Table 5.5 Sardinian Action Party (PSd'Az)

Year	% of vote	Seats
Chamber of Deputies		
1996		4 seats as part of Olive Tree Party Group
Regional Council		
1983[8]	12.3	–
1999 (13 June)	8.3	4/64

Other national or regionalist parties with representation include the Emilio and Romagna Freedom Party (one councilor); the Autonomous Lombardy Alliance (one Senate seat), Venetian Republic League (linked to Northern League) (2000: six representatives in Veneto Regional Council, with 11.9 per cent of vote).

Conclusion

As can be seen, Italy has a complex political system with great ethnic (national) and regional diversity, expressing itself in political parties and movements, special forms of devolution, and demands for secession in some places. While only a few of these nationalisms have caused concern to the Italian Government, those that have (particularly the Northern League, the South Tyrol People's Party, and the Valdostan Union) question the very existence of Italy as now constituted. While at first, the Italian state was reluctant to concede meaningful devolution, it has moved towards federalism since the 1990s, especially for the special regions.

Meanwhile, the echoes of Mussolini's fascism are present in the continuing strength of the National Alliance, which is strongly opposed to secessionist politics and the break-up of Italy. Paradoxically, the Alliance served along with the Northern League in Berlusconi's Government of 2001. This perhaps indicates that despite the rhetoric there is considerable give-and-take in Italian politics, underlined by the strong commitment to the EU, which encourages regionalism and linguistic diversity, but opposes secessions from member states.

6
Germany/*Deutschland*

Historical context

The German state ('Empire') dates from 1871, although German nationalism is at least a century older. After the period of Nazism (the 'Third Reich', 1933–45), Germany was divided in two by the victorious Allies, and its old capital, Berlin, divided into zones controlled by different Allies. Meanwhile, 'West Germany' had its capital in Bonn.

Although the desire for reunification was always there, it was muted. Many Germans considered that Germany was better relatively small, and that in any case the communist East Germany had gone beyond the point of return. However, the rapid collapse of communism in 1989 with the fall of the Berlin Wall speedily brought about the reunification of Germany, and the latent German nationalism was satisfied. This time, however, German nationalism was not to take a virulent form, but was harnessed to the greater aim of European integration. Working closely with the French, the West German Chancellor, Konrad Adenaeur in the 1950s had committed Germany to membership of the various European institutions which culminated in the European Community/Union. The old expansionism of the German Empire and Third Reich gave way to an intense development of Germany itself, with a purely economic domination over much of the European economy.

Nationalism in Germany is expressed today in the largely exclusive and ethnic nature of German citizenship, and in some expressions of extreme right-wing politics, including Neo-Nazism. The first German nationalists in the eighteenth century based their nationalism on pride in the German language and the inherent qualities of the German *volk*. When Germany became a state in 1871 as the German Empire, it was not a nation-state in the sense that all Germans belonged to it and that non-Germans were excluded. In the first case, the Germans of Austria and Switzerland remained outside Germany. In the second case, Germany included French, Polish and Lithuanian people, who were increasingly restless under German rule. The annexation from France of Alsace-Lorraine in 1870, despite the presence of many German speakers, who were however loyal to France, was an international question which continued to trouble the peace of Europe through to 1945. Given back to France, there was a brief period of Alsatian nationalism when the French government banned the Alsatian language from state schools. However, the development of Strasbourg as the home of the Council of Europe and seat of the European Parliament made Alsatians less separatist, and in 1980 the French began a process of regional devolution and bilingualism. In 1991 the Strasbourg local authority put all street signs into the Alsation language, which was not welcomed by the rest of France. German investment in the region has led to a revival of German-language education, and Alsatians put their loyalty first to Alsace or Lorraine, second to Europe and lastly to France.[1]

Neighbouring Saarland, also German-speaking, and originally part of Germany, was under League of Nations administration from 1920 to 1935, when it voted to join Germany. In 1945 it came under French occupation, but was allowed to vote for self-determination by the UN, and chose to join Germany in 1955, which was implemented in 1957. Poland and Lithuania achieved independence in 1918, but the independence of Czechoslovakia in 1918 brought around three million Sudeten Germans under the rule of a Slav state. Hitler annexed the Sudetenland in 1938, and proclaimed the *Anschluss* or union between Austria and Germany in the same year. The victory over Germany and Austria reversed these unions. Austria was restored but divided between the four Great Powers until independence in 1955, when it because a neutral state. The three million Sudeten Germans were expelled by Czechoslovakia in 1945 under the 'Beneš decrees' propounded by the Czechoslovak President Eduard Beneš. In 2002, the German Interior Minister Otto Schily and Bavaria's Prime Minister, Edmund Stoiber, called for the repeal of the decrees. Stoiber, married to a Sudeten German now resident in Bavaria said he would not support the Czech Republic's application to join the European Union (EU) if the decrees were not repealed. As the Christian Social Union (CSU)/Christian Democrats (CDU) candidate for Federal Chancellor, Stoiber's position took on some importance.

In 1940, the secret protocols of the Nazi–Soviet Pact brought the Baltic states of Lithuania, Latvia and Estonia within the Soviet Union, with the relocation of the German population to Poland and Germany. By the time the Baltic states regained their independence (1991), the German population had gone, but in recent years some claims have been made by Germans to recover lost property. This is more strongly seen in the former German Democratic Republic (East Germany) which was reunited with the German Federal Republic (West Germany) in August 1990, and to a lesser extent in Poland, which recovered its independence in 1945, only to come under Soviet control in 1948. Poland freed itself of this control in January 1990.

Apart from these manifestations of 'Greater German' nationalism, the focus of nationalism in Germany is the German state itself. Here, the relevant issues are German citizenship, immigrants and extreme right-wing politics.

Constitution (1949, amended)

Preamble
Conscious of their responsibility before God and Men, animated by the purpose to serve world peace as an equal part in a unified Europe, the German People have adopted … this Constitution. The Germans in the States of … [16 States] … This Constitution is thus valid for the entire German People.

Article 116 (Definition of a German, re-granting of citizenship)
(1) Unless otherwise provided by statute, a German within the meaning of this Constitution is a person who possesses German citizenship or who has been admitted to the territory of the German Reich within the frontiers of 31 December 1937 as a refugee or expellee of German ethnic origin or as the spouse or descendant of such a person.
(2) Former German citizens who, between 30 January 1933 and 8 May 1945, were deprived of their citizenship on political, racial or religious grounds, and their descendants, are re-granted German citizenship on application. They are considered as not having been deprived of their German citizenship where they have established their residence in Germany after 8 May 1945 and have not expressed a contrary intention.

The Constitution, or 'Basic Law' of Germany was adopted on 1949, although it uses features from previous constitutions. Of interest here are the Articles on Citizenship (116) (Definition of a German) and the Preamble as altered by the 36th Amendment (1990).[2]

The German state is strongly ethnic, for its citizenship is based on the 'right of blood' (*ius sanguinis*) rather than the 'right of soil' (*ius solis*).

The distinction is between a right based on heredity rather than on birth or residence. Germans are entitled to German citizenship if they can demonstrate descent from Germans, even if they are not residents of Germany. The significance of this is the rights which exiled Germans have to return to Germany as full citizens. Conversely, those non-Germans born in Germany or resident there have no automatic right to become German citizens, with some exceptions.

The Constitution is adopted by 'the German People', and gives rights to 'Germans' rather than 'citizens', although the distinction is not very clear. When the Constitution was drawn up in 1949, Germany was divided between the communist east and the non-communist west. Nevertheless, the Constitution gave citizenship to those in the east, and the pre-unification Preamble stated that 'The German People have also acted for those Germans who were not allowed to participate. The entire German People remains obliged to fulfil the unity and freedom of Germany in free self-determination.'

While these constitutional provisions can be largely explained by Germany's history, especially with regard to the period after 1945, the ethnic criterion for nationality actually goes back before the First World War, to the Reich citizenship law of 1913.[3] The Nazi 'Third Reich' (1933–45) built on this, but was explicitly racist, so that German citizens of Jewish descent were excluded from citizenship of Nazi Germany, and intermarriage of 'Aryans' and 'non-Aryans' was forbidden. Today, only extreme 'neo-Nazis' echo these sentiments, and usually the focus of attack are immigrants and asylum seekers, of whom Germany has a very large population (estimated at around 7 million by 1993, equivalent to 10 per cent of the former West German population and 1.5 per cent of the East German population.[4] In total foreign nationals represented 8.9 per cent of the population in 2000.)[5] In the period up to the 1990s, the main group was the 'Guest Workers' (*Gasterbeiter*) from the Mediterranean countries, especially Turkey, who were generally refused citizenship. In 1990 only 1423 Turks out of 1.9 million had been natu-ralised.[6] By 2001 it was estimated that Germany had 3.2 million Muslims out of a total population of 83 million,[7] but by then the naturalisation laws had been somewhat liberalised to give the right to apply for citizen-ship to legal non-criminal residents for at least eight years between the ages of 16 and 23, who had attended school in Germany for at least six years. If over 23, a residence of at least 15 years was required.[8] So far, rel-atively few have taken up this opportunity, partly because Germany and Turkey do not operate a dual-nationality system. So Turks have to give up their citizenship of Turkey if they become German citizens.

As in the rest of Europe, immigration and asylum seekers provide a powerful spur to nationalism, especially of the extreme variety. Violent incidents involving Germans and immigrants are quite common, and can result in fires and deaths. A relatively liberal policy on asylum seekers has attracted many from the Balkans as well as Asian and African countries. Only the Slavs, however, are close to German culture, and Germany has close economic links with Slovenia, Croatia and parts of Bosnia, where many Germans own businesses and property. Germany was quick to recognise the independence of the Balkan states, despite the misgivings of France and Britain. It may have felt a moral obligation to receive the displaced persons as a result of the wars which raged there subsequently.

Electoral nationalism

Germans vote overwhelmingly for mainstream parties of the centre-right and centre-left (CDU and Socialist Democrats (SPD) respectively). There is also a second mainstream conservative party, the Free Democratic Party (FDP), with 6.3 per cent of the vote in the federal elections of 1998 and 7.4 per cent in 2002. This party was in coalition with successive SPD and CDU/CSU governments from 1949 to 1998. In Bavaria, the Christian Democrats are replaced by the Christian Social Union (CSU), with which it is affiliated.[9] It is more conservative and nationalist than the CDU, with a strong Bavarian regionalist policy. However, there is no deviation from German nationalism in this, which unites all parties. This nationalism supports the ethnic character of the German nation and citizenship, the present boundaries of Germany and a strong belief in the EU. The advent of the Euro, however, in 2002 has split German public opinion on the virtues of European monetary integration, and this is reflected in splits in the mainstream parties. Nevertheless, German governments have been careful not to appear nationalist in the context of the EU, unlike Conservative governments and parties in Britain and France.

Parties with explicitly nationalist and/or racist characteristics are:

The Republicans *(Der Republikaner)*

The Republicans are an anti-immigration party established in 1983 by two disgruntled CSU Deputies who sought German reunification when the CSU was dealing with East Germany. In January 1989 it won 7.5 per cent in the Berlin regional elections under the leadership of a former SS officer. It stood in the European Parliament elections of June 1989 on an anti-integration platform and won 7.1 per cent of the German vote and six seats. In the 1992 Baden-Württemberg regional election of April 1992 it won 10.9 per cent and 15 seats. Thereafter, it faltered for a time, losing its European Parliament seats in June 1994, and its one Bundestag seat. In March 1996 it continued to be strong in Baden-Württemberg, with 9.1 per cent and 14 seats, but in the federal elections (Bundestag) of September 1998 it won only 1.8 per cent of the German vote and no seats. Similarly, in the European elections of June 1999 it polled only 1.7 per cent, and in the Baden-Württemberg regional elections of March 2001 it fell to 4.4 per cent of the vote. The 2002 Bundestag elections confirmed the poor performance of 1998.

German People's Union (*Deutsche Volksunion*) (DVU)

Dating from 1987, the DVU stands on an anti-immigrant anti-foreigner platform, and believes that Germans want a 'racially pure' country. In alliance with the National Democratic Party of Germany (see below), it won a seat in the Bremen state elections in September 1987. This increased to six seats in 1991, with 6.2 per cent of the vote. In 1992, it won six seats in Schleswig-Holstein, with 6.3 per cent of the vote. In May 1995, it lost its Bremen seats, and won only 2.5 per cent of the vote. In March 1996, it lost its seats in Schleswig-Holstein, with 4.3 per cent of the vote. In the former East German state of Saxony-Anhalt it did better in April 1998, with 12.9 per cent of the vote, and 16/116 seats. In the federal elections of September 1998 it won only 1.2 per cent of the vote, and no seats, but recovered somewhat in Bremen in June 1999, winning one seat and 3 per cent of the vote, but 6 per cent in Bremerhaven. In September 1999, it won five members in Brandenburg, so that it now had seats in three state legislatures. In the 2002 Bundestag elections, no seats were won.

National Democratic Party of Germany (*Nationaldemokratische Partei Deutschland*) (NPD)

Founded in 1964, its leader was found guilty of inciting racial hatred in 1965 and imprisoned, this small party won 4.3 per cent of the national vote in the 1969 elections, and obtained representation in several state legislatures around this time. By the federal elections of 1998, it had sunk to 0.3 per cent, and 0.4 per cent in the European Parliament elections in 1999. This lack of support was confirmed in the 2002 Bundestag election.

Conclusion

The electoral record of the nationalist parties in Germany does not indicate that these are a serious threat to the position of the mainstream parties, but in the context of the history of Nazism, any manifestation of nationalism and racism is taken seriously both at home and abroad. Loosely described as Neo-Nazis, parties with an anti-immigrant, anti-asylum seekers and anti-foreigner stance have hit the headlines at times, when accompanied by violence and arson directed at immigrants from the Mediterranean countries. This gives 'New Right' extremism in Germany its distinctive character, as does the provision in the German Constitution outlawing anti-system parties such as those deemed Neo-Nazi or Communist (Basic Law, Art.21 (2)). Despite this ban, as we have seen, parties which have been called 'Neo-Nazi' have had some success. The reasons for this are complex, and have been analysed at length by numerous authors.[10]

More generally than the extreme Right parties, the entire basis of the German state is based on an ethnic definition of the German nation, and the rights of 'Germans' in Germany. Although lately, the ethnic criterion has been relaxed for citizenship, the difference is marginal, and German nationalism still harks back to the philosophy of Johann Herder in the eighteenth century, who espoused a linguistic and ethnic definition of the German nation. But this is firmly controlled by the acceptance of the present boundaries of Germany and the restraints on German nationalism through membership of the EU, the Council of Union, NATO and the OSCE. Thus internationalism prevails over nationalism in contemporary Germany, and the manifestations of extreme or old-fashioned nationalism by non-mainstream parties have remained marginal in German politics. The testing point comes with the expansion of the EU and further integration. For Germany has now probably got more to lose than it has to gain from this, and has achieved a dominating position in Europe by force of numbers, its economy and trading relationships. Militarism is dead, as is German territorial expansionism. But German nationalism lives on, in the apparently effortless superiority of the German nation in Europe.

7
The Low Countries (Belgium/ *Koninkrijk België/Royaume de Belgique*, the Netherlands/ *Nederland*, and Luxembourg)

Historical context

These countries are grouped together in geography and history, but are very different in the context of nationalism. Nevertheless, it is possible to group them together as archetypal 'smaller European democracies', and two (Belgium and the Netherlands) are examples of 'consociational' or power-sharing democracies, although based on different social and political 'cleavages' (only Belgium is divided by ethnicity and language).[1] It is doubtful if there is a Belgian nation at all, since it is composed of two strong ethnic, linguistic and perhaps national groups, the Flemings in Flanders (60 per cent) and the Walloons or Francophones in Wallonia (30 per cent), and a small German-speaking population (10 per cent). The Netherlands (often erroneously called Holland[2]) is by contrast relatively unified ethnically and linguistically, but divided on religion. Even so, the Frisians of Friesland/*Fryslân* (411 000 in 2000[3]) are separated ethnically and linguistically from the Dutch, and have recently displayed nationalist politics and have achieved some cultural and political autonomy, Luxembourg is a political anomaly, a state of 432 000 people in an area of 998 square miles (2586 sq.km.), which has distinctive linguistic characteristics (Lëtzeburgisch) yet uses French and German as official written languages, with French the official language for administrative purposes. It might have easily been assimilated to France or Germany had not international and economic circumstances combined in its favour. It was given a kind of independence in 1815 under the sovereignty of the King of the Netherlands as Grand

Duke. It joined the Germanic Confederation from 1815 to 1867, gaining full independence in the latter year. To all intents and purposes united with Belgium and the Netherlands in economic matters today, it can hardly classify as a nation as generally understood, even if it has a national anthem and a national flag.

The struggle for Belgian independence (1830) is one of the first modern nationalist movements, coming at the same time as the national risings in Poland, Greece and Italy. What the Belgians sought was independence from Dutch rule, which had been imposed by the Congress of Vienna in 1815. For centuries they had been ruled by the Hapsburgs of Spain (1477–1713) and of Austria (1713–1815). When the Protestant Dutch in 1572 rebelled and declared their own confederation ('the United Provinces') (1579), the Catholic Belgians remained loyal to Spain, and then to Austria. The Dutch achieved independence in 1609, but this was not recognised by Spain until 1648, by which time the United Provinces had become a major power with strong trading, seafaring and colonial interests.

The Belgians only behaved in a nationalist way when they were transferred from Austrian to Dutch rule in 1815. This was clearly a threat to their Catholicism and the French language, which at that time was the official language. The Flemish (Dutch)-speaking majority in Belgium did not seek union with the Dutch, for it was religion rather than language which inspired their nationalism at this time. Later, as religion subsided as the prime force in politics, language was to divide the Belgians into two strong segments or quasi-nations, with a third linguistic minority (10 per cent), the German-speakers, in a small enclave.

The history of Belgium since the 1960s has been marked by extreme tension between the majority Flemish and the minority French-speakers, who had nevertheless dominated the state from the monarchy down. The Flemish struggled to achieve autonomy in Flanders, and equality of status in the Belgian state. After mass rallies in Flanders, Flemish was established as the sole official language in 1962, and in the following year Flemish, French and German were made Belgium's official languages in their respective regions. Universities, banks and political institutions including parties were split along linguistic lines.

This 'solution' led to bitterness, especially among the French-speakers, who resented the loss of their historic dominance. The Flemish proved insensitive to this, notably when they secured legislation in 1968 to split the fifteenth-century university of Louvain in two. The Dutch-speakers were given the original campus (re-named Katholieke Universiteit

Leuven) in Flanders, and the French-speakers were forced to re-establish themselves in a new university in Wallonia, the Université Catholique de Louvain at the new campus of Louvain-la-Neuve (1974), with the medical faculty in Brussels. The library books were divided in two between the universities between 1971 and 1979, even if most were in French.[4]

Finally, the 'Egmont Pact' of 1977 between the parties led to the establishment of a federal system based on Flanders, Wallonia and Brussels, with a small German-speaking region. Three of these were monolingual officially, but Brussels (*Brussel/Bruxelles*) was bilingual.

By then, it was questionable whether Belgium was a nation as normally understood. While there is no religious split (Catholics predominate in both Flanders and Wallonia), there is no Belgian language, and the divisions between the Dutch and French speakers have hardened. Federalism was established along extremely decentralised and consociational lines (see Constitution, below). National identification for Flemings is with Flanders more than with Belgium, although the Francophones and Brussels inhabitants tend to identify with Belgium predominantly.[5]

Constitutions

Belgium

Article 1 (Federal State)
[The Constitution adopted in 1970 makes Belgium a federal state, made up of Communities and Regions.]

Article 2 (Communities)
[There are three communities: the French Community, the Flemish Community, and the German-speaking Community.]

Article 3 (Regions)
[There are three regions: the Walloon Region, the Flemish Region, and the Brussels Region. Note that the population of Brussels Region are members of either the French or Flemish Communities and these control cultural and education matters within Brussels.]

Article 4 (Linguistic Regions)
[There are four linguistic regions: the French-speaking Region, the Dutch-speaking Region, the German-speaking Region, and the bilingual Region of Brussels (Capital). Each commune is part of one of these

linguistic regions. The boundaries of these regions can only be changed by a majority vote in each of the linguistic groups in each House of the Dutch Parliament, equal to at least two-thirds of the votes expressed.]

Article 30 (Choice of Language)
The use of languages in Belgium is optional: only the law can rule on this matter, and only for acts of the public authorities and for legal matters.

Article 33 (Sovereignty)
All power emanates from the nation.

Article 43 (Linguistic Groups)
Each House is divided into a French linguistic group and a Dutch linguistic group for cases determined by the Constitution [basically, boundaries of Linguistic Regions, and language matters.

Article 54 (Group Veto, Alarm Bell Procedure)
[Various procedures to protect the position of linguistic groups in the legislative process.]

Section II: The Senate
Article 67
[Details of indirect election of the 71 Senators by the Dutch electoral college: the French electoral college: the Flemish Community (Flemish Council); the Council of the French Community; and the Council of the German-speaking Community (the linguistic and national divisions of the country). The status of Brussels, the capital, as a bilingual city (*Brussel/Bruxelles*), is maintained by the guarantee that at least 7 Senators should be residents of the Brussels-Capital Region (1 Flemish speaker and 6 French-speakers).]

Article 68 (Group Balance)
[Details of how the share of seats between the linguistic groups is determined, and how each group chooses its representatives.]

Chapter IV (Communities, Regions)
Section I Bodies. Sub-section I (Community and Regional Councils)
Article 115 (Councils)
[Establishes the French Community Council, the Flemish Council and the German-speaking Council.]

Article 121 (Community Governments)
[Establishes the French, Flemish and German-speaking Community Councils.]

Section II Responsibilities
Subsection I Community Responsibilities
Article 127 (Decrees, Competencies)
The French and Dutch Community Councils establish by decrees cultural issues, education (with the exception of compulsory school age and minimum standards of diplomas, etc.). These apply in Brussels too, where all inhabitants are members of either the Dutch-language or French-language Communities.

Article 129 (Decrees on Language)
The French and Dutch Community Councils rule by decree on the use of language for administrative matters, public education, social relations between employers and their personnel in addition to corporate acts and documents required by law. Exceptions are those communes contiguous to another linguistic Region, where the law prescribes or allows the use of another language than that of the Region in which they are located.

Article 130 (German-speaking Community Council)
[Similar to powers of French and Dutch Community Councils, except for absence of administrative matters and social relations between employers and personnel. There is no power in Brussels.]

Article 135/6 (Region of Brussels-Capital; Linguistic Groups
in Brussels-Capital) and Article 166 (Brussels-Capital)
[Establishes the United Governing Bodies of Brussels, acting as an inter-Community consultation and coordination organ, and refers to the sections relating to the government of Brussels in the Constitution. For example, Article 128 (2) gives the two language communities in Brussels the right to make laws considered exclusive to these communities (i.e. those listed in Article 129).]

Article 137 (French and Flemish Community Council)

Article 138 (French Community Responsibilities)

Article 139 (German-speaking Community Council and
Walloon Regional Council)

Article 140 (Decrees of German-speaking Institutions)
[Details the complex powers of these bodies, and their relationship].

Article 167 (Shared Responsibility)
[Gives Community and Regional Governments the right to conclude treaties regarding matters that are within their responsibilities, subject to the approval of their Councils.]

This is unusual in a federal system, as it gives the regions and communities an international role. It also means that their consent is required for Belgian policy in EU matters in areas within their competence.

The extremely complex nature of this Constitution is the result of successive political crises dating back to the 1960s, when Flemish and Walloon nationalism threatened to destroy the Belgian state. The result is a finely crafted balance between the linguistic communities and territorial regions based on the principles of consociational democracy.[6]

But the complicated power-sharing constitutional arrangements have not entirely satisfied the Belgian population. Both Flanders/*Vlaanderen* in the north, and Wallonia/*Wallonie* in the south still have separatist movements and parties, whose aim is secure independence for these regions. On 29 November 1997, extreme Flemish nationalists declared a provisional government of the 'Republic of Flanders' with Gert Geens as President. This was followed by unofficial parliamentary elections in February 1998.[7] These nationalists are however, more separatist even than the main nationalist parties, the Flemish Bloc (*Vlaams Blok*) and the People's Union (*Volksunie*), who contest the official elections (see below).

The mainstream Belgian parties from the 1960s divided into separate Flemish and Walloon parties, whose relationship is always uneasy, and has led to the downfall of several Belgian Governments, dependent on coalitions across the language communities. The main flashpoints today are the status of Brussels, whose government was not brought under the federal system until 1993, and is still an uneasy French-majority city surrounded by the Flemish Region, and the remaining federal powers such as social security, which many Flemings consider involves a subsidy from them to the poorer Walloon Region. Devolving social security to the regions, however, would mean the effective end of the Belgian welfare state and the main reason for its existence. In contrast, the uneasy position of some border villages, such as Les Fourons/Vouron, a French-speaking part of the Flemish Region, are less prominent in politics than they were in the 1980s, when they brought down the Belgian Government in 1987.

The future of Belgium as a 'nation-state' is in doubt, even if the Belgian Constitution refers to 'The Nation' twice (Articles 33 and 193). Paradoxically (or perhaps logically) Belgium is at the centre of the EU, with Brussels housing its main institutions. If Belgium were to dissolve into the separate states of Flanders and Wallonia, this might be seen as a failure of the EU to protect the territorial integrity of its members. On the other hand, a 'Europe of the Regions' type of EU would be happy with the two independent regions of Flanders and Wallonia. The latter alternative, however, gets little support from the other member states, which are most unsympathetic to the break-up of state territories into independent regional units.

The Netherlands

The Netherlands does not face break-up, and its Constitution does not refer to language or ethnic groups. Friesland, however, is an historic nation, albeit split between the Netherlands, Germany and Denmark. Friesland in the Netherlands has been given a special form of devolution, and the official recognition of its language in administration and education. This has satisfied the 'nationalists' there, who are in any case very loyal to the House of Orange, the Dutch Royal Family.

There is another side to nationalism in the Netherlands: anti-immigration feeling. The Dutch controlled a vast colonial Empire until the 1960s, and a consequence of this is the modern wave of 'reverse colonialism': the immigration of the colonised to the mother country. All the former Empires of Europe face this development, but the Dutch and Belgians have proved very attractive to immigrants. In 2000, there were 43 890 applications from asylum seekers in the Netherlands, of which 13 per cent were successful. (In Belgium there were 42 690 applications and 33 per cent were recognised. This compares with only 38 590 in France (17 per cent recognised). Britain and Germany, however, top the league with 96 870 (29 per cent recognised) and 78 760 (12 per cent recognised) respectively.)[8]

Foreign nationals amounted to 8.3 per cent of the Belgian population in 2000 (slightly down on 8.9 per cent in 1990). They were 4.1 per cent of the population of the Netherlands (again, similar to that in 1990, which was 4.3 per cent). However, in some cities of the Netherlands and Belgium the proportion is very much higher, and this has led to political repercussions. In Rotterdam (Netherlands) and Antwerp (Belgium), for example, the immigrant population (first and second generation) is around 45 per cent.[9]

Electoral nationalism

Belgium

People's Union (Volksunie/VU)

The first Flemish nationalist party of modern times was founded in 1954 to promote Flemish autonomy, but it did not come to prominence until the 1960s, as shown in Table 7.1.

Table 7.1   Performance of the People's Union in regional and Parliament elections

Year	Seats	% of vote
House of Representatives (150 deputies)		
1965	12	
1969	20	
1974	22	
1977	20[a]	
1978	14[b]	
1981	20	
1985	16	
1987	16[c]	
1991	5.9	10
1995	4.7	5
1999	5.6	8
Flanders regional council (118 seats)		
1999	9.3	11[d]
European Parliament elections (25 MEPs)		
1989	5.4	1
1994	4.4	1
1999	7.6	2[e]
Brussels regional government (75 seats/6 parties)		
1995		1[f]
1999		0

Notes
[a] Enters coalition, but splits over 'Egmont Pact' on devolution (1978).
[b] Returns to opposition.
[c] In coalition, 1988–91.
[d] In alliance with Complete Democracy for the 21st Century/ID21.
[e] VU/ID21.
[f] Given portfolio in government.

Flemish Bloc (Vlaams Blok/VB)

The nationalist, anti-immigrant Flemish Bloc (VB) dates from 1978, and grew out of the Flemish People's Party, part of the People's Union (*Volksunie/VU*) and the Flemish National Party (1977) (see Table 7.2).

Democratic Front of French speakers (Front Démocratique des Francophones (FDF))

Dating from 1964, it sought to keep Brussels a French city, despite the fact that geographically it was within Flanders geographically, and had a strong

Table 7.2   Flemish Bloc in the elected bodies

Year	% of vote	Seats
House of Representatives (212 members to 1995; 150 from 1995)		
1991	6.6	12
1995	7.8	11
1999	9.9	15
Flanders regional council (118 seats)		
1995	12.3	15
1999	15.5	20
European Parliament (25 MEPs)		
1989	4.1	2
1994	9.4	2

Flemish-speaking minority. Flemish nationalists wanted Brussels to be included in the Flanders region set up under the 'Egmont Pact' of 1978. Instead, Brussels became a separate bilingual region, with all street signs in both Flemish and French. The FDF was in the coalition government which produced the Pact, and this seems to have contributed to the drop in their support at elections for the House of Representatives, from 11 seats in 1978 to six seats in 1981. This dropped to three seats in 1985, when two deputies left to join the Walloon Socialists. Then the FDF went into alliance with the Liberal Reformist Party (PRL), the latter having absorbed many members of the *Rassemblement Wallon*, an early (1968) Walloon nationalist party, which won 14 seats in the 1971 election. Another Francophone party, the Walloon Party (*Parti Wallon*), dating from 1985, sought a socialist Wallonia, but failed to make an impact at the polls. The combination of the FDF and the PRL, however, won 18 seats in the House of Representatives election in 1999, with 10.1 per cent of the vote. More importantly, the results in the Brussels and Walloon regional elections pointed to the importance of the FDF for the French-speakers (see Table 7.3).

Table 7.3   Results in the Brussels and Walloon regional elections

Year	% of vote	Seats
Brussels regional council (75 seats)		
1995	35	28 seats (in alliance with PRL; largest group)
1999	34.4	27
Walloon regional council (75 seats)		
1995	23.7	19 (2nd largest group)
1999	24.7	21

Netherlands

Fortuyn List

The anti-immigrant 'Fortuyn List'/*Lijst Pim Fortuyn* founded by the aca-demic-journalist Pim Fortuyn rose to prominence in 2002 when it won 35 per cent of the vote to control the Rotterdam city council with 17/24 seats on 6 March 2002 as shown in Table 7.4. Fortuyn was especially opposed to Muslims, whom he accused of being hostile towards Dutch culture, especially its liberal attitude towards homosexuals, of whom he was one. Muslims amount to 5 per cent of the population of the Netherlands as a whole, but are concentrated in the large cities. Fortuyn was murdered nine days before the elections of 15 May 2002, but his list stood, with some success. It won 17 per cent of the vote and 26 seats, giving it the right as the second largest party (after the Christian Democrats with 43 seats) to participate in the coalition government which traditionally operates along 'power-sharing' lines. This would normally lead to policies with a consensus across the party spectrum. What that meant in terms of nationalism and immigration was not clear. Fortuyn's successor was Mat Herben, a former journalist, and in the elections held on 22 January 2003 the Fortuyn List fell to 5.7 per cent of the vote and eight seats.

The Fortuyn 'phenomenon' illustrates the dangers of an easy categori-sation of all nationalist or anti-immigration parties as 'right-wing', 'fascist', 'racist' and so on. This was the line taken by most press and aca-demic commentators, but not all. For example, Neal Ascherson, writing in the *Observer*,[10] points out that Fortuyn

> had no time for neo-Nazis, welcomed non-whites into his party (although he argued that Holland could absorb no more immigrants) and loudly attacked Islam for its intolerance to gays. But he was part of the rebellion against the consensus politics that dominate so many

Table 7.4   The Performance of Fortuyn List in elections

Year	% of vote	Seats
Rotterdam City Council (24 seats)		
2002	35	17
Netherlands Parliament: Second Chamber		
(Tweede Kamer) (150 members)		
2002	17	26
2003	5.7	8

European states, a revolt against regimes that use the language of political correctness...

Frisian National Party (Fryske Nasjionale Partij/FNP)

The Frisian National Party, founded in 1962 to achieve further autonomy within a federal Europe has had no success in elections. It is affiliated to the European party grouping, the Democratic Party of the Peoples of Europe-European Free Alliance.[11]

Conclusion

Belgium and the Netherlands are both troubled by 'anti-system' nationalism, which have profoundly shaken their governments and states. In Belgium, linguistic nationalism has split the country into two main regions and 'communities', the Flemish and French-speakers. There is also a German-speaking community. The capital, Brussels, is profoundly split into two language communities, and has a complicated power-sharing government, as does the whole of the state. To some extent the monarchy holds the state together, as does the pressure of the EU. But the centrifugal force of ethnic and linguistic nationalism is powerful, and a possible outcome is a 'Europe of the Regions' including Flanders and Wallonia as members. That would leave the German-speakers and Brussels in an uneasy position outside these regions. It is also unlikely that Wallonia would benefit economically from independence, as it is to some extent subsidised by Flanders. So there is little desire for secession in Wallonia.

The Netherlands has been shaken by the anti-immigrant nationalism of the 'Fortuyn Group' in 2002, and its government is likely to take a more anti-immigrant line in future, especially if the Fortuyn Group is in the governing coalition. The peculiar form of consociational democracy practiced in the Netherlands was based on cooperation between Catholics, Protestants and Seculars, and it is questionable if that can be extended to Muslims, especially as they do not share the extremely permissive culture of the rest of the Netherlands. The Netherlands is not threatened by secessionists, but it is unhappy with the presence of many 'foreigners' of a different ethnic, cultural and religious character.

8

Scandinavia (Iceland/*Ísland*, Denmark/*Danmark*, Norway/*Norge*, Sweden/*Sverige*, Finland/*Suomi*)

Historical context

The Scandinavian countries[1] are alike in geopolitics (they occupy the most northerly part of the continent of Europe and have a common political history). Their majority populations have a common ethnicity and similar languages, but there are minority Eskimo, and Lapp (Sami) populations, which display nationalism. One estimate of the Sami population puts them at around 50 000, with 30 000 in Norway, 15 000 in Sweden, 5000 in Finland, and 2000 in Russia.[2] Another estimate (2000), however, puts the numbers higher: 105 000 in Europe, of which: 70 000 in Norway, 22 000 in Sweden, 8000 in Finland and 3000 in Russia.[3] The Eskimos in Greenland engage in electoral politics, but the Sami do not. Nevertheless, the latter are extremely active in politics generally, and in 1988 demanded the creation of a Sami parliament. In 1992 the Sami language was given equal status with Norwegian in Norway, but when Sweden and Finland entered the European Union (EU) in 1995 the Sami leaders demanded that the Sami people enter the EU as a separate people.[4]

The formation of nation-states in Scandinavia was a gradual process from the start of the nineteenth century to 1944, when Iceland became independent. For centuries the Crowns of Sweden and Denmark had controlled the area, with Sweden's Empire extending into Finland and the Baltic, notably present-day Latvia (Livonia) (1660–1720), Estonia (1561–1720) and part of Russia (Ingria) (1617–1720). Finland (Swedish from the twelfth century) was taken by Russia in 1809. For a time, until the mid-seventeenth century, Denmark extended into southern Sweden. Norway was independent until 1380, when a royal marriage brought it under Danish rule. In 1397 Norway, Denmark and Sweden were united under one sovereign (the Union of Kalmar), but in 1523 Sweden broke away to form its own state.

In 1814 the Norwegian Parliament accepted the Swedish monarch as King of Norway, but nationalism grew rapidly at the end of the nine-teenth century, so that in 1905 a constitutional crisis arose involving the monarchy's refusal to grant Norway its own consulates abroad. The Norwegian Parliament decided to break away from Sweden. This was supported by an unofficial referendum with a near-unanimous (99.95 per cent: 368 392 to 184) vote. A new monarch was found from the Danish royal family. Norwegian nationalism exists today in the form of continuing distrust of Sweden, and the reluctance to shed sovereignty by joining the EU. In November 1994, a referendum on EU membership failed by 4.4 per cent (52.2 per cent to 47.8 per cent, albeit down from the 7 per cent (53.5 per cent to 46.5 per cent) margin in the 1972 refer-endum. Denmark had joined the European Economic Community (EEC) in 1973, and Sweden and Finland joined in 1995.

Denmark like Britain has been Eurosceptic over the years. On 2 June 1992 a referendum rejected the Maastricht Treaty by 50.7 per cent to 49.3 per cent, but after various opt-outs were agreed, a referendum in 1993 endorsed the Treaty by 56.8 per cent to 47.2 per cent. The opt-outs are significant in the context of nationalism, for they allowed Denmark to opt out of the common currency, the common defence policy, coop-eration on immigration control and EU citizenship. A referendum specifically on whether to enter the current currency (Euro) was held on 28 September 2000, and the proposal was rejected.

A protocol of 1992 continued the prohibition against German acqui-sition of summer homes in Denmark. Ownership of such homes required a long-term residence qualification. So anti-EU and anti-German feeling indicate the continuing strength of Danish nationalism.

In history, the dispute with Germany dates back to the era of the Prussian state, and the notorious Schleswig-Holstein Question. Schleswig and Holstein were duchies held by the kings of Denmark from 1460, but were not part of the Kingdom. Holstein became a member of the Confederation of the Rhine in 1815, and its inhabitants were mainly German. When Frederick VII of Denmark died without an heir in 1863, Prussia fought Denmark and annexed the duchies in 1866. This situa-tion remained until 1920, when a plebiscite resulted in the northern part of Schleswig, populated mainly by Danes, being given to Denmark to become the province of Haderslev and Aabenraa. Southern Schleswig and Holstein remained part of Germany.

Relations with Germany deteriorated completely when Hitler invaded and occupied Denmark in April 1940. The Danes refused to cooperate with the Nazis, in particular over surrendering the small Jewish population. Despite the fact that the Nazis regarded the Danes as Aryans, they were subjected to repressive measures, including martial law. The reaction to this period was intense, and led the Danes to look north to fellow Scandinavians for international cooperation rather than to the emerging EEC. The Nordic Council (established in 1953) represented this cooperation, and includes as members Denmark (including the Faroe Islands and Greenland), Finland, Iceland, Norway and Sweden. The Council's secretariat in 1995 moved from Stockholm to Copenhagen to be close to the Secretariat of the Nordic Council of Ministers, a separate body. Denmark is thus the centre of Scandinavian international relations, which is another reason why the rival EU institutions based in Brussels have less appeal to its people.

After 1945, the old Schleswig-Holstein question re-emerged as a problem for Denmark and Germany. Now, however, these are both democratic regimes, and prepared to be accommodative. In South Schleswig (part of Germany, along with Holstein as the federal state of Schleswig-Holstein) there are around 50 000 Danish-speakers today, with 28 237 votes in 1992. This is considerably down from the period immediately after the Second World War. Then there was a strong pro-Danish movement with around 75 000 members in 1948, which won 71 864 votes in the general election of 1950.[5] Negotiations between Denmark and Germany, and including Britain as the Allied Power occupying that zone of Germany, led to the Kiel Statement of 1949. This stated that the Danes and Frisians had the right of national self-determination, and in the meantime possessed full civil rights, such as education in Danish. Kiel, the capital of Schleswig-Holstein, was the seat of the *Land* Parliament, and the Danish minority held four seats up to 1954. But new electoral laws meant that they failed to win a single member in the Kiel Parliament in 1954, despite winning more than 42 000 votes. The Danish Parliament expressed concern, and the obstacles were removed, and representation was renewed until 1964.

The German minority in Denmark is much smaller (*c.*20 000), and Danish Constitution gave the Germans voting for the Schleswig Party (1920) a seat in the Danish Parliament with 9721 votes in 1953. The Bonn–Copenhagen statements of March 1955 dealt with the minorities' position in both countries, and official policies changed from assimilation to multiculturalism. In the early 1990s, there were 53 Danish schools in Germany, with 5270 pupils. In Denmark, the German minority ran 18 private schools in 1989, with 1184 pupils.[6]

Lorenz Rarup, in the work by Sven Tägil which is here quoted, concludes that the minorities on both sides of the border accept their membership of the states in which they live, and do not seek to exercise the right of national self-determination, nor to challenge the border. Nevertheless, they are concerned to maintain their national identities through the use of their national language, their own schools, associations, churches and media (of course TV is freely available on a cross-border basis). The minorities vote in a national way, for their own parties. When Denmark joined the EEC in 1973, economic relationships became close but, as we have seen, suspicion of a German takeover remains and opt-outs have been granted to Denmark on closer integration. Danes are very nationalist when it comes to relationships with Germans.

In October 1995, the Danish People's Party was established 'to re-establish Denmark's independence and freedom to ensure the survival of the Danish nation and the Danish monarchy'. It opposes a multi-ethnic Denmark and immigration. It is opposed to membership of the EU, while supporting a free trade area. Its electoral history is one of rapid advance to the 12 per cent vote and 22 seats for the Danish Parliament in the election of November 2001 (see Table 8.1).

Other nationalist (anti-EU) parties in Denmark are the June Movement, formed after the referendum vote (2 June 1992) which rejected the Maastricht Treaty. It has won seats in the European Parliament. The Socialist People's Party (1958) also opposed the Maastricht Treaty, and has representation in the Danish and European Parliaments. The Red–Green Unity List (1989) is another anti-EU party with representation in the Danish Parliament campaigning in the September 2000 referendum against membership of the Euro.

The relations between the Scandinavian countries in the north today are close, but complicated by the fact that Norway, unlike Sweden and Finland, is not a member of the EU, and that Sweden, like Denmark (and Britain), refused to join the Euro in 2002. This means that 'European' identities are variable throughout Scandinavia, ranging from very weak in Norway to relatively strong in Finland, although in July 2002 it was reported that only one in five Finns 'care much for the EU', half the EU average.[7] Finland fears an influx of immigrants from the Baltic countries, especially Estonia, if these join the EU. Already illegal immigrants from Estonia are a sore in Finland. Relations between Sweden and

Finland have historically been as difficult as between Sweden and Norway. Finland was part of Sweden until 1809, then a Grand Duchy in the Russian Empire. It became independent in 1917, but peace with the emerging Soviet Union did not take effect until 1920, with the establishment of Finnish (and Swedish) neutrality.

The independence of Finland in the face of Stalin's expansionism is one of the miracles of modern European history. Finland fought a defensive war against the Soviet Union in 1939–40, but this ended in stalemate with a new demilitarisation agreement. With German aid in 1941 Finland beat off Soviet advances, but was punished in 1944 by the USSR with the loss of one-eighth of its territory. Russian–Finnish relations will be discussed further in the chapter on the Russia and the other nations of the former USSR.

Here, relations between Sweden and Finland involve mainly the presence of Swedish-speaking Finns and Ålanders (inhabitants of the Åland Islands, which lie midway between Sweden and Finland in the Baltic Sea).

In 1880, when Finland was under Russian control, Swedish speakers amounted to 294 900 or 14.3 per cent of the total population. In 1990, they were 296 700 but only 5.9 per cent of the population. 175 000 live in towns with 190 000 in and around the Finnish capital, Helsinki, and 100 000 in the northern area of Ostrobothnia.[8] The Ålanders (also part of Finland in Russia) amounted to 27 000 people in 1917 and to 23 000 people in Finland today. There are also 35 000 in Sweden, and a total of 65 000 in Europe as a whole.[9] They speak a form of Swedish closer to that of Stockholm than that of the other Swedish-speaking Finns. After the First World War the islands were the subject of a dispute between Finland, which continued control over them as successor to the Grand Duchy, and the islanders backed by Sweden, who demanded self-determination. A case was brought to the Permanent Court of International Justice, which had been established under the League of Nations in 1920. This awarded control to Finland in 1921, but safeguards for the population were upheld by the League, including autonomy and the use of the Swedish language. This was renewed in the autonomy statute of 1952, and extended by another statute in 1993. Only native Ålanders have the right of residence and the right to own land. It has been a separate member of the Nordic Council since 1970, and possesses its own flag and stamps. In 1991 it introduced its own currency. Ålanders have a 'sense of belonging to Swedish history'.[10] When Finland and Sweden joined the EU in 1995, the position of the islands again came to the fore. Duty-free tourism contributes 70 per cent of the national income of the islands, so they were allowed to remain outside the common market and sell duty-free goods. Other EU citizens are not allowed to buy property or set up industries in the islands. All this gave the Åland Islands something like 'full independence within the European Union'.[11]

More complex is the position of the Swedish-speakers in the mainland of Finland, amounting to around 300 000 people. These are mainly an urban elite today, concentrated in the capital Helsinki (Swedish: *Helsingfors*[12]), dating back to the time before 1809 when Finland was part of Sweden. There are also fishers and farmers whose antecedents go back to settlers of the thirteenth and fourteenth centuries, and recent immigrants from Sweden and Finns who have become Swedish speakers by choice. The 1919 Constitution of Finland (see below) states that Finnish and Swedish are both official languages and this applies also to local government and the right to use either language in public administration.

Constitutions

Iceland

Article 68
... The entitlement of foreign nationals to hold rights to real estate in the country shall be determined by law.

Temporary Provisions
Foreign nationals who, prior to the date of application of this constitutional law, have obtained the right to vote and have become eligible to elected to the Althingi [Parliament] or have obtained the right to hold public office, shall retain the said rights. Danish nationals who under Article 75 of the Constitution of 18 March 1920 would have obtained such rights had the law not been amended shall, from the date of entry into force of this constitutional law until six months after negotiations regarding the rights of Danish nationals in Iceland can start, also acquire the said rights and retain them.

N.B. See also the Danish Constitution, Section 87, below.

Denmark

Part IV (The Parliament). Section 28 (Membership)
... two Members shall be elected on the Faroe Islands and two Members in Greenland (see 'Electoral nationalism', below. These members do not belong to Danish parties).

Section 31 (Elections)
(5) Special rules for the representation of Greenland in the Parliament may be laid down by Statute.

Section 87 (Iceland)
Citizens of Iceland who enjoy rights with citizens of Denmark under the Danish-Icelandic Union (Abolition) etc. Act, shall continue the rights attached to Danish citizenship under the provisions of the Constitution Act.
[N.B. No mention is made of Schleswig in the Constitution, or of the rights of the German minority in Denmark there. Nor are there any provisions relating to property ownership by Germans, which formed a protocol to the Maastricht Treaty (see p. 127, above).]

Norway

Article 1
The Kingdom of Norway is a free, independent, indivisible and inalienable Realm.
[N.B. Nothing on the position of the Sami in the Constitution.]

Sweden

Chapter 2 (Fundamental Rights and Freedoms). Art. 7
[Prohibits dual nationality. N.B. Nothing on ethnicity or the rights of the Sami.]

Finland

Chapter 1 (Fundamental Provisions) Section 4 (The Territory of Finland)
The territory of Finland is indivisible. The national borders cannot be altered without the consent of the Parliament.

Section 17 (Right to one's language and culture)
(1) The national languages of Finland are Finnish and Swedish
(2) The right of everyone to use his or her own language, either Finnish or Swedish, before courts of law and other authorities, and to receive official documents in that language, shall be guaranteed by an Act. The public authorities shall provide for the cultural and societal needs of the Finnish-speaking and Swedish-speaking populations of the country on an equal basis.
(3) The Sami, as an indigenous people, as well as the Roma and other groups, have the right to maintain and develop their own language

and culture. Provisions on the right of the Sami to use the Sami language before the authorities are laid down by an Act...

Section 51 (Languages used in parliamentary work)
(1) The Finnish or Swedish languages are used in parliamentary work.
(2) The Government and other authorities shall submit the documents necessary for a matter to be taken up for consideration in the Parliament both in Finnish and Swedish. Likewise, the parliamentary replies and communications, the reports and statements of the Committees, as well as the written proposals of the Speaker's Council, shall be written in Finnish and Swedish.

Section 120 (Special Status of the Åland Islands)
The Åland Islands have self-government in accordance with what is specifically stipulated in the Act on the Autonomy of the Åland Islands.

Section 122 (Administrative divisions)
(1) In the organisation of administration, the objective shall be suitable territorial divisions, so that the Finnish-speaking and Swedish-speaking populations have an opportunity to receive services in their own language on equal terms.

Electoral nationalism

Iceland

No nationalist or ethnic parties.

Denmark

Danish People's Party/ Dansk Folkeparti (DF) (1995)
A breakaway from the Progress Party (founded 1972), which virtually disappeared, the DF is the main nationalist party in Denmark. Its first success was in the local elections of November 1997 when it won 6.8 per cent of the vote.

Party for People's Government/*Tjóðveldisflokkurin*, Faroe independist People's Party *Fólkaflokkurin*, Faroe Conservative Forward/*Siumut*, Greenland Social Democratic Eskimo Community/*Inuit Ataqatigiit*, Eskimo Community, Greenland communist, each of these parties has one member in the Danish Parliament elected in 2001.

Norway

While no explicitly nationalist or ethnic parties contest elections in Norway, the anti-EU parties can be counted as nationalist. These are the

Table 8.1   Danish People's Party and its growth

Year	% of vote	Seats
Parliament (Folketing) (179 members)		
1998	7.4	13
2001	12.0	22
European Parliament (16 seats)		
1999	5.8	1
June Movement (1992) (anti-Maastricht Treaty)		
European Parliament		
1994	15.2	2 (in Europe of Democracies and Diversities Group)
1999	16.1	3

Table 8.2   Norwegian Parliament and the performance of anti-EU parties (1989–2001)

Party	% of vote	Seats
Centre Party/Senterpartiet (SP)		
1989	6.5	11
1993	16.7	32
1997	7.9	11
2001	5.6	10
Socialist Left Party/Socialistisk Venstreparti/SV		
1989	10.1	17
1993	7.9	13
1997	6.0	9
2001	12.5	23

Centre Party/*Senterpartiet* (SP), the Socialist Left Party/*Sosialistisk Venstreparti* (SV) (see Table 8.2). Their electoral performance was strong when Norway was negotiating to enter the EU in 1993, and when the referendum of November 1994 rejected accession, the heat went out of the issue, and with it much of the vote for the anti-EU parties. The Socialist Left Party did well, however, in 2001, owing to the unpopularity of the minority Labour government.

Sweden

As in Norway, the nationalism of Sweden is represented by anti-EU parties. These are the Left Party/*Vänsterpartiet* (VP) (8.3 per cent of vote and

30 seats in the 349-seat Parliament/*Riksdag* in 2002), the Green Ecology Party/*Miljöpartiet de Gröna* (4.5 per cent and 17 seats in 2002) and New Democracy/*NyDemokrati* (*NyD*) (having won 24 seats with 6.7 per cent of vote in 1991, it had disappeared by 2002). The Swedish Social Democratic Labour Party/*Sveriges Socialdeokratiska Arbetarparti* (*SAP*), while officially in favour of joining the EU, was badly split, and the leadership allowed the anti view to be made in the party. In 2002 it stood as the Workers' Party-Social Democrats/*Arbetarepartiet-Socialdemokraterna* (*SD*), winning 39.9 per cent of the vote with 144 seats, and continued to lead the government.

Finland

Nationalist parties in Finland come in three types: (a) the party of the Swedish minority (Swedish People's Party); (b) the anti-EU parties and (c) two small 'patriotic' parties (League for a Free Finland, and the Patriotic National Alliance).

(a) Swedish People's Party/Svenska Folkpartiet (SFP)/ Ruotsalainen Kansanpuolue (RKP)

Dating back to 1906, before the independence of Finland in 1917, the SFP represents the Swedish population, which has been falling in size over the years. The parliamentary vote for the Party has thus fallen from 7.9 per cent in 1945 and 14 seats (its post-war peak) to 5.1 per cent and 11 seats in 1999 (see Table 8.3). Parties opposed to Finland joining the

Table 8.3 Finnish Parliament (Diet) (200 members) and the RKP

	% of vote	Seats
1991	5.5	12
1995	5.1	12
1999	5.1	11
Presidential election		
1994	22 (1st round)	
1994	46.1 (2nd round)	
2000	7.9 (1st round)	
European Parliament (16 seats)		
1996	5.1	1
1999	6.8	1

Table 8.4   Anti-EU parties and their performance in
Finnish and European Parliament

Year	% of vote	Seats
Finnish Christian Union (Suomen Kristillinien Liitto, SKL)		
Finnish Parliament		
1991	3.1	8
1995	3.0	7
1999	4.2	10
European Parliament		
1999	2.4	1
Green Union/Vihreä Litto (VL/VIHR)		
Danish Parliament		
1991	6.8	10
1995	6.5	9
1990	7.5	11
European Parliament		
1996	7.6	1
1999	13.4	2
Left Alliance/Vasemmistoliitto(VAS)/Vänsterförbundet (1990)		
Danish Parliament		
1991	10.2	19
1995	11.2	22
1999	10.9	20
European Parliament		
1996	10.5	2
1999	9.1	1

EU are the Finnish Christian Union (SKL) Green Union and Left Alliance as shown in Table 8.4.

The League for a Free Finland/*Vapaan Suomen Liitto(VSL)* is a right-wing nationalist party with 1 per cent of the parliamentary vote in 1995 and 0.4 per cent in 1999. The Patriotic National Alliance/*Isänmaallinen Kansallis-Litto (IKL)* is a right-wing nationalist party with no electoral success.

Conclusion

Nationalism in the Scandinavian countries is based on strong state and ethnic identity, with a contemporary dimension of suspicion of EU integration. Relations between the Scandinavian states are now good, where before they were uneasy, especially between Denmark and Norway, Norway and Sweden and Sweden and Finland. The difficult Schleswig-Holstein question, involving war between Denmark and Prussia/ Germany is now a good example of how minorities can be protected. The Sami population of northern Europe is not so easily dealt with as such a minority, and the Sami straddle three of the four states. Their ethnic, linguistic and cultural differences with the majority populations are large. They do not, however, cause much trouble politically, and have not mobilised electorally.

Electoral nationalism is present in all these countries in the anti-EU politics of many parties, and in the strong anti-EU vote in referendums. This type of nationalism is increasing. The Swedish population in Finland continues to express its interests in the SFP, which is however declining as the Swedish population falls. The Swedes have achieved political autonomy in the Åland Islands and bilingualism in Helsinki and the other areas where they have a strong presence.

9
Switzerland/*Schweiz/ Suisse/Svizzera*

Historical context

Switzerland is a special case for students of nationalism. Here is a state which is not a homogeneous 'ethnic' nation (it consists of at least three ethnic groups, German, French and Italian), but has features of a 'social' nation, and certainly an 'official' nation.[1] This makes it similar to Belgium, and the similarity increases when one compares their political systems, for both are 'consociational democracies' based on decentralised federalism. There is also a similarity in the presence of separatist or autonomist nationalism. In Switzerland this is found in the Jura region, where autonomists and nationalists have been active for many years.

The Jura is a largely French-speaking part of Switzerland, but was placed in the predominantly German-speaking Bern/Berne canton. It is split, however, into the Catholic north and Protestant south. This was to prove important when Jura nationalists tried to separate the Jura from Bern.

From the early nineteenth century the Jura was in conflict with Bern, which sent troops when autonomy was demanded. On top of the language difference, religion became a cause of conflict. Roman Catholic priests in the Jura were imprisoned or forced to seek refuge in France when Bern engaged in a Prussian-type Kulturkampf, or anti-Catholic legislation in the 1870s.

Electoral behaviour divided the Jurassians from the Bernese. The former rejected the new Bernese Constitution in 1893 by 9984 votes to 2189, but Germanisation continued. In 1947, a new militant Jura nationalism appeared when Bern refused to appoint a French speaker to a ministerial post in the canton. The *Rassemblement Jurassien* (*RJ*) was established in 1947, and pressure grew on Bern to give the Jura a separate canton. On the RJ's initiative, a referendum was held in 1959, but its implementation by the canton was not straightforward. In fact, it became a series of referendums in different parts of the canton, and one in the canton as a whole. The result did not satisfy the Jura nationalists, for only the northwest of the Jura, the Catholic part, voted to have its own canton. This left the rest of the Jura still under Bern, a mixed French–German and Catholic–Protestant area. The town of Moutier in Bern was separatist, however.

Now things began to get violent, and the *Front de Libération du Jura* (*FLJ*) engaged in terrorist acts. Another referendum, on 23 June 1974, showed the Jura people in favour of separation from Bern (by 36 802 to 34 057), but the rules were again turned against them, and five districts remained part of Bern. In 1990 the Jurassian Independentist Movement/ *Movement Indépendantiste Jurassien* (*MIJ*) was created, to campaign for complete independence from Switzerland of the six historic Jura districts. 'Independence Day' is celebrated annually on 23 June. In 1992, the vote against joining the EU in Switzerland was split between French speakers, who were mostly in favour of joining, and German speakers, who were mostly against. This strengthened the separatism of the Jura nationalists, who looked forward to independent Jura membership of the EU. The death of a young nationalist in 1993 sparked more violence, and an independent commission recommended the creation of a six-district Jura canton. This was turned down by Bern, however, and in 1994 an agreement to collaborate was reached between the Jura and Bern cantons, which was far from satisfactory from the nationalist point of view, since it retained the existing boundaries.

The RJ and Jurassian Unity/*Unité jurassienne* now (1994) united to form the Jurassian Autonomist Movement/*Mouvement Autonomiste Jurassien* (*MAJ*), which was more moderate than the MIJ, in that it accepted remaining part of Switzerland. All these bodies, and others, took part in an Interjurassian Assembly, a surrogate Parliament for the whole Jura. This passes resolutions, for example, favouring the creating of a South Jura Parliament, which as expected, is rejected by the Bern canton.[2]

The main sign of Swiss official nationalism is found in its relations with the outside world. Switzerland is isolationist and neutral in international relations. Most unusually in the global system, for long it was not a member of the UN. A referendum on 3 March 2002 backed UN membership by 55 per cent to 45 per cent and by 12 to 11 cantons. Switzerland has kept clear of North Atlantic Treaty Organization (NATO) and the EU, and has rejected membership of the latter in referendums on several occasions, most recently in March 2001 (see Table 9.3). It is, however, a member of the European Free Trade Association (EFTA), along with Iceland, Liechtenstein and Norway. A referendum rejected membership of the European Economic Area (EEA) in 1992. Switzerland is a member of various functional organisations, such as the International Criminal Police Organisation (ICPO/Interpol), and the International Telcommunications Satellite Organisation (INTELSAT).

There are a very large number of foreign workers (19 per cent in 1996), but a referendum proposing a restriction to 18 per cent was defeated in September 2000. The Swiss Democrats (1991) (see Table 9.1) and the Swiss People's Party are anti-EU, anti-immigrant parties. The latter was founded in 1971 and by the federal election in October 1999 had secured more votes than any other party, although the electoral system put it second in terms of seats.

Citizenship is almost impossible to obtain unless Swiss ancestry can be proved. This makes Switzerland along with Germany the most restrictive nation in Europe as far as naturalisation is concerned, although both are gradually becoming more liberal.[3] Referendums in 1994 and 2000 rejected relaxing restrictions on foreign ownership of property in Switzerland. At the same time, Switzerland has historically been a temporary refuge for exiles from other countries, although its borders were not entirely open for Jews fleeing Nazi Germany.

Despite not being a member of the UN at the time, Switzerland was the HQ of several UN agencies, including the UN Conference on Trade and Development (UNCTAD), the UN Institute for Training and Research (UNITAR), the UN Office of High Commissioner for Refugees (UNHCR), the UN Research Institute for Social Development (UNRISD), the Economic Commission for Europe (ECE), the International Labour Organisation (ILO), the International Telecommunication Union (ITU), the Universal Postal Union (Berne), the World Health Organisation (WHO), the World Intellectual Property Organisation (WIPO), the World Meteorological Organisation (WMO) and the World Trade Organisation (WTO). Geneva is also the HQ of the International Red Cross and Red Crescent Movement (1863). From 1920 to 1946 Geneva was the HQ of the League of Nations.

This anomaly is explicable when it is considered that neutrality is desirable for UN members whose jealousies often make it difficult to place UN agencies in a member state. Switzerland for its part welcomes the revenue which UN and other international spending produces within its borders.

The reasons for Switzerland's existence in the European state system are complex and relate to the balance of power between states which prevented any one of them annexing Swiss territory. The main threat came from the Hapsburgs of Austria. Dating from 1291, the Swiss Confederation was a kind of state which had no parallel in the rest of Europe. It had virtually no central government as understood elsewhere, and was instead a league of 'cantons' whose ethnic, religious and linguistic character was (and is) highly diverse. After a civil war in the mid-nineteenth century concerning the rights of Catholics, these were protected and more powers were given to the central government in 1848 and 1874, but even today it is difficult to compare the government of Switzerland with that in other states. There is no monarchy, elected president or Cabinet Government as understood in the rest of Europe, and an extensive use of the referendum to initiate and ratify policies.

Today, Switzerland is linguistically divided into German-speakers (64 per cent), French-speakers (19 per cent), Italians (8 per cent) and Romansch, a descendant of Roman (under 1 per cent). The last are in the southeast, within the canton of Grisons/Graubünden/Grischun (the three languages are French, German and Romansch).

In religion, Switzerland is divided into Roman Catholics (46 per cent) and Protestants (40 per cent). This division crosscuts with language, although the Calvinists have been based in Geneva/*Genève*, a French-speaking canton. There is no state-established church.

There are 26 cantons (including six cantons with half-representation in the States Council), whose basis is mainly linguistic today. In 1979 a new canton of Jura was formed after a strong political agitation by French-speakers in the predominantly German-speaking canton of Bern. This was a rare example of a breakdown of ethnic harmony in a model 'consociational' system. This system is especially suited to societies which are ethnically divided, and which cannot accept majority rule. Thus Switzerland operates a decentralized federal system with a Council of States and National Council as the central legislature (National Assembly), and a Federal Council of seven as the Government. This is elected by the Assembly for a four-year term and the head of state holds office in rotation from the main coalition parties for one year only.

Switzerland is an official and social nation in the sense that it has its own citizenship, flag, national anthem and national identity. While speaking languages found in other nations, the Swiss have distinctive forms of these languages. Thus Swiss German is different from German in Austria and Germany. Swiss Protestantism is different from other Protestants, although similar to Calvinism in the Netherlands, Hungary and Scotland.

Constitution[4]

Preamble
In the name of God Almighty!
We the Swiss People and Cantons...

Article 1 (Swiss Confederation)
The Swiss People and the Cantons of... (26 cantons) form the Swiss Confederation.

Article 4 (National Languages)
The National Languages are German, French, Italian, and Romansch.

Article 18 (Freedom of Language)
The freedom of language is guaranteed.

Article 37 (Citizenship)
(1) Every person who has the citizenship of a Municipality and of the Canton to which it belongs, has Swiss citizenship.

Article 38 (Acquisition and Loss of Citizenship)
(1) The Confederation shall regulate the acquisition and the loss of citizenship through descent, marriage and adoption. Moreover, it shall regulate the loss of Swiss citizenship on other grounds, and the reinstatement of citizenship.
(2) It shall set minimum requirements for the naturalisation of foreigners by the Cantons and grant naturalisation permits.
(2) It shall facilitate the naturalisation of stateless children.

Article 40 (Swiss citizens domiciled abroad)
(1) The Confederation shall encourage links among Swiss citizens domiciled abroad, and their links with Switzerland. It may support organisations which pursue this goal.

Article 55 (Participation of the Cantons in Decisions of Foreign Policy)
(1) The Cantons shall participate in the preparation of decisions of foreign policy which concern their powers or their essential interests.
(3) The position of the Cantons shall have particular weights when their powers are concerned. In these cases, the Cantons shall participate in international negotiations as appropriate.

Article 56 (Relations between the Cantons and Foreign Countries)
(1) The Cantons may conclude treaties with foreign countries within the scope of their powers.

Article 62 (Education)
(1) Education is a cantonal matter [but professional and university education is for the Confederation}.

Article 70 (Languages)
(1) The official languages of the Confederation are German, French, and Italian. Romansch shall be an official language for communicating with persons of Romansch language.
(2) The Cantons shall designate their official languages. In order to preserve harmony between linguistic communities, they shall respect the traditional territorial distribution of languages, and take account of the indigenous linguistic minorities.
(5) The Confederation shall support the measures taken by the Cantons of Grisons and Ticino to maintain and to promote Romansch and Italian.

Article 72 (Church and State)
(1) The regulation of the relationship between church and state is a cantonal matter.
(2) The Confederation may…take measures to maintain public peace between members of the various religious communities.

Electoral nationalism

(1) Swiss Democrats/*Schweitzer Democraten (SD)*, *Démocrates Suisses (SD)*, *Democratici Svizzeri (DS)* (1961) National Council (200 members)
Won 1 seat in 1967 elections, 4 seats in 1971, 2 in 1979.

Table 9.1   Swiss Democrats and the elections

Year	% of vote	Seats
1983	3.5	4 (joint list with Swiss Republican movement)
1987	2.9	3
1991	3.4	5 (joint list with Ticino League[4]).
1995	3.1	3 (stood alone)
1999	1.8	1

(2) Swiss People's Party/*Schweizer Volkspartei (SVP)*, *Union Démocratique du Centre (UDC)*, *Unione Democratica di Centro (UDC)*, *Uniun Democratica dal Center (UDC)*(1971)
Campaigns against EU and EEA membership. Largest party in terms of votes in 1999, and second in seats.

Table 9.2   SVP/UDC and their election performance

Year	% of vote	Seats
1983	11.1	23
1987	11.0	25
1991	11.9	25
1995	14.9	29
1999	22.5	44

Table 9.3   Referendums on joining EU, EEA and UN

	% Yes	% No	Cantons (Yes)
1986 (UN)	24.3	75.7	0
1992 (EEA)	49.7	50.3	7/26
2001 (EU)	23.2	76.8	0
2002 (UN)	54.6	45.4	13/26

Table 9.4   Referendums on relaxing restrictions on foreign ownership of property and number of foreign workers to 18%

year	% Yes	% No	Cantons (Yes)
1994	46.4	53.6	6/26
2000	36.2	63.8	0

Conclusion

Switzerland is both one of the most nationalist states in Europe and one of the most internationalist. The paradox is difficult to explain except by reference to its peculiar history and geography. Threatened by Hapsburg overlords, in 1291 three Swiss cantons banded together to defend themselves, and were soon joined by other parts of the region. Later, Protestantism (Calvinism and Zwingliism) was a distinctive feature of the Swiss, although there were also Catholics, especially in areas such as the Jura. It was the Jura that was to prove troublesome to the confederation, and the rift between French and German speakers was serious for a while. It is still unresolved in the Jura region.

The geography of Switzerland also explains its independence. Landlocked and impenetrable except through high mountain passes, it was difficult to conquer and almost impossible to govern. It was also not very attractive as a possession, as its natural resources were limited to dairy products, forestry and clocks. It was useful in the European state system as it separated the Empires of France, Germany and Austria and made it difficult for them to use Swiss territory against each other.

Switzerland's nationalism is most clearly seen in its long-standing opposition to joining the EU and, until recently, the UN. It has also expressed opposition to foreign ownership of Swiss property, to foreign workers and to liberal citizenship laws. But this nationalism is of the multicultural, consociational variety, decentralised to the level of the cantons with their own languages and religions, and a very weak central government by the standards of other European states.

Its internationalism is well known, from the establishment of the Red Cross in Geneva in 1864, to the plethora of international bodies located in Switzerland today. The signs are that Switzerland is moving away from isolationism, with membership of the UN, but not the EU. Like the Scandinavians, the Swiss are non-imperial nations, and do not seek an aggressive world role. This gives them an advantage over the nations in Europe whose nationalism is confused by their imperialism. No secessionists now trouble the Swiss state, and no former colonies rise up to seek their revenge, or to be unwelcome as immigrants. This does not make the Swiss particularly liberal, as their long-term opposition to votes for women shows (women received the vote for federal elections in 1971, and the first woman cabinet minister was appointed in 1984). But it does show a side to nationalism which is no threat to either citizens or foreigners.

10

'Mitteleuropa' (Austria/*Osterreich*, Hungary/*Magyarország*, the Czech Republic/*Česká Republika* and Slovakia/*Slovenská Republika*)

Historical context

Central Europe (or '*Mitteleuropa*' in German) was historically the domain of the Hapsburg Empire, which succumbed to the Allied victory and nationalism in 1918. At that point, Austrian imperialism was replaced by nation-states of a kind. Apart from the four states in this chapter, the Hapsburgs lost control of the south of Poland to the new nation-state of Poland, the north of Italy had already gone to Italy by 1866, and Slovenia, Croatia and Bosnia-Hercegovina formed part of the new Kingdom of the Serbs, Croats and Slovenes (from 1929, Yugoslavia). Hungary ruled the eastern Carpathian region, which went to Poland in 1918. Lwów was its centre (called by its German name, *Lemberg* by the Hapsburgs; *Lvov* by the Russians and *Lviv* by the Ukrainians).[1] This region was lost to the USSR in 1945, and became part of the independent Ukraine in 1991. These areas are dealt with separately in other chapters.

To reduce the complexity of this area to one chapter is of course to simplify, but they belong together because of their common experience of long-term Hapsburg rule. This legacy is still present today, as the Hapsburg lands differ in culture from those ruled by the Ottomans (Turks) and Romanovs (Russians). Although today they are based on the principle of nationhood, the imperial history is only too evident in the nations under scrutiny.

In the contemporary world, Austria is a small (8.1 million; 32 378 sq. miles/83 859 sq.km.) state. At its height (1911) Austria-Hungary[2] had

49.5 million people and 241 300 sq.miles/615 300 sq.km. This was a severe loss, of territory, population and prestige. It had one good side, however. It relieved Austria of governing a sprawling and rebellious collection of nations, of whom the Austrian Germans were but one, but not a majority in the Empire (10.6 million; the largest group were Slavs with 20.8 million).

Now Austria became a German nation-state, and according to the Austrian-born Hitler, Vienna was its national centre. He annexed Austria to Germany in 1938 (the *Anschluss*) on this basis. Today, Austrian nationalism is associated with the Austrian Freedom Party, described by many as 'Neo-Nazi'. The party has little in common with the original Nazis, although some members have expressed admiration for Hitler. It is essentially an anti-immigrant, anti-EU party, and so similar to other parties of that kind in Europe. It has an uneasy relationship with the Slovenian minority in the province of Carpathia, whose Governor is the former Freedom Party leader, Jörg Haider. Haider's Government has denied equal status for the Slovenian language, and has Germanised Slovenian place-names. Haider's electoral success (the Austrian Freedom Party came first in the 1999 Austrian elections, with 52 seats in the Austrian Parliament) caused a major incident in the EU, when member-states boycotted Austria for a while. This was lifted in September 2000, and the boycott did little for the democratic credentials of the EU as it appeared to deny Austrians the right to make their own decisions.

Hungary is a fairly small (10 million; 35.920 sq.miles/93 032 sq.km.) nation-state which in 1918 was reduced to a homogeneous nation (with the exception of small territorial minorities and a sizeable Roma (Gypsy) population with no territorial base). Three million ethnic Hungarians live outside Hungary, including 2.1 million[3] in Romania, but Hungary itself is 92 per cent Hungarian. Its nationalism today is latent electorally, but there is a general nostalgia for the 'Greater Hungary' before 1918, and sympathy for the many ethnic Hungarians who live in Romania and who suffered ethnic discrimination there.[4] This came to a head in the latter years of Ceauşescu's rule in Romania, when Transylvanians sparked the movement which toppled the communist regime (1989). Discrimination against ethnic Hungarians was prevalent in Romania, even after the transition to democracy. Hungary has been concerned about the plight of the Hungarians in Romania, and has passed a 'Law on Hungarians Living in Neighbouring Countries', which gives ethnic Hungarians in Romania special rights to employment and social security in Hungary. While this has sometimes been condemned in Romania, the governments of Hungary and Romania have signed agreements on the Hungarians in Romania in 1996 and 2001. These accept the special rights of ethnic Hungarians in Romania and Hungary, while binding Hungary to a policy of abstaining from nationalist and irredentist activity in Romania.

On the edge of the Vojvodina region in Serbia where some 457 000 ethnic Hungarians live, Belgrade engaged in the notorious siege and bombardment of Vukovar (1991), partly in Croatia. Vojvodina itself is an Autonomous Province of Serbia, like Kosovo, but unlike that troubled area, nothing has been heard of it in international affairs. Hungary today has an interest in this region, although talk of regaining it and other lost lands such as Slovakia and Transylvania is in the realm of wishful thinking, and not voiced officially. 60 per cent in a 1990s survey said that there were 'parts of neighbouring countries that really should belong to Hungary', but only 3 per cent agreed that 'When ethnic conflicts affect the rights of Hungarians living in neighbouring countries, our government should threaten military action if necessary.'[5]

The Czech Republic and Slovakia are among the most recent states in Europe, having begun in 1993, although this was the result of the break-up of Czechoslovakia, established in 1918. The latter was a combination of the ancient regions of Bohemia, Moravia, Slovakia, Ruthenia and part of Silesia, Each of these could be counted an ethnic nation, with varying degrees of national consciousness.[6] In particular, there is Moravian nationalist movement, which came to prominence in the first multi-party elections held in Czechoslovakia in 1990. There were some electoral successes, and nationalist demonstrations in the Moravian capital, Brno. The few Silesians in Moravia, joined these nationalists, while also linking up with their co-nationals in Poland. But the movement for independence died down on the independence of the Czech Republic, which showed more sensitivity to Moravia. Eventually Moravian nationalism switched to espousing regional representation in the EU, when the Czech Republic joined.[7] The Czech Republic (10.3 million; 30 450 sq.miles/78.866 sq.km.) is about 60 per cent of the area of the former Czechoslovakia, and two-thirds of its population (Slovakia: 5.4 million; 18 923 sq.miles/49.012 sq.km.).

The decision to split up was a voluntary one, unlike the imposed dismemberment of Austria and Hungary in 1918. The details of this episode are somewhat controversial, as no referendums were held to sanction the establishment of the Czech and Slovak states. Instead the decisions were taken at parliamentary and executive level, at the federal level in Prague, and at the republic levels at Prague and Bratislava. The strains between the Czechs and Slovaks had been evident for some time, and the establishment of a federal system in 1990 (the Czech and Slovak Federative Republic) was not sufficient to hold it together. The national differences between Czechs and Slovaks are complex, and some would say minimal. However, there are national features of a linguistic, ethnic and historic nature, which were compounded in modern times by economic and social differences. In particular, the Czechs were the wealthy partners, who espoused free enterprise solutions, while the Slovaks were relatively poor and more state-minded in economic terms. This difference, in the circumstances of the fall of communism in 1989, exposed the incompatibility between the two parts of the Czechoslovak state. Nevertheless, the relationship between them today is mainly friendly, although tensions remain over citizenship rights and the Roma minority who are now mainly stateless persons, and amount to around 800 000 in both parts of former Czechoslovakia. Considerable international pressure has been put on the Czech and Slovak states to ameliorate their position, and the most potent influence is that of the EU, to which both states are applicant members.

The Czech Republic is faced with demands from some German politicians[8] for compensation for the three million Sudeten Germans who were deprived of citizenship and property and expelled from Czechoslovakia in 1945 under the Beneš Decrees.[9] The small Hungarian minority was treated likewise. Due to boundary changes there are now many Hungarians in Slovakia: 650 000, or 10.5 per cent[10] of the population, and concentrated in certain areas where their percentage is much higher. These have to fight the fact that although minority rights are guaranteed in the Constitution, the official language of Slovakia is Slovak, and echoes of past Hungarian overlordship of Slovakia are not welcome. The Hungarian Coalition Party represents them in the Slovak Parliament, with 20 deputies and 11.2 per cent of the vote in the 2002 elections (somewhat higher than the percentage of Hungarians in the population!).

Constitutions

Austria

The Constitution of Austria does not define an Austrian citizen, but Austrian law lays down the rules for naturalisation, which are very restrictive and based on the right of descent (*ius sanguinis*). In this it resembles Germany and Switzerland. In the days of the Hapsburg Empire such a right would have maintained a multi-ethnic citizenship, but today it gives an effective monopoly to Germans. Others have to have 30 years' residency before they can claim automatic citizenship. After 10 years' residency an application can be made from those with a good knowledge of German. Refugees get an expedited treatment, for Austria is sympathetic to stateless persons and those driven out by the Nazis. Citizenship for foreigners who reside and invest at least $1 million is favoured, and for academics appointed to university chairs in Austria.

Hungary

Article 5 (State Goals)
The State of the Republic of Hungary shall defend ... the territorial integrity of the country, and its national borders as established in international treaties.

Article 6 (Peace)
(1) The Republic renounces war as a means of solving disputes between nations and shall refrain from the use of force and the threat thereof against the independence or territorial integrity of other states.

Article 68 (Minorities)
(1) The national and ethnic minorities living in the Republic of Hungary participate in the sovereign power of the people: they represent a constituent part of the State.
(2) The Republic of Hungary shall provide for the protection of national and ethnic minorities and ensure their collective participation in public affairs, the fostering of their cultures, the use of their native languages and the use of names in their native languages.
(3) The laws of the Republic of Hungary shall ensure representation for the national and ethnic minorities living within the country.
(4) National and ethnic minorities shall have the right to form local and national bodies for self-government.
(5) A majority of two-thirds of the votes of the Members of Parliament present is required to pass the law on the rights of national and ethnic minorities.

Article 69 (Citizenship)
(4) A majority of two-thirds of the votes of the Members of Parliament present is required to pass the law on citizenship.

Article 70 (Electoral Rights)
(1) All adult Hungarian citizens residing in the territory of the Republic of Hungary have the right to be elected and the right to vote in ... minority self-government elections ...

(2) Persons residing in the territory of the Republic of Hungary as immigrants who do not have Hungarian citizenship also have the right to vote in local government elections ... as well as the right to participate in local referenda and popular initiatives.

Article 70A (No Discrimination)
(1) ... without discrimination on the basis of race, colour ... language, religion ..., national or social origins ...

Citizenship law (1993)

Section 2 (2)
... a Hungarian citizen who is simultaneously also the citizen of another state shall be regarded as a Hungarian citizen for the purposes of the application of the Hungarian law.

Section 3 (1)
(1) The child of a Hungarian citizen shall become a Hungarian citizen at birth.
(2) The Hungarian citizenship of the child of a non-Hungarian parent shall derive with retroactive effect from the date of birth, if the other parent is a Hungarian citizen ...
(3) Until the contrary is proved, the following shall be regarded as Hungarian citizens:
(a) Children born in Hungary of stateless persons residing in Hungary;
(b) Children born of unknown parents and found in Hungary.

Acquisition of Hungarian Citizenship. Naturalisation

Section 4
[Conditions include 8 years' residence (shortened to 3 years if married to or adopted by a Hungarian citizen, or parent of a Hungarian citizen, or refugee), clean criminal record, assured livelihood and residence in Hungary, passing examination in basic constitutional studies in the Hungarian language, unless exempted.]

The Czech Republic

Preamble
We, the citizens of the Czech Republic in Bohemia, Moravia, and Silesia at the time of the renewal of an independent Czech state, being loyal to all good traditions of the ancient statehood of Czech Crown Lands[11] and the Czechoslovak State ...

Citizenship law (not in Constitution)

In 1969 Czech citizenship was introduced as a separate category from Czechoslovak citizenship. This was based on the principle of *ius soli*, essentially based on residence in the Czech part of the country. On the dissolution of Czechoslovakia in 1993, the question of Czech citizenship arose again, and new laws had already passed through the Czech Parliament in 1992 in anticipation of the split. Slovaks in the Czech Republic were not considered 'Czechs' unless they had *ius soli* and had to apply for Czech citizenship. Meanwhile, they were deprived of all civic rights, including voting and social security, and were subject to deportation. This was a more restrictive view of citizenship than that taken by Slovakia at the same time.

The other casualties of the new citizenship law were the Roma (Romanies/Gypsies) who suddenly became stateless persons, and equally deprived of rights and had nowhere else to go. While international pressure has led to amelioration of their position, this is still an unfortunate result of national self-determination in Czechoslovakia.

Slovakia

Preamble
We, the Slovak nation, mindful of the political and cultural heritage of our forebears, and of the centuries of experience from the struggle for national existence and our own statehood, in the sense of the spiritual heritage of Cyril and Methodiu and the historical legacy of the Great Moravian Empire, proceeding from the natural right of nations to self-determination, together with members of national minorities and ethnic groups living on the territory of the Slovak Republic...

Article 3
(1) The territory of the Slovak is united and indivisible
(2) The borders of the Slovak Republic can be changed only by a constitutional law.

Article 6
(1) Slovak is the state language on the territory of the Slovak Republic.
(2) The use of other languages in dealings with the authorities will be regulated by law.

Article 12 (Equality)
(2) ... regardless of race, colour of skin, language, creed and religion... affiliation to a nation or ethnic group... descent...

Part 4 The Rights of National Minorities and Ethnic Groups: Article 33
Membership of any national minority or ethnic group must not be to anyone's detriment.

Article 34

(1) The comprehensive development of citizens representing national minorities or ethnic groups in the Slovak Republic is guaranteed, particularly the right to develop their own culture, together with other members of the minority of ethnic group, the right to disseminate and receive information in their mother tongue, the right to associate in national minority associations, and the right to set up and maintain educational and cultural institutions. Details will be set up in a law.

(2) [Citizens belonging to national minorities or ethnic groups have, under conditions defined by law]

    (a) The right to education in their own language,

    (b) The right to use their language in dealings with the authorities,

    (c) The right to participate in the solution of affairs concerning national minorities and ethnic groups.

Electoral nationalism

Austria

Freedom Party of Austria/*Freiheitliche Partei Österreichs* (FPÖ)

The Freedom Party dates back to 1956 but came to prominence only in the 1983, when it won 12 seats and joined the coalition government (see Table 10.1). At this time the Austrian leadership of the party was moderate, but already the Carinthian section was campaigning against bilingual education (German/Slovene) in Carinthia. This led to Jörg Haider's rise to power as national leader in 1986, and the electoral rise of the party was rapid. Haider became governor of Carinthia in 1989 in a coalition with the Austrian People's Party, a well-established conservative, anti-EU party which had participated in most of Austria's coalition governments since the war.

After its success in the 1999 Austrian parliamentary elections, when it came second, seven members of the Freedom Party joined the coalition with the Conservatives (the People's Party/ÖVP). This gave rise to an unofficial boycott of Austria by the EU, and Haider withdrew from the leadership to Carinthia, where he remained Governor. In September 2002, the Freedom Party coalition ministers withdrew, after Haider and other hardliners complained about their moderate policies in government. As the main anti-immigrant, anti-EU, pro-Austrian German party, the Freedom Party today represents Austrian nationalism in its most traditional and extreme form, although its support has been badly hit by its internal squabbles and erratic actions in power.

Table 10.1   Austrian Parliament: Bundesrat (183 members)

	% of vote	Seats
1986	9.7	–
1990	16.6	–
1994	22.6	42
1995	21.9	40
1999	26.9	52 (same as Austrian People's Party)
2002	10.2	19
European Parliament: direct elections (21 MEPs)		
1996	27.5	6
1999	23.5	5

Hungary

No obvious nationalist party, but various Roma parties and groups formed the Hungarian Romany Alliance in 2001 to contest the 2002 parliamentary elections. In view of the fact that few Romanies have the vote, this was a symbolic move.

Czech Republic

The nearest to a nationalist is the Republican Movement/*Republikáni Miroslava Sládka (RMS)*, the successor to the bankrupt Association for the Republic-Czechoslovak Republic Party (SPR-RSČ). The RMS rejects Sudeten German claims for restitution, but is paradoxically also anti-Semitic. It seeks measures against 'unadaptable' minorities such as the Roma, even to the length of building a wall around them. However, its electoral success is minimal with 3.9 per cent of the vote in the Chamber of Deputies election in 1998, and no seats. There are also two Romany organisations (Romany National Congress and Romany Civic Initiative).

It should be remembered that the parties which engineered the break-up of Czechoslovakia in 1992 could be considered nationalists. These were the Civic Democratic Party/*Občanská Demokratická Strana (ODS)* and the Christian Democratic Union-Czechoslovak People's Party/ *Křestánskodemokratická Unie-Československá Strana Lidová (KDU-ČSL)*.

Moravian nationalism (the Moravian National Party/*MNS*, since 1997 merged with the Bohemian-Moravian Centre Union/*ČMUS*) to form the Moravian Democratic Party) won some electoral successes in 1990, and linked up with Silesian nationalists in Moravian and Poland, but it is no longer a significant electoral force.

Slovakia

Slovak National Party/*Slovenská Národná Strana (SNS)*

Dating back to 1871, and hence one of the oldest nationalist parties in Europe, the SNS was launched in 1989 in its present form. It was quickly bound up with the move to make Slovakia an independent state, with the concomitant cultural nationalism of making the Slovak language the exclusive official language, with schools teaching in Slovak even where there are Hungarian majorities. It attacked the 1995 Slovak–Hungarian friendship treaty and supported constitutional amendments to make the learning of Slovak a civic duty for all citizens. In 2001 it advocated 'reservations' for 'unadaptable' Romas, who would have to undergo education to become good citizens. In 2002, it won only 3.3 per cent of the vote, and no seats (see Table 10.2).

Table 10.2 Slovak Parliament (National Council) (150 members)

Year	% of vote	Seats
1992	7.9	9 (joined in coalition with HZDS, but resigned a year later)
1994	5.4	9 (joined coalition again)
1998	9.1	14 (went into opposition)
2002	3.3	–

Movement for a Democratic Slovakia/Hnutie za Demokratické Slovensko (HZDS)

The main nationalist party in Slovakia, led by Chairman Vladimír Mečiar, was established in 1991 issued a nationalist appeal, 'For a Democratic Slovakia'. By late 1992 it was demanding an independent Slovakia, after the Czech government made apparently unacceptable conditions for continuing the federation. It led the government from

1992 (with a short break in 1994) to 1998 as shown in Table 10.3. By 2000 it was sounding less nationalist, and supported Slovakia's candidature for membership of the EU, but dipped in support in 2002 to 19.5 per cent of the vote and 36 out of 150 seats in the National Council elections.

Table 10.3   National Council elections (150 members)

Year	% of vote	Seats
1994	34.9	61
1998	27.0	43
2002	19.5	36

Presidential elections (candidate: Vladimír Mečiar)
1999 (2nd round) 42.8 per cent (defeated)

Party of the Hungarian Coalition/Strana mad'arskej koalície/Magyar Koalício Pártja (SMK) (1998) (a combination of three ethnic Hungarian parties)

Table 10.4   National Council elections

Year	% of vote	Seats
1998	9.1	15
2002	11.2	20

Conclusion

Nationalism gave rise to the states of the former Austrian Empire, and today nationalism is still very much alive, but in a different form. Most of the nation-states of Europe are satisfied with their post-imperial existence, and look forward to joining the EU. Their national aspirations relate to the loss of national territory and concern about the existence of minorities and immigrants within their borders. But moderation and prudence prevail, and only Austria and Slovakia appear to have crossed the boundary between acceptable and unacceptable nationalism by today's standards.

Even so, the extreme nationalists of today are not nearly as nationalist as their pre-war counterparts, who were often racists along the lines of the Nazi Party in Germany and Mussolini's Fascist Party, and sought dictatorship rather than democracy. Without exception, today's extreme nationalists are democrats and many accept that the EU is the way ahead for their nations. Their anti-immigrant stance is echoed in every country in Europe, and Euroscepticism is also widespread in every member-state.

The boundaries of the state system of Europe as now constituted are not challenged by any government or party in the area of the former Hapsburg Empire, unlike in the period up to 1945. Imperialism is dead, and nationalism is the norm. But it is a satisfied nationalism, and compatible with supranationalism, up to a point. War on grounds of nationalism in Europe, as in the two World Wars of the twentieth century, is effectively ruled out.

11
The Balkans[1]

Historical context

(Former) Yugoslavia

The history of the Balkans is one of mind-boggling complexity, and has been described in innumerable books, articles and broadcasts. Here, only a brief summary is given, with the intention of moving swiftly to the two main focuses of this book, the contemporary constitutional context and recent electoral nationalism.

In one interpretation, the nationalism of the Balkans today is but a continuation of centuries of ethnic struggle, coming to a height in the 1990s. In another interpretation, what we see today is a novel working out of changes peculiar to the late twentieth and early twenty-first centuries, with external international factors as important as internal 'ethnic' factors.[2] Another possible interpretation relates to mass psychology, which combines biological and contextual explanations. In the case of Yugoslavia, this is presented by a Serb psychiatrist now based in Australia, Dusan Kecmanovic.[3] While these interpretations are all valid, up to a point, here the discussion is limited to the most immediate manifestations of nationalist behaviour in the post-war (i.e. from the late 1990s) Balkans.

The break-up of Empire is the first clue to nationalism in the Balkans (known before 1914 as the 'Balkan Question'). First, it was the gradual erosion of the Turkish (Ottoman) Empire from 1878 to its final collapse in 1918, which gave rise to nation-states in the region. Then it was the end of the Austrian (Hapsburg) Empire in 1918, which saw the rest of the region organised on national grounds. Last, the collapse of Soviet communism from 1989 shook up the state system to such an extent that Yugoslavia and Albania collapsed as communist systems, even if they were not within the Soviet bloc. Within that bloc, nationalism was released in Bulgaria and Romania, with effects on Greece, Turkey and Hungary. Only Yugoslavia, however, disintegrated as a state to the extent that most of its constituent parts seceded. All that remained after 1992 was the new Federal Republic of Yugoslavia, consisting of Serbia and Montenegro, two states dating back to at least the nineteenth century, but with an ancient pedigree (Serbia and Montenegro were recognised as fully independent of Turkey in 1878).

The reason for the disintegration of Yugoslavia is not far to find. At the centre of Yugoslavia was a latent imperialism, that of 'Greater Serbia'. This had aspirations to control all the other nations making up the federation, but had been kept under control by the Croat dictator of Yugoslavia, Josep Broz-Tito ('Tito') (1892–1980). He also repressed Croat nationalism, which had some aspirations for a 'Greater Croatia', combining Croats in neighbouring Bosnia-Hercegovina with Croatia.

When the Serb leader, Milošević, refused to reconstruct the political and economic system of the federation along the lines desired by Slovenia and Croatia in the early 1990s, the only alternative for these complainants was secession. Milošević resisted further decentralisation on the grounds that it was retrogressive. His 'modernising' programme was rational in view of the extremely fragmented nature of the Yugoslav federation, but it failed to correspond to the realities of the 1990s. He resisted the nationalisms of nations other than the Serb, and he attempted to keep the Yugoslav Communist Party in power when all over Europe communism was collapsing. So he was doomed to failure. He was not at first a Serb nationalist, but on a visit to Kosovo/*Kosova* in 1989, commemorating the infamous Battle of Kosovo (1389), when the Serbs were defeated by the Turks, he was subjected to Serb claims there that they suffered persecution by the Moslem Kosovans. He promised to put a stop to that, and removed Kosovo's autonomy.

This triggered a Civil War and 'ethnic cleansing' in the interests of ethnic Serbs in Croatia, Bosnia-Hercegovina[4] (hereinafter, 'B-H') and Kosovo. Milošević's actions sent danger signals to all the non-Serb nations of the federation that constitutional guarantees could easily be revoked by Serbia. That proved to be the case when Milošević and his supporters ignored the Constitution with regard to the Presidency of the federation and installed their own puppet as President. Attempts to save the federation failed when Slovenia and Croatia declared their independence (25 June 1991).

In a year or so, all the republics except Serbia and Montenegro had left Yugoslavia for good. Serbia, with almost 10 million people out of the total of 10.6 million dominates the Federation. This figure includes Kosovo (2 million) and Vojvodina (2.2 million), the former around 90 per cent ethnic Albanian, and the latter containing 457000 Hungarians. Kosovo's Assembly was suspended by Serbia in 1990, along with that of Vojvodina, but Kosovo's Assembly was re-established in 2001 (see Table 11.4). Voyvodina remains without devolution, but ethnic Hungarians are guaranteed seats in the Federal and Serbian legislatures. Serbia has its own President and National Assembly and provides 108 out of the 138 members of the Federal Assembly.

Montenegro is an ancient kingdom, with independence from the fourteenth century. It later succumbed to the Turks, but was granted independence by international treaty in 1878, along with Serbia. It joined the Kingdom of the Serbs, Croats and Slovenes (later Yugoslavia) in 1918, and stayed with Yugoslavia in 1991–92 when the other components seceded. Since then, Montenegro has been split between separatists and federalists, with the former gaining control in 2001. Five seats out of the 77 members of the Montenegrin Assembly are reserved for ethnic minorities (mainly Albanians). Serbs and Montenegrins are usually described as in the same ethnic group, but Montenegrins consider themselves a nation. Since the separatists have gained control, 'Serbs' and 'Montenegrins' tend to mean federalists and separatists respectively. The process of separation from Yugoslavia is on going, but Serbia after Milošević is much more accommodating to Montenegrin nationalism, and there is a possibility that federation will survive the advent of liberal democracy in Yugoslavia.

The sudden collapse of the old Yugoslavia has been attributed to the triumph of nationalism over federation, but it was not quite as simple as that. Communism collapsed in Slovenia and Croatia, and the Yugoslav state could not reform itself in time to survive as a capitalist, democratic state. Nationalism was the only alternative to communism in these circumstances.

Only Slovenia is an almost homogeneous nation-state, although its tiny (0.5 per cent) Hungarian and Italian minorities are today protected in the Slovenian Constitution (see below). There are extreme nationalists in Slovenia, but they are weakly represented in the Slovenian Parliament (see below). Slovenia was the first republic to leave Yugoslavia, and it was the most prosperous. Its orientation is European, not Balkan, a legacy of its Hapsburg heritage. On 23 March 2003, in a referendum on joining the European Union (EU), 89.6 per cent voted Yes and 10.4 per cent voted No.

Croatia followed Slovenia to independence. But unlike the homogeneous Slovene nation-state, Croatia was only 78 per cent Croat, with 12 per cent Serb on independence. Croatia followed a nationalist line in its first post-communist Constitution in December 1990. This was strengthened when Croatia went independent in May 1991. Croatia adopted a Constitution, which made Croatian with the Latin script official, and offered citizenship to all ethnic Croats in other states. In the April/May 1990 democratic elections a nationalist (Christian Democratic Union/*HDZ*) President, Franjo Tudjman, was elected. Croatia's ethnic Serb minority rejected independence and fought against the government with the aid of the Yugoslav Federal Army and ethnic Serb troops. In January 1992 a ceasefire was declared, but by this time the Serbs were in control of the ethnically Serb areas, which they declared the Republic of Serbian Croatia. In 1993, The Croatian Government fought back, with the aid of the UN and the US, and by May 1995 had recovered the lost territories. About 150 000 Croatian Serbs fled, with another 95 000 later in the decade when all Serb-controlled areas were reintegrated into Croatia.

In a sense, Croatia had invited Serb retaliation for it had engaged in discrimination against the Serb language, the Cyrillic script and Serb nationality generally, despite its liberal-style Constitution. This Constitution, however, was based on the dominance of Croat ethnic nationalism, and the Serbs were well aware of that, despite Constitutional guarantees (see Constitutions, below). In line with this, Tudjman followed a 'Greater Croatia' policy, with the aim of annexing the Croat-inhabited parts of Bosnia-Hercegovina, and he tried to secure a deal with Milošević to that end, with Serbia taking the rest. International opinion would have none of it, however, and the Dayton Peace treaty of December 1995 settled instead for a division of B-H into the Bosniac-Croat Federation and the Serb Republic (see Constitutions, below). The death of Tudjman in December 1999 led to a moderation of Croatian nationalism when the opposition coalition of the Social Democratic Party of Croatia and the Croatian Social Liberal Party won a victory (3 January 2000) with 68 out of 151 seats in the Chamber of Representatives to become the largest bloc. Croatia's sights are now set on joining the EU, and for that a moderate nationalism is required.

B-H has no national majority at all, being split almost equally into Muslims, now called Bosniacs (44 per cent), Serbs (31 per cent) and Croats (17 per cent). Only the first had a principal loyalty to the new Bosnian state, with the others looking to Serbia and Croatia respectively as their 'nations'. As it turned out, no nation-state was possible in Bosnia, and an effective partition along national lines took place, after UN-intervention and American pressure. This might be considered a 'national' solution of a kind, but it only made sense if the constitution was consociational, as in Switzerland and Belgium. The conditions for such a system were not present, however.

Serbia was in the most unfortunate position from the nationalist point of view. Its 'Greater Serbia' aim was understandable if the ideal is a nation-state, but that meant uniting with Serbs in Croatia and Bosnia in particular, where approximately 1.8 million Serbs lived. Serbia itself, with 9.3 million people, was only 66 per cent Serb, and in Kosovo (part of Serbia, although autonomous) the ethnic Albanians are 90 per cent (*c.* 2 million) of the total. In Vojvodina, there is a Hungarian minority of 350000 people. In this situation, the nationalism of Serbia is almost impossible to satisfy without a complete shake-up of the geopolitical structure or a considerable ethnic migration.

Nationalism in the contemporary politics of the former and present-day Yugoslavia is different from what it was in the 1990s. The militant leaders in Serbia are out of office, with the leader Slobodan Milošević on trial in The Hague for War Crimes. Yugoslavia is ruled by the Democratic Opposition of Serbia under President Vojislav Koštunica, an opponent of Milošević. His policy is one of accommodation with international opinion, and moderation on national questions. Nevertheless, he opposes the Kosovan desire for independence, and so to that extent may be considered a Greater Serbian nationalist.

B-H remains a constitutional curiosity, with effective partition between Muslims (Bosniacs) and Croats on the one hand (51 per cent of the territory but 61 per cent of the population in 1991, including all of the multinational Sarajevo) and Serbs on the other (49 per cent of territory and 33 per cent of the 1991 population) in the *Republika Srpska*. This was obviously weighted against the Serbs, who had previously occupied much more (70 per cent) of the territory.

A curious overall government was installed, with three Heads of State, and a divided Parliament with two chambers The House of Peoples has 10 members from the Bosniac-Croat Federation and five from the Bosnian Serb Republic. The 42-member House of Representatives is similarly split on national grounds, and the two territories (Bosniac-Croat and Serb) each have their own parliaments. This effectively divides the Croats and Muslims from the Serbs, and is the result of the American-brokered Dayton peace agreement of December 1995, involving Serbia as well as the representatives of B-H. This is a kind of consociationalism with a very weak central government (analogies are sometimes drawn with Switzerland) and may be the only practical solution in the short term. It is certainly not a classic nationalist or consociational solution, and probably would not survive the withdrawal of the international military presence.

Kosovo (Albanian *Kosova*) (part of Serbia) is split between Serbs loyal to Belgrade, Albanians who seek the restitution of autonomy and Albanians who seek independence (a few want to join Albania). After the period of 'ethnic cleansing' imposed on Albanians by the Serbs, the reverse is now underway, with Kosovan Serbs on the retreat. As in Bosnia, international (UN) forces keep the peace, but internal changes have helped. Belgrade's change of regime in 2000 encouraged moderate Albanian nationalists in Kosovo, who are now in the ascendant. However, a contemporary democratic–nationalist solution to Kosovo would certainly be independence from Serbia. Historic Serb nationalism, however, sees Kosovo as the heartland of Serbia, with the battle of Kosovo (1389) similar in nationalist mythology to the Hungarian battle of Mohacs (1526), when the Turks beat the Magyars. The Turks have gone from Hungary, but their religious legacy lingers on in Serbia in the Kosovan Muslims.

Macedonia is the remaining breakaway republic of Yugoslavia, with a multinational population. Macedonians (66.5 per cent of the republic in 1997) are present in Greece too (around 100000, though Macedonian nationalists claim that there are over 1 million[5]), which has its own Macedonian districts. There are also Macedonians in Bulgaria (182000; nationalists claim 500000) and in adjoining areas of Yugoslavia and Albania. Greece tried to block Macedonian independence and used sanctions to stop it using the name Macedonia, hence the compromise for international purposes, 'Former Yugoslav Republic of Macedonia (FYROM)'. For internal use, however, including the Constitution, the title is 'The Republic of Macedonia'.

The main national trouble, however, has been between the 'Macedonian' Christian Slav majority and the ethnic Albanian Muslims (23 per cent). The Democratic Party of Albanians (DPA) withdrew its support from the ruling coalition in November 2000, and civil war broke out in February 2001. After that, splits between moderates and extremists took place in several parties when a new six-party coalition, which included the DPA, was formed in May 2001. Then North Atlantic Treaty Organization (NATO) sent in troops to oversee a ceasefire, and efforts to secure an accommodation between the nations and religious groups intensified. In short, the presence of ethnic Albanians outside Albania and Macedonians in both Greece and Macedonia has prevented a 'national' solution in this part of the Balkans. It might appear that Albania is the national (and natural) home for 'Albanians' and Greece the national home for 'Greeks', but such an idea is simplistic. National loyalties are only one of the loyalties involved (others are religion, language and political ideology). Nevertheless, the conflicts on national grounds in Kosovo and Macedonia will continue until a logical and acceptable conclusion is reached. At the start of the twenty-first century, this appears to be one based on national self-determination.

Albania/*Republika e Shqipërisë*

Albania was independent from 1912, when it broke away from Turkey. Unfortunately from the national point of view, Albanians are spread across several states with under half in Albania itself. There are 3.4 million people in Albania of whom 3 million (90 per cent) are ethnic Albanians. But there are 2.1 million Albanians in Serbia, mainly in Kosovo,[6] 460 000 in Macedonia, 75 000 in Turkey, 60 000 in Greece, 50 000 in Montenegro and 20 000 in Italy.[7]

Seventy per cent of Albanians are Muslims, but there are 20 per cent Greek Orthodox, and 10 per cent Roman Catholic. It will be seen that religion and ethnicity do not coincide entirely.

Albania's problem from a national point of view is to balance its national interest as a state with its ethnic nationalism. The confusion following the demise of Yugoslavia and the Kosovo crisis made Albania the recipient of numerous refugees fleeing the Serb terror. It was also bound up in Macedonian politics, where almost half a million Albanians resided. Albanian parties developed when democracy was introduced in 1991, and ethnic Albanian claims to a flag, education in Albanian and autonomy-complicated relationships with the ethnic Macedonians. But Albania itself was anxious to avoid entanglements in other states, especially when there was a mass exodus to Italy of its citizens in 1991. Then the government collapsed in 1997 over financial scandals, leading to renewed emigration. So holding Albania together took precedence over nationalist aims to unite all Albanians in a Greater Albania.

Greece/Hellenic Republic/*Elleniki Demokratia*

Greece gave rise to one of the earliest nationalist movements in the nineteenth-century Europe, with a 'War of Independence' against the Turks in 1821. After great power intervention in 1827, it gained independence in 1829. This did not satisfy Greek nationalism, however, as many Greeks still resided in the Ottoman (Turkish) Empire in Macedonia, Crete and other territories. After the Balkan Wars (1912–13), Greece recovered most of these areas. As we have seen, Greece today is in conflict with the FYROM, whose use of the name 'Macedonia' as an independent state is denied by Greece as a claim on its territory, as indeed it is by Macedonian nationalists. European Commission (EC) recognition was therefore denied until the compromise title of FYROM was adopted in 1993, and admission was gained to the UN. Nevertheless, the dispute between Macedonia and Greece continued, with the closure of the trade route from Macedonia to the port of Salonika. This was lifted after UN and US mediation in October 1994, when Macedonia modified its national flag and affirmed that it had no territorial claims on Greece. Greece said it would 'never recognise a state bearing the name of Macedonia or one of its derivatives', but for the moment the clumsy FYROM title seems to suffice. Nevertheless, this is often avoided outside Greece in favour of 'Republic of Macedonia/*Republika Makedonija*'.

The main national dispute today is with Turkey, especially with regard to Cyprus. Cyprus is divided between Greeks (588 000), who make up 85 per cent of the Republic of Cyprus (the southern state), and Turks, who are 12 per cent of the southern state, and monopolise the Turkish Republic of Northern Cyprus.[8] The division of Cyprus was the result of two developments: (1) the attempt in 1974 of the military regime in Greece to annex Cyprus to Greece and (2) the subsequent invasion of northern Cyprus by Turkey, leading to its occupation of one-third of the island. The result is that Cyprus consists of two states divided by a military boundary. Only Turkey recognises the Turkish Republic of Northern Cyprus. The Republic of Cyprus wishes to join the EU, but the division of the island is likely to make this difficult. Turkey is also a candidate, but its dispute with Greece over Cyprus is likely to result in Greece's veto on its membership, and its record on civil rights, especially with regard to its Kurdish minority is poor.

Bulgaria/*Republika Balgariya* and Turkey/*Türkiye Cumhuriyeti*[9]

These are coupled together because their nationalisms are intertwined. Bulgaria formed part of the Turkish (Ottoman) Empire, but its nationalism emerged early in the nineteenth century alongside that of Greece. It achieved autonomy under the Turks in 1878 as a result of international decisions at the Congress of Berlin. It declared independence in 1908, and fought in both Balkan Wars (1912–13) against Turkey. It was defeated in the second Balkan War (1913), and again in the First World

War, when it sided with Germany and Austria. This did not destroy its independence, however, as the Turkish Empire was dismantled in 1918, rather than restored. In 1941 it again sided with Germany, but was defeated and occupied by Russia, whose control through a client communist regime lasted until 1990. Since then, the main issue concerning nationalism has been the Turkish minority, amounting to around 900 000 or 9.4 per cent of the population in 1997. This divide is reinforced by religion (the Bulgarians are mostly Bulgarian Orthodox Christian) and language (the Bulgarian speak a Slavic tongue). Bulgaria is a Slavonic nation, while Turks speak Turkish, with four dialects present in 'Turkey-in-Europe', and among the ethnic Turks in other European countries.[10]

The Turkish population of Bulgaria has been subject to attack ever since the British Liberal leader Gladstone issued his famous pamphlet *The Bulgarian Horrors and the Question of the East* in 1876. In this he demanded that the Turks in Bulgaria should clear out 'bag and baggage' from 'the province they have desolated and profaned' (Bulgaria).[11] Turkey had massacred, raped and tortured thousands of Christians, after these had risen in rebellion. In return, the Great Powers intervened to give Bulgaria independence under the Treaty of Berlin (1878).

In modern times, Bulgaria expelled 250 000 'Muslims of Turkish origin' in 1950–51, when Turkey supported the UN in Korea. This was of course the result of Bulgaria being a communist country after 1944. Bulgaria tried to assimilate the Turks to Bulgarian culture and names, and agreed in 1968 to allow emigration of 100 000 Turks to Turkey. When this reached 310 000 by 1989, Bulgaria closed the border.

The advent of liberal democracy in January 1990 was accompanied by a proclamation that 'everybody in Bulgaria would be able to choose his name, religion, and language freely'. After that ethnic tension subsided.

Relations with Greece meanwhile were complicated when Bulgaria recognised the independence of Macedonia (FYROM) in 1992. Bulgaria considered that all Macedonians were ethnically Bulgarians, another curiosity of nationalism in this area. Greece appealed to its EC partners to limit or stop aid to Bulgaria, but the latter's admission to the Council of Europe (COE) indicated that most countries in the rest of Europe were friendly. Bulgaria deflected Turkish attempts to bring it in to an anti-Greek anti-Serb alliance. Once again, nationalism and internationalism interacted, with the attractions of EU membership limiting the ethnocentric behaviour, which might otherwise have prevailed. A Turkish Democratic Party (DKP) was formed in 1993, but was denied registration in 1996 on the grounds that the constitution forbad ethnic parties.

Nevertheless, the Internal Macedonian Revolutionary Organisation (VMRO), the Bulgarian branch of the Macedonian nationalist movement with the same name, represents people originating in the historic Macedonia. It won two seats in 1997, but failed to win any in 2001.

Romania/Rumania/*România*

Romania (population 22.5 million) originated in the union of the principalities of Wallachia and Moldavia in 1859 under a native Prince, subject to the sovereignty of the Turkish Empire. After allying with Russia against Turkey in the Russian–Turkish War (1877–78), the Treaty of Berlin recognised Romanian independence, with its Prince as King. Similarly, having joined the Allies against the Central Powers in 1916, Romania was rewarded with Bessarabia, Bukovina, Transylvania and Banat, a very mixed bag ethnically. The Second World War saw Romania on the Nazi side, and it was penalised at its end when Bessarabia, Bukovina, Banat and part of Transylvania were transferred to its neighbours, the USSR, Yugoslavia and Bulgaria. The main national problems today are the presence of Hungarians in Transylvania (7.1 per cent of the total population) and the anomalous position of Moldova, an ethnic Romanian state that is not part of Romania. Based on the historic province of Bessarabia, it became part of the Soviet Union in 1924, after a brief period of independence (1917–19), followed by annexation to Romania in 1919 under the Versailles Peace Treaty. This was reversed in 1940 when the Soviet Union formed the Moldavian Soviet Socialist Republic out of Bessarabia. Romania was affected by the collapse of the Soviet Union and the establishment of the independent state of Ukraine, for Moldova and Bessarabia straddle both these states.

The former Soviet Republic of Moldavia declared its independence in August 1991, and Romania has sought to unite with it. But Moldova is only 65 per cent ethnic Moldovan, with Ukrainians 14 per cent, Russians 13 per cent and three other ethnic minorities. At a referendum in 1994 Moldova rejected union with Romania, and its parliament voted to join the Commonwealth of Independent States (CIS), the successor to the USSR and dominated by Russia. Thus Moldova retains a precarious independence, sandwiched between Romania and Ukraine, with protection from Russia.

Meanwhile, part of Moldova declared its independence as the Transdniester Republic/Transnistria in December 1991, and rejected union with Romania in a referendum on 6 March 1994. The area consists largely of Russians and Ukrainians. Romania has refused to recognise this secession, and Russian and Organization for Security and

Co-operation in Europe (OSCE) intervention has led to a ceasefire and plans for autonomy. A referendum in Transdniester on 24 December 1995 voted by 81 per cent for independence, however, and Moldova granted the republic a 'state-territorial formation in the form of a republic within Moldova's internationally recognised border'. Moldova and Transnistria agreed to this in May 1997 but Russian troops remained in the breakaway province. A President was elected in December 1996, followed by a legislature in December 2000. This election consisted mainly of independent candidates, and in May 2001 there was an agreement between Romania and Transdnistra to coordinate taxes and remove customs barriers. In December 2001 the President was re-elected, who has proposed making the Russian language official and joining the Russian-Belarus Union.

The other issue of nationality concerns the 2.1 million[12] Hungarians living in Romania (mainly in Transylvania). Transferred thither in 1918 as a penalty on the war-loser Hungary, their position is of some concern to Hungary (see Chapter 10), since they have suffered at the hands of successive Romanian governments, whether monarchic or communist. These have followed the classic nationalist strategy of trying to assimilate minorities to the majority culture, in this case based on ethnicity, language and religion, a potent mixture. Even after 'democracy' was instituted in 1990, local governments in Transylvania proceeded to eliminate Hungarian road signs and to restrict 'anti-Romanian' public meetings. The central government appointed Romanian prefects in Hungarian areas, curbed Hungarian-language education, and made the display of the Hungarian flag or the singing of the Hungarian national anthem a criminal offence.

Some progress towards Romanian–Hungarian reconciliation was made in 1996, when Hungary renounced any territorial claims on Romania, and Romania guaranteed rights for Hungarians in Romania. This was denounced by nationalists in both states, but progress was made throughout the late 1990s, especially as both Hungary and Romania wished to join NATO (Hungary joined in 1999, and Romania is in the affiliated Euro-Atlantic Partnership Council (EAPC), established in 1997). So once again internationalism has modified nationalism.

Constitutions

All the countries in the region have liberal democratic constitutions, but only that of Greece dates further back than 1991 (to 1975). In this account, only the aspects relevant to nationalism and ethnicity are discussed.

The Federal Republic of Yugoslavia (1992, amended 2000)

Preamble

Mindful of the freedom loving, democratic and nation-building traditions, historical ties and shared interests of the state of Serbia and the state of Montenegro; arising from the unbroken community of Yugoslavia and voluntary association between Serbia and Montenegro...

Article 2

(1) The Federal Republic of Yugoslavia shall be composed of the Republic of Serbia and the Republic of Montenegro.

(2) The Federal Republic of Yugoslavia may be joined by other member republics...

Article 3

(3) The boundaries between member republics may be changed only subject to their agreement, in accordance with the constitutions of the member republics.

Article 4

(1) The Federal Republic of Yugoslavia shall have a flag, a national anthem, and a coat-of-arms.

Article 7

(1) Within its competencies, a member republic may maintain relations with foreign states, establish its own missions in other states, and join international organizations.

Article 11

The Federal Republic of Yugoslavia shall recognize and guarantee the rights of national minorities to preserve, foster and express their ethnic, cultural, linguistic and other peculiarities, as well as to use their national symbols, in accordance with international law.

Article 15

(1) In the Federal Republic of Yugoslavia, the Serbian language in its ekavian and ijekavian dialects and the Cyrillic script shall be official, while the Latin script shall be in official use as provided for by the Constitution and law.

(2) In regions of the Federal Republic of Yugoslavia inhabited by national minorities, the languages and scripts of these minorities shall also be in official use in the manner prescribed by law.

Article 17

(2) A Yugoslav citizen shall be simultaneously a citizen of one of the member republics.

(5) Yugoslav citizenship shall be regulated by law (see below).

Article 23

(3) Every person taken into custody must be informed immediately in his mother tongue or in a language which he understands of the reasons for his arrest...

Article 45

(1) Freedom of the expression of national sentiments and culture and the use of one's mother tongue and script shall be guaranteed.

(2) No one shall be obliged to declare his nationality.

Article 46

(1) Members of national minorities shall have the right to education in their own language, in conformity with the law.

(2) Members of national minorities shall have the right to information media in their own language.

Articles 47–49 [more rights for national minorities]

Article 50

Any incitement or encouragement of national, racial, religious or other inequality as well as the incitement and fomenting of national, racial, religious or other hatred and intolerance shall be unconstitutional and punishable.

Article 66

(3) The right of asylum shall be guaranteed to foreign citizens and stateless persons who are being persecuted... for participation in movements for... national liberation...

Citizenship

Yugoslavia (1997)

Yugoslav citizenship law today dates from 1997, and from January 1997 to November 2001 more than 176 000 individuals had acquired Yugoslav citizenship. At the same time, there were more than 400 000 refugees in Yugoslavia, nearly all ethnic Serbs (245 000 from Croatia, 143 500 from Bosnia). Serbia hosted 377 131 refugees and Montenegro 14 418.[13] Given that Yugoslavia did not recognise the break-up of the previous Federal Republic and considered all its inhabitants to be entitled to Yugoslav citizenship, there is a predisposition to let these citizens continue as such in the new Yugoslavia. Matters are not that simple, however, and less than half of the refugees from the old Yugoslavia have been granted citizenship.

Despite the fact that Yugoslavia is one state, Serbia and Montenegro operate separate citizenship laws, the former dating from 1979 and the latter from 1999. This is because of the curiosity that citizenship pertains to the constituent republics as well as to the federation (Article 17(2)). (The same provision is found in Switzerland, as we have seen, where there is dual federal and cantonal citizenship.) The effect of this is to introduce a host of anomalies, which are beyond the scope of this work, but can be followed in various publications and web sites on the subject.[14]

Slovenia (1991, amended 1997, 2000)

Article 3
Slovenia … is founded on the permanent and inalienable right of the Slovene nation to self-determination.

Article 5
… It shall protect and guarantee the rights of the autochthonous Italian and Hungarian national communities. It shall maintain concern for autochthonous Slovene national minorities in neighbouring countries and for Slovene emigrants and workers abroad and shall foster their contacts with the homeland …

Article 11
The official language in Slovenia is Slovene. In those municipalities where Italian or Hungarian national communities reside, Italian or Hungarian shall also be official languages.

Article 61 (Expression of National Affiliation)
Everyone has the right to freely express affiliation with his nation or national community, to foster and give expression to his culture and to use his language and script.

Article 62 (Right to Use One's Language and Script)
Everyone has the right to use his language and script in a manner provided by law in the exercise of his rights and duties and in procedures before state and other bodies performing a public function.

Article 64 (Special Rights of the Autochthonous Italian and Hungarian National Communities in Slovenia)
The autochthonous Italian and Hungarian national communities and their members shall be guaranteed the right to use their national symbols freely … to establish organisations … as well as activities in the field of public media and publishing … education and schooling in their own languages … The geographic areas in which bilingual schools are compulsory shall be established by law …

The two national communities shall be directly represented in representative bodies of local self-government and in the National Assembly ... The rights of both national communities and their members shall be guaranteed irrespective of the number of members of these communities ...

Article 65 (Status and Special Rights of the Romany Community in Slovenia)
The status and special rights of the Romany community living in Slovenia shall be regulated by law.

Organisation of the State (a) The National Assembly
Article 80 (Composition and Election)
... One deputy of the Italian and one deputy of the Hungarian national communities shall always be elected to the National Assembly.

Citizenship law

Unlike Yugoslavia, the new independent successor states are not keen to grant citizenship to former citizens of Yugoslavia who are from outside their borders. Nevertheless, Slovenia operated an open policy on obtaining citizenship until 25 December 1991, but after that was restrictive. Non-Slovene families were evicted in increasing numbers as the decade wore on, and 130 000 former residents (mostly Croats, Bosniacs and Serbs) were erased from the register of permanent residents due to their non-Slovene or mixed ethnic origin. About 90 000 left Slovenia and the remaining 40 000 were stateless persons, with no rights to state-run education and social security.[15] International pressure has been applied, particularly by the International Helsinki Federation for Human Rights (Vienna) and the EU is watchful of ethnic discrimination in applicant states. Nevertheless, Slovenia is a true nation-state, with 99 per cent of its population Slovene.

Croatia (1990 with amendments)

Chapter 1 (Historical Foundations): The millennial identity of the Croatian national and the continuity of its statehood, confirmed by the course of its entire historical experience ... [there follows a long historical account of Croatia of some controversy].

... the Republic of Croatia is hereby established as the national state of the Croatian people and a state of members of autochthonous national minorities: Serbs, Czechs, Slovaks, Italians, Hungarians, Germans, Austrians, Ukrainians and Ruthenians and others who are citizens, who are guaranteed equality with citizens of Croatian nationality and the realization of national rights in accordance with the democratic norms of the United Nations and countries of the free world.[16]

Article 10 (Citizens Abroad)
(1) The Republic of Croatia protects the rights and interests of its citizens living or staying abroad, and promotes their links with the homeland.
(2) Parts of the Croatian nation in other states shall be guaranteed special concern and protection by the Republic of Croatia.

Article 12 (State Language)
(1) The Croatian language and the Latin script shall be in official use in the Republic of Croatia.[17]
(2) In individual local units, another language and the Cyrillic or some other script may be introduced into official use along with the Croatian language and the Latin script under conditions specified by law.

Article 15 (Rights of Foreigners, Cultural Rights)
(1) Members of all nations and minorities have equal rights in the Republic of Croatia.
(2) Members of all nations and minorities are guaranteed freedom to express their nationality and use their language and script, and cultural autonomy.

Article 39 (Intolerance)
Any call for or incitement to war, or resort to violence, national, racial or religious hatred ... shall be prohibited and punishable by law.

Article 43 (Association)
(1) Everyone shall be guaranteed the right to free association for the purposes of protection of their interests or promotion of ... national, cultural ... convictions and objectives. For this purpose, citizens may freely form political parties, trade unions, and other associations ...
(2) The exercise of this right shall be restricted by the prohibition of any violent threat to the ... independence, unity and territorial integrity of the Republic.

Article 45 (Electoral Rights)
(2) In elections for the Croatian Parliament and the President of the Republic, the Republic ensures suffrage to all citizens who at the time of the elections find themselves outside its borders, so that they may vote in the states in which they find themselves or any other way specified by law.[18]

Citizenship law (1991–93)

Article 2
The citizen of the Republic of Croatia who is at the same time a foreign citizen, shall be, before the authorities of the Republic of Croatia, deemed to be exclusively a Croatian citizen.

Article 3
Croatian citizenship shall be acquired:
1. By origin [i.e. adopted];
2. By birth in the territory of the Republic of Croatia.

Article 8
A foreign citizen who files a petition for acquiring Croatian citizenship shall acquire Croatian citizenship by naturalisation if he or she meets the following prerequisites: five points are listed but only one [5. that a conclusion can be drawn from his or her conduct that he or she is attached to the legal system and customs persisting in the Republic of Croatia and that he or she accept the Croatian culture] applies to.

Article 16
A member of the Croatian people who does not have a place of residence in the Republic of Croatia can acquire Croatian citizenship if he or she meets the prerequisites from Article 8, paragraph 1, point 5 of this Law ... and issues a written statement that he or she considers himself or herself to be a Croatian citizen.

Bosnia-Hercegovina/Bosnia and Hercegovina (B-H/B and H) (1995)

Preamble
... Inspired by the ... Declaration on the Rights of Persons Belonging to National or Ethnic, Religious and Linguistic Minorities ... Recalling the Basic Principles agreed in Geneva on 8 September 1995, and in New York on 26 September 1995, Bosniacs, Croats, and Serbs, as constituent peoples (along with Others), and citizens of B and H hereby determine that the Constitution of Bosnia and Hercegovina is as follows

Article I (B and H)
Paragraph (Continuation)
The Republic of B and H, the official name of which shall henceforth be 'B and H', shall continue its legal existence under international law as a state, with its internal structure modified as provided herein and with its internationally recognized borders ...

Paragraph 3 (Composition)
B and H shall consist of two Entities, the Federation of B and H and the Republika Srpska (hereinafter 'the Entities').

Paragraph 7 (Citizenship)
There shall be a citizenship of B and H, to be regulated by the Parliamentary Assembly, and a citizenship of each Entity, to be regulated by each Entity, provided that:
(a) all citizens of either Entity are thereby citizens of B and H.

Article IV (Parliamentary Assembly)
Paragraph 1 (House of Peoples)
The House of Peoples shall compose 15 Delegates, two-thirds from the federation (including five Croats and five Bosniacs) and one-third from the Republika Srpska (five Serbs) ...

Article V (Presidency)
The Presidency of Bosnia and Hercegovina shall consist of three members: one Bosniac and one Croat, each directly elected from the territory of the Federation, and one Serb directly elected from the territory of the Republika Srpska.
[There follows a complex set of rules about the workings of the consociational system].

Citizenship law

Article I, Paragraph 7 instituted dual citizenship, with the Republic of B and H citizenship in practice weaker than that of the 'Entities'. Indeed, until late 2001, B-H citizenship procedures lacked a unified identification card, registration, and so on. International pressure led to these being introduced to bring B-H into line with international practice, but most citizens identify with the Entities rather than the Republic of B-H, since the former are ethnonational and exercise the powers of the police, and most revenue and expenditure powers.

Macedonia

Preamble
Taking as starting points the historical, cultural, spiritual and statehood heritage of the Macedonian people and their struggle over centuries for national and social freedom as well as the creation of their own state ... Macedonia is established as a national state of the Macedonian people, in which full equality as citizens and permanent co-existence with

the Macedonian people is provided for Albanians, Turks, Vlachs, Romanies and other nationalities living in the Republic of Macedonia.

Article 3

(4) The Republic of Macedonia has no territorial pretensions towards any neighbouring state.

Article 7

(1) The Macedonian language, written using its Cyrillic alphabet, is the official language of Macedonia.

(2) In the units of local self-government where the majority [(3) talks of 'a considerable number'] of the inhabitants belong to a nationality, in addition to the Macedonian language and Cyrillic alphabet, their language and alphabet are also in official use, in a manner determined by law.

Article 48

(1) Members of nationalities have a right freely to express, foster and develop their identity and national attributes.

(2) The Republic guarantees the protection of the ethnic, cultural, linguistic and religious identity of the nationalities.

(3) Members of the nationalities have the right to establish institutions for culture and art, as well as scholarly and other associations for the expression, fostering and development of their identity.

(4) Members of the nationalities have the right to instruction in their language in primary and secondary education, as determined by law. In schools where education is carried out in the language of a nationality, the Macedonian language is also studied.

Article 49

(1) The Republic cares for the status and rights of those persons belonging to the Macedonian people in neighbouring countries, as well as Macedonian expatriates, assists their cultural development and promotes links with them. In the exercise of this concern the Republic will not interfere in the sovereign rights of other states or in their internal affairs.

Article 78

(1) The Assembly establishes a Council for Inter-Ethnic Relations [the members are appointed on the Proposal of the President, Art. 84].

(2) The Council consists of the President of the Assembly and two members each from the ranks of the Macedonians, Albanians, Turks, Vlachs and Romanies, as well as two members from the ranks of

other nationalities in Macedonia [the Council makes proposals which the Assembly must consider].

Citizenship law

Macedonia operated a liberal Citizenship Law until 2003, under which citizens could also hold citizenship of another state.[19] This allowed Macedonians, Albanians, and so on who were citizens of other states to hold Macedonian citizenship simultaneously and to move freely to Macedonia. The result has been a large number of immigrants from Albania and Serbia, especially Kosovo, many of whom have gained Macedonian citizenship. From 2003, however, only one citizenship was generally allowed, although bilateral agreements have been made with Serbia and B-H (but not Albania) for reciprocal dual nationality. At the same time, the 15 years' residence qualification for Macedonian citizenship has been reduced to 10 years.

Albania (1991)

Article 4 (Human Rights, Minorities)
The Republic of Albania recognizes and guarantees the fundamental human rights and freedoms, those of national minorities, admitted in the international documents. [No other references are made to nations or national minorities.]

Citizenship law

Albania operates a 'dual nationality' system of citizenship, and supports the protection of ethnic Albanians outside its borders (of whom there are around 3 million, including over 2 million in Kosova and 460 000 in Macedonia). But it does not encourage them to apply for Albanian citizenship, and its prime aim in foreign policy is cooperation with other states in the region.

Greece (1975)

In the name of the Holy and Consubstantial and Indivisible Trinity, the Fifth Constitutional Assembly of Greece votes.
[There are no references to nations, nationalities or ethnic groups in the Constitution. According to the nationalist leaders of the 2 per cent of the population that is non-Greek (mainly Macedonians and Turks) this has allowed for a denial of their national rights and a policy of assimilation and discrimination. The Government does, however, recognise a

religious minority, the Muslims in Thrace as an ethnic minority, although 'Turks' as such are not recognised as citizens. Ethnic Turks (i.e. non-citizens) have the right to buy and sell houses, and to conduct certain businesses. No language other than Greek is officially recognised, and indeed the use of the Macedonian language and religion has been banned, and Macedonian place names have been changed.[20]]

Citizenship law

According to Macedonian nationalist leaders in Greece, Greece is using its Citizenship laws to pursue 'ethnic cleansing' of Macedonians in Greece. The offending article (Art. 20 of the Law on Citizenship of the Republic) that 'a Greek citizen who is abroad and works or is against the national interests of Greece' may lose his/her citizenship. This is used if Macedonians express their nationality by participating in Macedonian associations, especially in the US, Canada and Australia.

Bulgaria (1991)

Article 11 (Political Parties)
(4) There shall be no political parties on ethnic, racial, or religious lines ...

Chapter Two. Fundamental Rights and Obligations of Citizens: Article 25 (Citizenship)
(1) A Bulgarian citizen is anyone born of at least one parent holding a Bulgarian citizenship, or born on the territory of the Republic of Bulgaria, should he not be entitled to any other citizenship by virtue of origin. Bulgarian citizenship shall further be acquirable through naturalisation.
(2) A person of Bulgarian origin shall acquire Bulgarian citizenship through a facilitated procedure.

Article 36 (Language)
(1) The study and use of the Bulgarian language is a right and obligation of every Bulgarian citizen.
(2) Citizens whose mother tongue is not Bulgarian shall have the right to study and use their own language alongside the compulsory study of the Bulgarian language.
(3) The situations in which only the official language shall be used shall be established by law.

Article 44 (Association)
(2) No organization shall ... incite racial, national, ethnic or religious enmity ...

Article 54 (Culture, Creativity)
(1) Everyone shall have the right to ... develop his own culture in accordance with his ethnic self-identification, which shall be recognized and guaranteed by the law.

Chapter Three. National Assembly: Article 65 (Eligibility)
(1) Eligible for election to the National Assembly is any Bulgarian citizen who does not hold another citizenship ...
[Behind these legal provisions lies a strong Bulgarian ethnonationalism. No nations or ethnic groups are recognised or allowed to form parties, etc. Muslims and Turks in particular have little protection in Bulgaria, and Macedonians in Bulgaria complain that they are not recognised as a minority nationality with rights. There are religious divisions interacting with national ones here, and a history of conflict with Turkey, Greece and Macedonia. Pressures from international organisations such as the Council of Europe, the EU, Human Rights Watch and Amnesty International are likely to modify old attitudes.]

Romania (1991)

Article 1 (State Principles)
(1) Romania is an ... indivisible Nation State.

Article 3 (Territory)
(1) The territory of Romania is inalienable.
(2) The frontiers of the Country are sanctioned by an organic law ...
(4) No foreign populations may be displaced or colonized in the territory of the Romanian State.

Article 13 (Language)
In Romania, the official language is Romanian.

Article 30 (Expression)
(7) Any defamation of the country and the nation, and instigation to ... national, racial, class or religious hatred, any incitement to discrimination, territorial separatism ... shall be prohibited by law.[21]

Article 32 (Education)
(2) Education of all grades shall be in Romanian. Education may also be conducted in a foreign language of international use, under the terms laid down by law.
(3) The right of persons belonging to national minorities to learn their mother tongue, and their right to be educated in this language are guaranteed; the ways to exercise these rights shall be regulated by law.[22]

(7) The State shall ensure the freedom of religious education, in accordance with the specific requirements of each religious cult. In public schools, religious education is organised and guaranteed by law.

Article 37 (Association, Political Parties, Unions)
(2) Any political parties or organisations which, by their aims or activity, militate against ... the sovereignty, integrity or independence of Romania shall be unconstitutional.

Article 127 (Language in Courts)
(1) Procedure shall be conducted in Romanian.
(2) Citizens belonging to national minorities, as well as persons who cannot understand or speak Romanian, have the right to take cognisance ... through an interpreter ...

Article 59 (Election, National Minorities)
(2) Organisations of citizens belonging to national minorities, which fail to obtain the number of votes for representation in Parliament, have the right to one Deputy seat each, under the terms of the electoral law.[23] Citizens of a national minority are entitled to be represented by one organisation only.

Electoral nationalism

Serbia

Principal parties: Socialist Party of Serbia/Socijalistička Partija Srbije (SPS) *(1990)*

The successor to the League of Communists of Yugoslavia, and chaired by Milošević until put on trial in the Hague for War Crimes in June 2001, this is considered a Serb nationalist party on account of its actions on behalf of Serbs in Yugoslavia generally, although it is a socialist (communist) party. It fell from power in 2000, when Milošević won around 37 per cent of the vote in the federal Presidential election, and in federal parliamentary elections at the same time the SPS/Yugoslav United Left (JUL) alliance won only 44 seats out of 138, with 14 per cent of the vote.

Democratic Party/Demokratska Stranka (DS) *(1990)*

A nationalist party, advocating intervention in support of Serb nationalists in B-H. Later, apparently turned against nationalism when it opposed Miloševi´c, and joined the Democratic Opposition of Serbia in

2000. Its leader, Ziran Djindi´c, became Prime Minster of Serbia in
January 2001.

*Democratic Party of Serbia/*Demokratska Stranka Srbije (DSS) *(1992)*

Originally nationalist, it moved away from Milošević in 1997, and
joined the Opposition Government in 2000, but withdrew in 2001. Led
by Vojislav Koštunica, it opposes sending Serbs to the War Crimes
Tribunal.

Table 11.1   The Federal Republic of Yugoslavia

	% of vote	Seats
President (elected 24 September 2000)		
Vojislav Koštunica (Democratic Party of Serbia)	50.2	
Slobodan Milošević (Socialist Party of Serbia)	37.2	
Tomislav Nikolic (Serbian Radical Party)	5.9	
Vojislav Mihajiloviá (Serbian Renewal Movement)	3.0	
Federal Assembly: Chamber of Citizens (138 Members: 108 from Serbia and 30 from Montenegro) (elected 24 September 2000):		
Serbia		
Democratic Opposition of Serbia (DOS)[24]	43.9	58
Serb Socialist Party/Yugoslav United Left	32.9	44
Serb Radical Party (nationalist)	8.7	5
Socialist Party of Montenegro	2.2	28
Serb Renewal Movement	2.2	–
Serbian Peoople's Party of Montenegro	–	2
Union of Vojvodina's Hungarians	–	1
Montenegro		
Socialist People's Party of Montenegro	–	19
Democratic Serb Opposition	–	10
Socialist Party of Serbia/Yugoslav United Left	–	7
Serbian Radical Party	–	2
Serbian People's Party of Montenegro	–	1
Serbian Renewal Movement	–	1
Democratic Party of Socialists of Montenegro	–	boycott

*Serbian Radical Party/*Srpska Radikalna Stranka (SRS) *(1991)*

Advocates the creation of a Greater Serbia. After a strong start electorally,
it fell from 34 seats in the federal lower house in 1992 to 16 in 1996.
In the Serbian lower house it fared better, with 29.3 per cent of
the vote and 82 seats out of 250 in 1998, but after Milošević's fall, it got
only 8.5 per cent of the vote and 23 seats in December 2000.

Serbian Renewal Movement/Srpski Pokret Obnove (SPO) *(1990)*

A moderate nationalist party under the chairmanship of Vuk Drašković, in opposition to Milošević, it won 15.4 per cent of the vote in the first round of the 1997 Presidential elections, coming third. In the Serbian Parliamentary elections it won 45 seats with 20 per cent of the vote. At the election in September 2000, when Milošević fell from power, the SPO presidential candidate got only 3 per cent of the vote, and was reduced to 4 per cent of the vote in the Serbian Assembly, winning no seats.

National minority parties

These include the Party of Democratic Action/*Partija Demokratske Akcije* *(PDA)*, representing Muslims. It won three seats in the Serbian Assembly in 1997, one federal lower house seat in 1996, and three seats in the Montenegrin Assembly in the same year. Its leader, Rasim Ljajić, became Minister for National and Ethnic Communities in the federal government of 2000. The party is also represented in, Kosovo and other Yugoslav regions.

Union of Vojvodina's Hungarians/Savez Vojvodjanskih Madjara (SVM)/Vajdasági Magyar Szövetsége (VMSz) *(1994)*

Campaigns for the restoration of Vojvodina's autonomy, which had been abolished by Miloševi'c, it was one of several Hungarian parties operating in the region. It won four seats in the Serbian Assembly in 1997 and 2000, and one federal lower house seat in the latter year. Its leader, Jozef Kasza, was appointed a Deputy Prime Minister in the DOS Government of Serbia, and another Hungarian became Minister of Agriculture.

Table 11.2   President

Year	President
1989–97	Slobodan Milošević (Socialist Party of Serbia (SPS): communist).
1997	Milan Milutinović (ex-SPS)

Table 11.3   Serbian National Assembly (250 members): 2000 election

	% of vote	Seats
Democratic Opposition of Serbia (18 parties)[25]	63.9	176
Socialist Party of Serbia	13.5	37
Serb Radical Party (nationalist)	8.6	23
Serb Unity Party (nationalist)	5.3	14
Serb Renewal Movement	3.7	–
Yugoslav Left (communist)	0.4	– (5% threshold)
Others	4.6	–

Kosovo/Kosova (part of Serbia, but with its own Assembly since 2001)

The Kosovo Assembly (120 members) elections on 17 November 2001 had 16 lists and the main winners were three ethnic Albanian lists and one Serb list. As might be expected, the Albanian parties advocate independence for Kosovo, and the Serbs oppose it. In 2001 these voted for Coalition Returning/*Koalicija Povratak* (*KP*). However, the Albanians are split between the moderate Democratic League of Kosovo/*Lidhja Demijkratike e Kosovës* (*LDK*) and the militant Democratic Party of Kosovo/*Partija Demokratike e Kosovës* (*PDK*). The following minorities are represented by one seat each: the Turks, the Ashkali and the Roma.

Table 11.4   Kosovo Assembly (120 members): 2001 election. Parties winning more than one seat[26]

	% of vote	Seats
Democratic League of Kosovo (Moderate)	46.3	47
Democratic Party of Kosovo (Separatist)	25.5	26
Coalition Returning (Serbian)	11.0	22
Alliance for the Future of Kosovo	7.8	8
Motherland	1.2	4
Kosovo Democratic Turkish Party	0.9	3
New Initiative for a Democratic Kosovo	0.5	2
Ashkali Albanian Democratic Party of Kosovo	0.4	2

Montenegro

There is a nationalist (pro-independence) party in Montenegro, the Democratic Party of Socialists of Montenegro/*Demokratska Partija Crne Gore (DPSCG)*, which succeeded the League of Communists of Montenegro in 1991. It favoured federation with Serbia until the late 1990s, and now supports independence.

President

Milo Djukanović (reformist: favours independence). Elected 1997.

Table 11.5   Montenegro Assembly (77 seats): 2001 election

	% of vote	Seats
Democratic Party of Socialists/Social Democratic Party (DPSCG/SdPCG) (favours independence)	42.0	36
Serbian People's Party of Montenegro/ Socialist Peoples Party of Montenegro/Serb People's Party (SNPCG) (anti-independence)	40.6	33
Liberal Union of Montenegro (LSCG) (pro-independence)	7.9	6
Others (Democratic Union of Albanians; Democratic Alliance of Montenegro (both Albanian))	9.5	2

Slovenia

Table 11.6   Slovenian National Assembly

Year	% of vote	Seats
Presidential election (1997)*		
Milan Kučan (no party)		55.6
Janez Podobnik (Slovenian People's Party)		18.4
National Assembly: State Chamber (90 members)**		
1992	9.9	12
1996	3.2	4
2000	4.4	4

Notes
*   Six other candidates stood.
**   The only overt nationalist party is the Slovenian National Party.

Croatia

Presidential elections

Franjo Tudjman won the presidential election in 1992 with 56.7 per cent of the vote. He had been made President in 1990 by election of his party, the Christian Democratic Union (HDZ), which is usually described as nationalist. He was re-elected by a landslide in 1997. On his death in

December 1999, there was a reaction away from nationalism and Stjepan Mesić of the Croatian People's Party (HNS) won the first round of the 2000 presidential election with 41.1 per cent and with 56.0 per cent at the second round. This time, the nationalist (HDZ) candidate won only 22.5 per cent of the vote in the first round, and was eliminated.

Table 11.7 Parliament (Sabor) (up to 151 members, including up to six to represent Croatians abroad, and five to represent ethnic minorities whose share of the population is at least 8%): 2000 election

	% of vote	Seats
(a) Social Democratic Party/(b) Croatian Social Liberal Party/ (c) Littoral and Highland Region Alliance/(d) Slavonian-Baranian Croatian Party		
	38.7	71
		(a) 44
		(b) 24
		(c) 2
		(d) 1
Croatian Democratic Union (HDZ)	26.7	46
United List (ZL) (5 parties or a centrist nature)	14.7	25
(a) Croatian Rights Party ('xenophobic'[27])/ (b) Croatian Christian Democratic Union		
	5.2	(a) 4
		(b) 1
Serbian National Party (Serb minority)	–	1
Hungarian Democratic Community (Hungarian minority)	–	1
Non-partisan representatives of minorities	–	2
Representatives of Croatian abroad	–	6

Republic of Bosnia-Hercegovina

Presidency

The presidency is elected by three ethnic groups (Bosniacs, Serbs and Croats). The elections in September 1998 saw the election of the candidates of (a) Bosniacs: Party of Democratic Action (SDA), with 87 per cent of the vote; (b) Serbs: Socialist Party of the Serbian Republic (SPRS) in 'Sloga' alliance, with 51.2 per cent of the vote; and (c) Croatian Democratic Union (HDZ), with 52.9 per cent of the vote. All of these could be considered nationalist candidates, but the moderate Sloga alliance proved too much for the more nationalist SPRS, which withdrew from the ruling coalition in January 2000. Seven other parties were represented with one seat each.

House of the Peoples

(Upper House: 15 members, 10 from the Federation and five from the Republic of Sprska: indirectly elected by legislatures of the constitutent 'entities'.) No details.

Table 11.8   Parliament: (A) House of Representatives (42 members: 28 elected by the Federation of Bosnia-Hercegovina and 14 elected from the Republic of Srpska): 2000 election

	% of vote	*Seats*
Party of Democratic Action (SDA) (Bosniac nationalist)	18.8	8
Social Democratic Party/Social Democrats (SDP)	18.0	9
Serb Democratic Party (SDS)(Serb nationalist)	17.8	6
Croatian Democratic Union (HDZ)(Croatian nationalist)	11.4	5
Party for BiH (SBiH) (moderate Bosniac nationalist)	11.4	4

Federation of Bosnia and Hercegovina (i.e. Bosniacs and Croats)

President and Vice-President elected by the legislature

Alternatively a Bosniac and a Croat. 13 other parties were represented, with one to three seats, some with only regional support.

Table 11.9   Parliament: (A) House of Representatives (140 members): 2000 election

	% of vote	*Seats*
Party of Democratic Action (SDA) (Bosniac nationalist)	26.8	38
Social Democratic Party (SDP)	26.1	37
Croatian Democratic Union (HDZ) (Croatian Nationalist)	17.5	25
Party for BiH (SBiH) (moderate Bosniac nationalist)	14.9	21

House of the Peoples

(74 members, at least 30 Bosniacs and 30 Croats.) 2000 election. No details.

Serbian Republic (Republika Srpska)

President: Mirko Sarović (Serbian Radical Party) (hardliner)

Elected with 53 per cent of vote (2000). Seven other parties were represented, with one to four seats.

Table 11.10 People's Assembly (83 members): 2000 election

	% of vote	Seats
Serb Democratic Party (SDS) (Serb nationalist)	36.1	31
Party of Independent Social Democrats (SNSD)	13.0	11
Party of Democratic Progress (PDP) (moderate) (Chairman became Prime Minister)	12.2	11
Party of Democratic Action (SDA) (Bosniac nationalist)	7.6	6
Party for Bosnia and Hercegovina (SbiH) (moderate, mainly Muslim)	5.2	4
Social Democratic Party of Bosnia and Hercegovina (mainly Muslim but inter-ethnic list)	5.0	4

Chamber of Deputies (14 members)

No details.

Macedonia

President: Boris Trajkovski (Internal Macedonian Revolutionary Organisation (VMRO-DPMNE) (nationalist). 'Elected December 1999, with 52.9 per cent of vote'

Table 11.11 Parliament (120 members)

	% of vote	Seats
1994		
Internal Macedonian Revolutionary Org. (VMRO)	boycott	
Democratic Alternative (DA)	–	–
Social Democratic Alliance of Macedonia (SDSM)	48.3	58
Party of Democratic Prosperity (Albanian)(PPD)	8.3	10
Democratic People's Party (NDP)	3.3	4
Liberal Party of Macedonia (LPM)	24.2	29
Socialist Party of Macedonia (SPM)	7.5	9
Others	8.4	11
1998		
VMRO	(28.1)	
DA	(10.1)	62
SDSM	25.2	27
PPD		14
PDSH	(19.3)	11
Liberal Democratic Party (LDP) (includes LPM)	7.0	4
SPM	4.7	2
Others	5.0	–

In May 2001 a six-party national unity government was formed including the DPA, PDP, VMRO-DPMNE, LPM LDP and PDP, to be joined later by the SDSM. Strains between Slav and Albanian parties continued, and in the 2002 elections the nationalists (VMRO-DPMNE) were overtaken by the Social Democratic Union of Macedonia (SDSM), formerly communist but now 'European' Social Democratic, and considered to be more moderate than the nationalists. Nevertheless, it was formerly in coalition with the nationalists on an anti-Albanian platform.

Albania

President

Prof. Rexhep Mejdani (elected by Parliament, 1997) (non-party).

Table 11.12   People's Assembly (140 members) (parties with two or more seats)

	% of vote	Seats
1996		
Socialist Party of Albania (PSSH)	20.4	10
Democratic Party of Albania (PDSH)	55.5	122
Albanian Republican Party (PRSH)	5.7	3
Albania National Front (PBK)(nationalist)	5.0	2
Human Rights Union Party (PBDNJ)(Greek minority)	4.0	3
Movement of Legality Party (PLL) (monarchist)	2.1	–
1997		
PSSH	52.8	99
PDSH	25.7	29
Social Democratic Party (PSD)	2.5	8
PBDJ	2.8	4
PBK	2.3	3
PLL	3.5	2
Democratic Alliance (AD)	2.8	2
2001		
PSSH	41.5	73
PDSH/PBK/PRSH/PLL list	36.8	46
Party of Democrats (PD)	5.1	6
PSD	3.6	4
PBNJ	2.6	3
AD	2.5	3

Greece

President: elected by Parliament (ceremonial)

Constantine Stephanopolous

Chamber of Deputies (300 members)

It is difficult to identify nationalist parties as such in Greece, and the former support for *enonis* with Cyprus in no longer a political issue, although antagonism with Turkey is, and also opposition to closer EU integration. The ruling party is the Pan Hellenic Socialist Movement (PASOK) (43.8 per cent of the vote and 158 seats in 2000). Next is New Democracy (ND), a conservative party, with 42.7 per cent and 125 seats in 2000. There are no national minority parties in Greece, which is a homogeneous nation-state.

Bulgaria

President

Georgi Parvanov (Bulgarian Socialist Party/BSP), elected 2001. The main thing to notice in the context of nationalism is the relatively strong position electorally of the Turkish minority, represented by the Movement for Rights and Freedom.

Table 11.13 National Assembly (240 members)

	% of vote	Seats
1994		
Bulgarian Socialist Party (BSP)	43.5	125
Union of Democratic Forces (SDS) (conservative)	24.2	69
People's Union (NS) (agrarian – conservative)	6.5	18
Movement for Rights and Freedom (DPS) (Turkish)	5.4	15
Others	20.4	13
1997		
SDS	52.3	123
NS		14
BSP	22.0	58
DPS	7.6	19
Bulgarian Euroleft (BE)	5.5	14
Others	12.6	12
2001		
National Movement Simeon II (NDST)(conservative)	42.7	120
SDS/NS	18.2	51
BSP	17.1	48
DPS	7.5	21
Others	13.5	–

Romania

President

Ion Iliescu (Social Democratic Party/*PSD*), elected 2000, with 66.8 per cent of the vote. The nationalist (Party of Greater Romania) candidate came second in the first round with 28.3 per cent of the vote, and obtained 33.2 per cent on the second round.

Table 11.14   Parliament (Chamber of Deputies) (346 members)

	% of vote	Seats
1992		
Social Democratic Party (PSD) (socialist)	27.7	117
Democratic Convention of Romania (CDR)(cons.)	20.0	82
Democratic Party (PD)(social democratic)	10.2	43
Hungarian Democratic Alliance of Romania (RMDSz)	7.5	27
Party of Great Romania (PRM) (nationalist)	3.9	16
National Liberal Party (PNL)	2.6	–
Others	30.7	43
1996		
CDR	30.2	97
PSD	21.5	91
PD	12.9	53
RMDSz	6.6	25
PNL	with CDR	25
PRM	4.5	19
Others	24.3	18
2000		
PSD	36.6	155
PRM	19.5	84
PD	7.0	31
PNL	6.9	30
RMDSz	6.8	27
CDR	5.0	–
Others	17.3	–

(19 ethnic minority parties were each given one seat in the Chamber in the 2000 elections, these represented Albanians, Armenians, Bulgarians, Croats, Ruthenians, Tatar Turkish Muslims, Slovaks and Czechs, Germans, Greeks, Italians, Jews, Lipova Russians, Poles, Roma, Serbs, Slav Macedonians, Turks, Ukrainians and a General Union of Ethnic Associations[28].)

Noteworthy is the big rise in support for the nationalist Party of Great Romania (PRM), from 3.9 per cent of the vote and 16 seats in 1992 to

19.5 per cent and 84 seats in 2000. It is strongly against the use of the Hungarian language in Romania, and seeks to ban the Hungarian Democratic Alliance of Romania/*RMDSz*. This, however, has held steady at around 7 per cent of the vote and 25–27 seats.

Conclusion

The fact that the states in the Balkans are with only two exceptions (Slovenia and Greece), multiethnic in makeup, makes the application of the principles of nationalism problematic. 'One nation, one state' cannot be applied, but many states seek to do so, sometimes by 'ethnic cleansing'. This has invariably led to a great deal of violence in the area, especially in the former Yugoslavia. Only the intervention of international forces has made peace possible, followed by democracy. But democracy in these circumstances cannot be a simple majoritarian one, and a range of devices from the representation of ethnic minority parties to out-and-out power sharing has been tried. In Bosnia-Hercogovina, internal partition into two states along ethnic lines has been imposed by international decree. This seems a halfway house to total independence, which cannot be long delayed. In Serbia, Kosovo and Voyvodina defy the notion of a Serbian nation-state, and echo the 'Greater Serbia' claims of the past. Kosovo has international protection and autonomy has been restored. Serb–Albanian conflict there is continuing, albeit modified by moderate nationalists now in power in Serbia and Kosovo. But Kosovo's eventual independence from Serbia seems inevitable, if denied so far by international opinion, which wishes to see democracy safely established in Serbia. The Hungarian minority in Vojvodina seems to be dormant, with Hungary itself wary of getting involved in Balkan affairs. In time, however, the reunion of ethnic Hungarians (including in Transylvania in Romania) seems to be inevitable for the proper functioning of a 'Europe of the Nations'. Romanians themselves are divided between their state and that of Moldova, which has so far resisted any union of Romanians (it is only 65 per cent Romanian, with 14 per cent Ukrainian and 13 per cent Russian). Moldova is in a very precarious position, sandwiched between Ukraine and Romania, and curiously dependent on Russian support for its survival as an independent state. A 'European' solution might be in order here, but the prospects for entry to the EU are distant indeed, as they are for most Balkan states apart from Greece (already a member since 1981), Slovenia and Croatia, which are relatively well-developed and peaceful, and high up on the EU waiting list.

In general, the prospects for democratic nationalism are better in the early twenty-first century than they have ever been. Ethnic cleansing is in the past (even if the return of those 'cleansed' remains problematic), and democracy has been established everywhere. But the 'nation-state' ideal is inappropriate nearly everywhere. More suitable is power-sharing (consociationalism), or national minority representation and constitutional guarantees. As we have seen, quite a lot has been achieved in these directions.

12
Poland/*Polska*

Historical context

Poland is one of the most nationalist nations in Europe,[1] the result of
the dismemberment of the Polish state in the eighteenth century by the
Kingdom of Prussia and the Empires of Austria and Russia. This gave rise
to a nationalist reaction, culminating in uprisings in 1793, 1830 and
1863. But it was not until 1918 that Poland recovered its statehood. Its
boundaries remained difficult to agree on, however. Germany retained
East Prussia, and the port of Danzig/*Gdansk*, a German town, was put
under international control, along with the adjoining 'Polish Corridor'
giving Poland access to the sea there. Lithuania was largely under Polish
control, including what is its capital today, Vilnius/Pol. *Wilna/*
Russ.*Vilna*). Another of today's states, Belarus, was at that time largely
within Poland (but not its capital, Minsk), and the Ukrainian city of
today, L'viv/Polish *Lwow*/German *Lemberg*, was part of Poland along
with its hinterland.

There followed a tormented period in Polish history involving external wars with Russia, Germany and Austria, and a difficult relationship
with Lithuania, whose nationalism was incompatible with that of
Poland, because of competing territorial claims. Internal problems also
arose, leading to a dictatorship under the national liberator Pilsudski
in 1926. Some of these were expressed in anti-Semitism, which was
prevalent in Poland at this time. Another German–Russian (now
'Nazi-Soviet') pact at Poland's expense was concluded in 1939, which led
to the dismemberment of the nation, German control followed, and
then Soviet occupation.

The boundaries of Poland after 1945 were mostly satisfactory from a
nationalist point of view, and included areas of Germany with strong

Polish populations, and even those parts almost entirely German, such as Danzig (now Gdansk), the western borderlands with Germany and East Prussia. Familiar German names disappeared, to be replaced with Polish ones.[2] But Wilna/Vilna/Vilnius stayed part of the Lithuanian Soviet Socialist Republic, although it had been part of Poland from 1920 to 1940. It remains as the capital of the independent Lithuania, and some problems of its Polish minority have surfaced in Lithuanian politics (see Chapter 13). Forced transfers of Poles from the 'Marchlands' of the Soviet Union after 1945 reduced the number of Poles outside Poland, although over one million remained in the Soviet Union in the last Census of 1989.[3] According to another source (Minahan) there are (2000 est.) 1.2 million Poles in Ukraine, 414 000 in Belarus, 265 000 in Lithuania and 245 000 in Germany.[4] This might appear to be a problem for Polish nationalism, but with the exception of Lithuania and perhaps Germany (on account of German claims to compensation for lost lands) and Russia (on account of Poland's membership of the North Atlantic Treaty Organization (NATO)), there are no tensions between Poland and foreign states. Within Poland itself, Germans are 1.2 million or 3.1 per cent of the population, and other national minorities amount to 2 per cent of the population, although these are not identified in the Census. Most are Ukrainians, Byelorussions and Lithuanians. A Council of National Minorities was set up in 1991. The German minority[5] in Poland has been politically active since the demise of communism, and has been represented by a party, the German Minority of Lower Silesia/ *Mniejszość Niemiecka Slaksa Opolskiego/MNSO*, which obtained seven members of the Polish Parliament (Lower House/*Sejm*) in October 1991, four in 1993 and two in 1997 and 2001. This is despite the fact that the party obtained only 0.4 per cent of the Polish vote in 2001, for minority parties are exempt from the 5 per cent threshold for representation.

There is an autonomist movement in Silesia (*Ruch Autonomii Slaska*), which seeks an autonomous Silesia in a federal Poland and in a Europe of the Regions, and its language is Silesian, not German.[6] Silesia straddles Moravia (Czech Republic), so this is a 'lesser' Silesia.[7] The Czech Silesians (44 000 in 1991) however speak a language akin to Czech, Moravian and Polish, and most Germans in the region were expelled in 1945 (48 000 remain). Religion is not a salient national division in Poland, since the Roman Catholic Church accounts for 95 per cent of the population.

Democratic nationalism was thwarted by the establishment of a communist regime in 1948, which soon gave rise to uprisings in the traditional Polish fashion, directed against Russian domination.

Nationalism expressed itself in the Catholic Church (a Polish Pope, John Paul II, was appointed in 1978), the Solidarity trade union movement, and national culture, notably the cinema.

Soviet forces started to withdraw in 1991, and in 1992 Poland's National Defence Committee announced that Poland had no natural enemies, and no territorial claims on neighbouring states. This is the situation prevailing today, and Poland looks to the west for its national fulfillment. It joined NATO in 1999 and is a candidate member of the European Union (EU).

Nationalism today is largely satisfied and there are no nationalist parties as such in Poland. Anti-immigration and racist parties are absent, and anti-EU parties are based on issues other than national sovereignty (such as abortion and farming interests). This does not mean that Poland has ceased to be nationalist. Antipathy to Germans, Russians and Lithuanians remains, and any threat to Poland's territory and independence would meet with the same resistance today that it did in previous centuries.

Constitution

Preamble
Having regard to the existence and future of our Homeland ... We, the Polish Nation ... Beholden to our ancestors for their labours, their struggle for independence achieved at great sacrifice ... Hereby establish this Constitution ...

Article 4
(1) Supreme power in the Republic of Poland shall be vested in the nation.

Article 27
Polish shall be the official language in the Republic of Poland. This provision shall not infringe upon minority rights resulting from ratified international agreements.

Article 34
(1) Polish citizenship shall be acquired by birth to parents being Polish citizens. Other methods of acquiring Polish citizenship shall be specified by statute [see Citizenship Laws, below].

Article 35
(1) The Republic of Poland shall ensure Polish citizens belonging to national or ethnic minorities the freedom to maintain and develop

their own language, maintain customs and traditions, and to develop their own culture.

(2) National and ethnic minorities shall have the right to establish educational and cultural institutions, institutions designed to protect religious identity, as well as to participate in the resolution of matters connected with their cultural identity.

Citizenship laws

(a) by birth: children born or found in the territory of Poland, if both parents are not known, whose citizenship cannot be established, or who are stateless.

(b) by descent: regardless of the country of birth if at least one parent is a Polish citizen.

(c) by naturalisation: eligible to apply after 5 years permanent residence. Dual citizenship: not recognised.

Electoral nationalism

As mentioned above, there are no nationalist parties as such in Poland, but there is a German minority party in Lower Silesia, which has representation (2 seats) in the Polish Lower House of Parliament, and some local councillors. Anti-immigrant parties do not exist, and Poland has a liberal asylum law. There are anti-EU parties, but these do not stress issues of national independence, rather religious and economic interests.

Conclusion

The struggle for Polish independence is one of the most heroic national struggles in European history. As recently as during the Second World War, this independence was again destroyed. The boundaries of the Polish state are still problematic, in view of the large number of Poles in neighbouring states. However, Poland has renounced all claims to territory elsewhere, and has achieved boundaries which on the western side at least are generous to it. Its future as a European nation-state seems secure, with the endorsement of international institutions such as NATO and the UN.

13
The Baltic Nations (Lithuania/*Lietuva*, Latvia/ *Latvija*, and Estonia/*Eesti*)

Historical context

An atlas of Europe before 1918 does not show Lithuania or Latvia. The former corresponds to what was then the Duchy of Courland, and the latter was Livonia. Russia controlled both, as well as Estonia (Estland), and had done so since the eighteenth century. Before that, Sweden was the ruler. The present-day state boundaries do not correspond exactly to these historic divisions, but there is no doubt that ethnic divisions between them have existed for a long time, and marked them off from Russia.

The development of nationalism in the Baltic nations was essentially a phenomenon of the nineteenth century, and followed a classical sequence of intellectual nationalism, middle class nationalism and finally working class nationalism.[1] What impelled this 'belated' nationalism was the shortsighted 'Russification' policy of Tsar Alexander III (Tsar from 1881 to 1894). This meant the imposition of the Russian language and the Russian Orthodox Church, and created a reaction among the non-Russians of the Empire. It led directly to the nationalisms of the Baltic nations.

The collapse of Russia and Germany in 1918 gave the Baltic nations the opportunity their nationalists had been waiting for. It was Allied policy to weaken German influence in Eastern Europe and curtail the spread of communism from Russia. Given the presence of nationalists in the Baltics it made democratic sense to set up nation-states wherever possible. Poland was an obvious candidate for statehood, and so it now appeared were the Baltics. Unfortunately, Poland and Lithuania were competitors for territory, and Poland was able to secure much of Lithuania on the basis of its historic claim. Thus Vilnius, the present-day capital of Lithuania, was within Poland from 1918 to 1939. So was much of Belarus and Ukraine.

Latvia and Estonia were less trouble, although the former overlapped ethnically with Lithuania, and the latter with Russia. The Nazi–Soviet Pact of 1939 soon resulted in the disappearance of all three Baltic states, to be reconstituted as Soviet Republics. This was the situation until the latter years of Gorbachev's rule, when multiparty elections were allowed for the first time. In Lithuania, the nationalists won control of Parliament in February 1990, and proceeded to declare independence. Gorbachev responded with force, but his own fall later that year resulted in the demise of the Soviet Union. In a referendum on 9 February 1991, Lithuanians voted by 90.5 per cent to back independence. Given that Lithuania was only 80 per cent ethnically Lithuanian, many non-Lithuanians must have voted Yes.

The Lithuanian initiative soon spread to Latvia and Estonia. The Latvian Supreme Soviet (then Communist-controlled) condemned the 1940 annexation, and proclaimed a 'free and independent state of Latvia', but as part of a new Soviet Union. The newly formed Latvian Popular Front won a majority in the multiparty elections of March–April 1990, and a referendum on independence showed that 74 per cent of the voters were in favour. Again, the voting showed that not only the 'ethnic nation' was in favour of independence. Only a little over half of the population were ethnic Latvians, with a third Russian and 4 per cent Belarussian. Independence was declared on 21 August 1991, and was recognised by the Soviet Union on 10 September 1991.

Latvia has been dominated by poor relations between the ethnic Latvians and the Russian speakers. Citizenship and voting rights depend on the ability to pass tests in the Latvian language, and minorities must attend Latvian-language schools by 2004. This has polarised politics, so that Latvians and Russians support different parties. The latter have been increasing in support, but are excluded from government (see below, under Electoral Nationalism).

Estonia had annulled the 1940 annexation as far back as 12 November 1989, before the demise of the Communists. It called for eventual independence in March 1990, and adopted the name 'Republic of Estonia' in May. In a referendum on 3 March 1991, 77.8 per cent voted in favour of independence. This was accepted in September by the USSR Supreme Soviet. As in the other Baltic countries the percentage for independence was much higher than the percentage of the population which was Estonian (this was only 61.5 per cent). Throughout the Soviet Union, people were disillusioned with Moscow rule and communism, and not even Gorbachev could stop the disintegration of the Union. But it was the failed 'coup' on 19 August 1991 that set the seal on the Soviet Union. After that all the republics broke away, and those which had already declared independence, like the Baltics, were recognised.

This brief chronology cannot account for the strength of nationalism at this time. Clearly, the events of 1989–91 did not come out of the blue, and there were signs that nationalism was stirring in the Baltic countries, especially in cultural events and demonstrations. Most impressive was 'The Baltic Way', when two million people (2/5 of the entire native population) linked hands across the three countries on 23 August 1989, in a chain stretching from Vilnius, by Riga to Tallinn, demanding independence.[2]

The Soviet Union might have survived had things been handled differently. Gorbachev, an advanced and liberal thinker in many ways, could not accommodate nationalism in his scheme of things. When even the communists in the Baltics asked for autonomy, he responded with force and then with procrastination. He could not see that his acceptance of democracy in the communist bloc was equivalent to the demise of communism and its 'Empire'.

The Baltic communists were not at all sure of their ground at first, and looked to a reconstituted Soviet Union, rather than to total independence. But they used the language of nationalism, which was very difficult to accommodate with Gorbachev's brand of communism. He latterly accepted that the USSR should be reconstituted as a 'union of confederal democratic states', but it was too late. There was no trust left. At the end of the day, it was Russian old-guard communists who killed the Soviet Union, with their attempt to turn the clock back in the coup against Gorbachev in August 1991. After that, Ukraine declared its independence (December), and the other republics followed immediately. But it was the Baltic nations which first showed the way to the disintegration of the Soviet Union, and to the triumph of nationalism over communism. Contemporary politics in the Baltic states is now controlled by the native people, not by Russia, and their constitutions reflect this.

Constitutions

Lithuania (1992)

Preamble

The Lithuanian Nation, having established the State of Lithuania many centuries ago, having based its legal foundations on the Lithuanian

Statutes and the Constitutions of the Republic of Lithuania, having for centuries defended its freedom, having preserved its spirit, native language, writing, and customs, embodying the inborn right of each person and the People to live and create freely in the land of their fathers and forefathers ... by the will of the citizens of the reborn State of Lithuania, approves and declares this Constitution.

Article 10
(2) The State borders may only be realigned by an international treaty of the Republic of Lithuania which has been ratified by four-fifths of the Parliament members.

Article 12
(1) Citizenship of the Republic of Lithuania shall be acquired by birth or on other bases established by law [see Citizenship Laws, below].
(2) With the exception of cases established by law, no person may be a citizen of the Republic of Lithuania and another state at the same time ... (Citizenship Law amended, September 2002, to allow dual citizenship).

Article 14
Lithuanian shall be the State language.[3]

Article 37
Citizens who belong to ethnic communities shall have the right to foster their language, culture, and customs.

Article 42
(2) The State shall support culture and science, and shall be concerned with the protection of Lithuanian history, art, and other cultural monuments and valuables.

Article 45
Ethnic communities of citizens shall independently administer the affairs of their ethnic culture, education, organisations, charity, and mutual assistance. The state shall support ethnic communities.
Note: in May 2002, Article 119 of the Constitution was amended to allow foreigners to run and vote in local elections, effective from 2004.

Citizenship law (1991, amended 2002)

Article 1 (Citizens of the Republic of Lithuania)
The following persons shall be citizens of the Republic of Lithuania:
(1) Persons who were citizens of the Republic of Lithuania prior to 15 June 1940, and their children and grandchildren, provided they have

not acquired citizenship of another state; (amended, September 2002, to permit dual citizenship).

(2) Persons who were permanent residents on the territory of the Republic of Lithuania in the period from 9 January 1919 to 15 June 1940, as well as their children and grandchildren, provided on the day of entry into force of this Law they have been permanent residents in Lithuania, and are not citizens of another state ... (amended September 2002).

Article 5 (Retaining Citizenship of the Republic of Lithuania)
Residence by a citizen ... in a foreign state shall not of itself result in the loss of citizenship of the Republic of Lithuania.

Article 12 (Conditions for Granting Citizenship of the Republic of Lithuania)
A person, upon his or her request, may be granted citizenship ... provided he or she ... meets the following conditions of citizenship:
(1) Has passed the examination in the Lithuanian language (can speak and read Lithuanian);
(2) For the last ten years has had a permanent place of residence on the territory of Lithuania;
(3) Has a permanent place of employment or a constant legal source of support on the territory of the Republic of Lithuania ...
Persons meeting the conditions ... shall be granted citizenship ... taking into consideration the interests of the Republic of Lithuania.

Article 17 (Retention of the Right to Citizenship of the Republic of Lithuania)
The right to citizenship of the Republic of Lithuania shall be retained for an indefinite period for:
(1) Persons who had citizenship of the Republic of Lithuania until 15 June 1940 and are at the present time residing in other states [provided they have not repatriated from Lithuania];
(2) Children of persons who had citizenship ... [as above], who were born in Lithuania or in refugee camps but are at the present time residing in other states; and
(3) Other persons of Lithuanian origin who are residing in foreign states or on the territories governed by said states ... Said persons together with members of their families may enter the Republic of Lithuania without visas and reside in Lithuania without having the requirements of the Law on Immigration applied to them ...

Latvia (1922; significantly amended 1998)

Article 3 (Territory)
The territory of the State of Latvia, within the borders established by international agreements, consists of Vidzeme, Latgale, Kurzeme and Zemgale.

Article 4 (Language, Flag)
The Latvian language is the official language in the Republic of Latvia ...

Article 114 (Minorities)
Persons belonging to ethnic minorities have the right to preserve and develop their language and their ethnic and cultural identity.[4]

Citizenship laws (1994, 1998, 2002)

Similar to those of Lithuania, for example, granting citizenship to ethnic Latvians, and those who possessed Latvian citizenship prior to1940. For naturalised citizens, a language test in Latvian was required. The main group of non-citizens on independence was Russians, who comprised one-third of the population (905 500 out of 2.7 million). By 1998, this had reduced to 700 000, and of this total 452 000 had failed to become Latvian citizens, mainly because of the language requirement.

A liberalisation of the laws was made in 1998 after a referendum in which 53 per cent voted in favour. But it was still necessary to pass a test in Latvian, which many of the older Russians were unable or unwilling to do. From May 2002, it was not necessary for those seeking public office (as in national elections) to speak fluent Latvian, but attendance at Latvian-language schools is mandatory. The liberalising changes were introduced after strong pressure from abroad, particularly from the Organization for Security and Co-operation in Europe (OSCE), North Atlantic Treaty Organization (NATO) and the European Union (EU) (Latvia seeks entry to the last two, and is already a member of the first, as are Lithuania and Estonia).

Once Latvia joins the EU, Latvian citizenship will mean EU citizenship, and this should persuade the Russian minority to learn Latvian to become citizens of the EU (the alternative is to be outside the EU, with Russian citizenship or as stateless persons).

Estonia (1992)

Preamble
Unwavering in their faith and with an unswerving will to safeguard and develop a state which is established on the inextinguishable right of the Estonian people to national self-determination and which was proclaimed on February 24, 1918 ... the Estonian people adopted, on the basis of Article 1 of the Constitution which entered into force in 1938, by Referendum held on June 28, 1992 the following Constitution.

Article 6 (Language)
The official language of Estonia is Estonian.

Article 8 (Citizenship)
(1) Every child with one parent who is Estonian shall have the right, by birth, to Estonian citizenship.
(2) Everyone who as a minor lost his or her Estonian citizenship shall have the right to have his or her citizenship restored.
(4) No person may be deprived of Estonian citizenship because of his or her persuasion.
(5) Conditions and procedures for the acquisition ... of citizenship shall be determined by the Law on Citizenship.

Article 12 (No Discrimination)
(1) ... No one may be discriminated against on the basis of nationality, race, colour, sex, language, origin, creed .... .

Article 36
(3) Every Estonian shall have the right to settle in Estonia.

Article 37 (Education)
(4) Everyone shall have the right to instruction in Estonian. Educational institutions established for minorities shall choose their own language of instruction.

Article 55 (Foreign and Stateless Persons)
Citizens of foreign states and stateless persons present in Estonia are obligated to respect the Estonian constitutional system of government.

Article 57 (Right to Vote)
(1) The right to vote shall belong to every Estonian citizen who has attained the age of eighteen.

Article 79 (President: Election)
(3) Any Estonian by birth, who is at least forty years of age, may be presented as a candidate for President of the Republic.

Language laws

These have been tightened since independence, so that business people, public servants and local government workers must speak Estonian in order to continue in employment. This is the reverse of the situation in the Soviet Union, when Russian was the official language in Estonia. The state does not support Russian-language schools, despite the very strong presence of Russians in Estonia.

Citizenship laws (1995)

As in Lithuania and Latvia, Estonia recognises as citizens those (and their children) who were citizens before 1940, and those by birth if one parent is Estonia. Non-Estonians can be naturalised as citizens if they fulfil several conditions, including knowledge of the Estonian language. As Estonian is a non-Slav, Finno-Ugric language, this is a barrier for many Russians, who in 1998 were 28 per cent of the population (in 2000 this was down to 25.6 per cent[5]). Estonian is the first language of only 64 per cent of the population, but in 2000, Estonians accounted for 68 per cent of the population.

Dual nationality is not recognised, but it is not forbidden, as only one Estonian parent is required for citizenship. Dual citizens can hold public office, and non-citizens can vote in local elections. Around 300 000 of the population of 1.4 million are non-citizens, most of whom are Russians with permanent or temporary residence permits. By 2001, 116 000 had received citizenship through the naturalisation process. Around 220 000 persons (17 per cent of the population) were stateless.

Like the other Baltic states, Estonia has come in for a lot of criticism from western countries because of its treatment of the Russian minority. In order to understand Baltic attitudes to citizenship and minority rights, it must be remembered that these states were forcibly annexed by the Soviet Union in 1940, with mass deportations shortly after. Then Russification proceeded, with discrimination against the native languages. It is not surprising that these nations wish to redress the balance today.

At the same time, the presence of so many 'aliens' without civic rights in democratic countries is an affront to contemporary notions of human rights, and the pressures from international institutions are strong to encourage the liberalisation of the citizenship and language laws. Russia has been hostile to these countries, and has exaggerated the plight of ethnic Russians for political reasons, especially its hostility to NATO, which is recruiting members in the Baltics. Luckily, the most extreme forms of nationalism are absent in these states, as we shall see.

Electoral nationalism

Lithuania

All the parties in Lithuania are nationalist to a degree, if by that is meant support for the secession of Lithuania from the USSR. Even former communists are as nationalist as others in that respect. Curiously, the party which led Lithuania to independence, the Lithuanian Reform Movement/*Sajudis*, under Vytautus Landsbergis,[6] no longer exists, and its successor, the Homeland Union-Lithuanian Conservatives (*Tevynes Sajunga-Lietuvos Konservatoriai/TS-LK*) is very weak today, and was reduced to nine seats in the 141-member Parliament (*Seimas*) in October 2000. A breakaway from this party joined the Lithuanian Liberal Union (*Lietuvos Liberalu Sajunga/LLS*) in 1999, and in the 2000 elections obtained 17.3 per cent and 34 seats. In January 2003, Rolandas Paksas, former LLS chairman, won the presidential election with 55 per cent of the vote, after a campaign described as 'populist or nationalist in nature', with Paksas as the 'Le Pen of the Baltics'.[7] Despite this taunt, his campaign spokesman said that Paksas was 'entirely for Lithuania's membership in the EU'.[8] Nevertheless, the right-wing coalition formed in January 2003, was more anti-Russian than the previous Social Democratic coalition

Other nationalist parties are very small. The Lithuanian Poles (*c.* 8 per cent of the population) are represented by the Lithuanian Polish Union (*Lietuvos Lenjku Sajunga/LLS*) which has two seats with 1.9 per cent of the vote. It proclaims its loyalty to Lithuania while promoting Polish education.

Latvia

Latvia has a more virulent nationalism than Lithuania, being more anti-Russian. The Latvian National Independence Movement (*Latvijas Nacionala Neatkaribas Kustiba/LNNK*) was founded in 1988, and spearheaded the independence movement. On independence it stated that welfare benefits should be limited to ethic Latvians, and that non-Latvians should amount to not more than 25 per cent of the citizenry (they are 45 per cent of the population). It opposed liberalising the naturalisation laws. This extremism has not paid off at the polls, however, and after a series of name changes (it is now Fatherland and Freedom-Latvian National Conservative Party (*Tevzemei un Brvibai-Latvijas Nacionala Konservativa Partija/TB-LNNK*)), it won only 5.4 per cent of the vote and seven seats of the 100 seats in the Parliament (*Saeima*) in the 2002 elections, down from 14.7 per cent of the vote and 17 seats in the 1998 elections.[9]

In contrast, the party which is the main voice of the Russian-speakers in Latvia, for Human [Equal] Rights in a United Latvia, came second in 2002, with 18.9 per cent of the vote and 24 seats, up from 14.1 per cent and 16 seats in 1998, when it stood as the National Harmony Party

(*Tautas Saskanas Partija/TSP*). Despite its strength, none of the other five parties in the Parliament will cooperate with the pro-Russian party, so it is excluded from the coalition headed by the centre-right New Era party (23.9 per cent of the vote and 26 seats). This indicates the continuing strength of bad feeling between Latvians and Russians in Latvia.

Estonia

The post-1988 movement for independence was led by the Estonian Popular Front (EPF), headed by Edgar Savisaar, a former communist functionary. This transformation from communism to nationalism was commonplace throughout the communist bloc, but in the Baltic nations, especially Estonia and Latvia, the anti-Russian feelings ran deep. Savisaar became prime minister of the independent Estonia from 1990 to 1992, but by then the Popular Front had split into various parties, one of which was the Estonian Centre Party/*Eesti Keskerakond* (*EKe*), which Savisaar chaired. This won 12.2 per cent of the vote with 15 seats in the 101-member Parliament (*Riigikogu*) in 1992. Its presidential candidate came third, with 23.7 per cent of the vote at the same time. By the elections of 1999, the EKe was first with 23.4 per cent of the vote and 28 seats, but the coalition formed then did not include the party.[10]

Today, the 'nationalists' in Estonia are either strongly anti-Russian or ethnic Russians themselves. The Fatherland Union/*Isamaaliit* (*IML*) best exemplifies the former, and came second in the 1999 parliamentary elections with 16.1 per cent of the vote and 18 seats. It joined the three-party coalition with the Moderates and the Reform Party but had left the coalition by 2002.

The Russians (30 per cent of the population) are mainly represented by the United People's Party of Estonia/*Eestimaa Ühendatud Rahvapartei* (*EÜRP*), the Russian Unity Party (RUP), and the Russian Party of Estonia/*Vene Erakond Eestis* (*VEE*). Given that only Estonian citizens can vote, and that most ethnic Russians are not citizens, it is surprising that these parties get votes and seats. In 1999, the EÜRP got 6.1 per cent of the votes and six seats in alliance with the RUP. The VEE won 2 per cent of the vote, but no seats, in 1999. Clearly, these votes and seats do not represent the true strength of the Russian minority in Estonia, and the Constitution makes no provision for the representation of ethnic minorities.

Today, Estonian politics is still dominated by issues of nationality and independence. Russians represent a threat, whether at home or abroad. This is understandable, given Estonia's history, but contemporary politics are more complex. Russia has moderated its hostility, even if there is no friendship. Europe attracts Estonia, as it does the other Baltic countries, and for this western opinion has to be taken into account. This opinion is critical of Estonia on grounds of human rights 'violations' relating to its Constitution and citizenship laws. But the Constitutions and citizenship laws of these countries do not differ greatly from that of Estonia's or of the other Baltic states. What differs is the size of the problem, with very large ethnic minorities whose resistance to learning the language of the 'host' nation is considerable. Few ethnic Russians wish to return to Russia, however, and the price of citizenship is to learn the language of the nation-state they wish to remain a part of.

Conclusion

The Baltic states are fiercely nationalist, in the face of Russian oppression in the recent past. They are extremely small by traditional standards of nationhood and economic viability (Lithuania: 3.7 million; Latvia: 2.4 million; Estonia: 1.4 million). But in contemporary politics, size is not important in comparison to the aims of national self-determination and viability in global economics. The first leads to democracy on a national basis, and the latter to a place in the global market place. International institutions support both these aims, through the principles of the UN, OSCE, Council of Europe (CoE), and so on, and the trading unions such as the EU.

The Baltic nations achieved statehood in 1918, against all the odds as perceived only a few years earlier. The loss of this independence was simply the result of a cynical pact between apparent opposites, the Nazis and the Soviet communists. No one predicted that these nations would recover their independence by 1991, since no international interest was taken in them, and their populations seemed dormant as far as nationalism was concerned. That this was an illusion, with the nations inherently strong, and the empires inherently weak, was demonstrated in Europe generally, and especially in the Baltics, after 1988.

14
Russia-in-Europe,[1] Belarus and Ukraine

Historical context

Russia is both a nation and an empire, but its evolution from one to the other took centuries, and did not cease entirely after the USSR broke up in 1991. Its historical origins are obscure, and seem to be to the west of the present-day Russia, in Kiev/*Kyiv*, now the capital of Ukraine. The shift eastward to Moscow (Muscovy) in the fourteenth century, when Poland took Byelorussia (hereafter, Belarus) and Ukraine, marks the special character of Russia as an eastern Slav nation. The development of St Petersburg, however, by Peter the Great (ruled 1682–1724) marked a turning towards Europe and the expansion of Russia into the Baltic (1721). This landward extension of Russia made it an empire, with many nations and ethnic groups coming under its control.

The distinction between the Russian and non-Russian parts of the empire was not always clear, even to its citizens, let alone foreigners. But this was not unusual in Europe in multinational states and empires. Thus, 'England' and 'English' was loosely applied to the United Kingdom of Great Britain and Ireland and its citizens until recently, and 'Spain' and 'Spanish' similarly covered Basques and Catalans. Of course, this usage was generally acceptable before the rise of nationalism in these areas, which took place strongly from the nineteenth century. In the Russian Empire, the Tsar-imposed 'Russification' inspired a reaction in the non-Russian nations, which increased in intensity in the late nineteenth century.

The communists were more sensitive to nationality and nationalism, and Lenin and Stalin both proclaimed the right of national self-determination. When this was taken up by the Baltic nations and Ukraine, however, the communists were prepared to fight against it. Even so, the Constitution of the Soviet Union recognised the right of the constituent republics, which were organised on the basis of nationality, to secede from the Union. But it was not possible in practice for these to do so, under the principles of Soviet unity, which had theoretically 'solved' the national question by substituting class rule for national rule. Nevertheless, the Soviet Union was a multinational union, with many languages and cultures having official recognition. Overall, however, Russia was the core nation, and Russian was the language of the central state and army. So it was possible to conceive of the USSR as a system founded on 'internal colonialism', with the colonies the non-Russian nations/republics. This was of course officially denied, but under Gorbachev, it seemed to be substantiated when it was admitted in 1989 that the Baltic states and Bessarabian Moldavia had been illegally annexed in 1940, something which of course the native inhabitants there had always known.

This triggered the break-up of the Soviet Union, to many people's surprise, including experts.[2] Even then, some denied the importance of nationalism in that.[3] There seems no doubt that but for the strength of national identity and nationalism, the Soviet Union could have survived as a reconstituted liberal–democratic state. But since it was a multinational empire, with a history of colonial oppression as well as of communist dictatorship, when one was rejected the other had to go too. The same was true in Yugoslavia and Czechoslovakia. Even non-communist countries such as Spain and Portugal found that the overthrow of dictatorship revealed the repressed nationalisms within their countries.

Russia remained a multinational state after the demise of the USSR, for of its 145 million people, only 87.5 per cent were Russians. The remainder was made up of Tatars/Tartars (3.5 per cent), Ukrainians (2.7 per cent), ethnic Germans (1.3 per cent), Chuvash/Chavash (1.1 per cent), and so on, making up more than 130 nationalities in total. Few of these could be considered nationalist, with the notable exception of the Chechens (*c*. 1 million), who formed 79 per cent of the Chechen Republic (Chechnya) within the Russian Federation. Russians amounted to 11 per cent of the population of Chechnya. The struggle between the Chechens and the Russians for independence became one of the most bitter in Europe, and is still being waged today. It is based on ethnic nationalism on the part of the Chechens, which is often the most virulent type. Ukrainian nationalism, on the other hand, is multi-ethnic and can be classified as 'civic' in nature. The Russian Federation is one of the last unresolved areas of internal colonialism in Europe. One missing factor in the solution of its problem is an international presence, which has gone a long way to settling the problems of former Yugoslavia, which were equally bitter and apparently intractable. Russia has refused to countenance Chechen independence, for reasons which may be connected to its economic resources (oil/oil pipelines) and the fear that to give way to one secessionist nation might mean giving way to others. Yet a nationalist answer to these questions still looks better than a colonial answer (even if modified by federation) in the twenty-first century.

Russian nationalism has been expressed in two ways since independence. A traditional 'Great Russian' nationalism was expressed by the Liberal Democratic Party of Russia (LDPR), chaired by Vladimir Zhirinovsky. Founded in 1990, when the Soviet Union still existed, it seeks to restore the boundaries of that state, even to the reconquest of Finland (lost to the Russian Empire in 1918). For a while this nationalism found considerable support in Russia. Zhirinovsky won 6.2 million votes (7.8 per cent) in the presidential elections of 1991 (see Table 14.1), and was the strongest party in terms of votes in the State Duma (parliamentary) elections in 1993, with 22.8 per cent of the vote, but was second in terms of states with 64 seats. Zhirinovsky's eccentricities (including anti-Semitism, while admitting in 2001 to having a Jewish father) alienated moderate voters, who gave the party only 11.4 per cent of the proportional vote in the 1995 State Duma elections, and 51 seats (but this still made it the second party in terms of seats) (see Table 14.2). Further troubles beset the party, and in 1999 it slumped to 6 per cent of the proportional vote and 17 seats. In the 2000 presidential elections Zhirinovsky came fifth, with 2.7 per cent of the vote.

This seems to indicate the collapse of virulent Russian nationalism/ imperialism, but this could be misleading, since Zhirinovsky was a very unattractive nationalist leader. Mainstream politicians, such as the president elected in 2000, Vladimir Putin, have been vigorous in their defence of the Russian Federation against secessionists, especially in Chechnya, and can be counted as Russian nationalists. Their attitude towards other nations, especially the Baltics, is distinctly hostile at times. Many Russians today regret the passing of the USSR, and are Great Russians at heart. The former Communist Party of the Soviet Union (CPSU), now called the Communist Party of the Russian Federation (CPRF), is an ethnic nationalist party advocating a 'Slavic Union' of Russia, Ukraine and Belarus, and it opposed the war in Chechnya. But there is an increasing realisation that the clock cannot be turned back. Most of the new states of the former USSR are in harmony with Russian nationalism as long as it maintains a non-expansionist policy, which is now prevalent.

A more complex case is that of Belarus. Belarusans/*Belarusy* were mainly, but by no means solely, the inhabitants of the Byelorussian Republic of the Soviet Union. There, they amounted to 8.2 million of the population of 10 million (78 per cent). But another 3.5 million Belarusans were living in Russia, Ukraine, Poland, Lithuania and Latvia. Belarus declared its State Sovereignty on 27 July 1990 (a rather ambiguous act at this time) and independence after the failed coup in August 1991, and the name Belarus was adopted. But the rulers of Belarus were not keen on the dissolution of the USSR, and were especially ready to join the Commonwealth of Independent States (CIS) which succeeded it, and promote its capital, Minsk, as its headquarters. Belarus's first president, Alyaksandr Lukashenka, was pro-Russian and moreover was a reluctant democrat, if he was one at all. Democratic elections were delayed for years, and referendums used to sanction the use of Russian as a second official language, and economic integration with the Russian Federation. In May 1997, a union charter was signed between Belarus and Russia, though Belarus nationalists demonstrated against it. In December 1998, the presidents of Russia and Belarus agreed to have common policies on economic, foreign and military affairs. Belarus reverted to Stalinism, but not without opposition from nationalists, whose demonstrations in October 1999 had to be put down with force. So the 'national revolution' in Belarus is far from complete.

In fact, Belarusans, also known as 'White Russians', are ethnically similar to Russians, though their language is separate, and probably would not have left the Soviet Union had it not disintegrated around them. But they certainly showed the desire for 'sovereignty' as early as mid-1990, more than a year before the Soviet Union's demise.

This cannot be said of Ukraine, for its nationalism has a long history. It came under Russia in part only in the early eighteenth century, having been under Poland since the sixteenth century, with a brief period of independence in the seventeenth century. On the disintegration of Poland in 1795, it was entirely under Russia. Nevertheless, like Poland it never lost its nationalism, and declared its independence from Russia in 1918. But it was invaded by Poland, which also claimed it, and only became part of the USSR as a constituent republic on 30 December 1922, after a struggle involving not only nationalists but also communists against anti-communist 'White Russians'. By this time, Poland was re-established as a nation-state, but including Western Ukraine, and Czechoslovakia included Carpatho-Ukraine (Ruthenia). These states did not give the Ukrainians the autonomy they desired, and which had been promised in the post-First World War agreements.

Before the Second World War the Nazi occupiers of Czechoslovakia granted autonomy to Ruthenia, and hoped the Ukrainians there and in Poland would reciprocate by fighting on their side. But the Nazis also made a deal with Hungary to enable them to annex Ruthenia, which they did in March 1939, and another deal in September 1939 with Russia to give them Western Ukraine. An uprising of Ukrainian nationalists in June 1941 was put down by the Nazis. So the Ukrainians found themselves inside a pincer movement from both east and west, something that had also happened to the Poles.

Ukraine's nationalism was suppressed under Stalin, but its national identity was respected within the Soviet system, at least as far as language and education were concerned. There was even a kind of autonomy within the Soviet federal system. This kept alive the nation, although it was subject to communist authoritarianism and central power. The collapse of that authoritarianism and power under Gorbachev released Ukrainian nationalism from its inhibitions, and once more a kind of independence was declared (16 July 1990). But this was not a secession from the USSR, which came only after the failure of the coup against Gorbachev on 24 August 1991. This was a deathblow to the Soviet Union, and came as a surprise to most people at home and abroad. But Ukrainians overwhelmingly (by 90.3 per cent in a turnout of 83.7 per cent) endorsed this secession in a referendum on 1 December 1991, and Belarus and Russia announced the demise of the Soviet Union on 8 December.

Ukraine, which was established as an independent state, was not a homogeneous nation. Ukrainians amounted to 73 per cent of the population, and they were split culturally between Eastern and Western Ukrainians. The former were more Russified, while the latter (based in Galicia and Ruthenia) had been under Austrian rule until 1918, where nationalism was more tolerated than in Russia. These differences have continued to the present.

Russians are 22 per cent of the population of Ukraine, and of course spoke Russian rather than Ukrainian. Nevertheless, Ukrainian was made the official language in 1990. However, it would be a mistake to think that the ethnic Russians owed their prime loyalty to Russia, for most voted for Ukrainian independence. Ukraine, for its part, was liberal in its citizenship policies, and did not seek to exclude Russian speakers from citizenship, even if they did not know Ukrainian (see Citizenship Laws, below). In a short time, most were able to master Ukrainian, which is in any case closer to Russian than the Baltic languages.

The Crimea/*Krym* was a more difficult area, however, and there the concentration of Russians and Tatars/Tartars voted for autonomy in

1991, and soon after that for independence this was revoked in May 1992, and Crimea was made an Autonomous Republic (*Respublika Krym*) of Ukraine, with protection for its languages and cultures. A referendum in 1994 supported dual Ukrainian–Russian citizenship, but this was not granted in the 1996 Constitution. In 1999 more power was granted over property and the budget. This seems to have satisfied moderate opinion in Crimea, and support for pro-Russian parties has declined (see Electoral Nationalism, below).

Another national problem area is the Donbass region of Eastern Ukraine, which is composed largely of ethnic Russians. A referendum there in June 1994 supported closer economic ties with Russia, and making Russian an official language. The new Ukrainian Constitution of 1996 did not grant this, however. The Donbass region is made up of two of Ukraine's 24 provinces (Donetska/Donets'k and Luhanska/Luhans'k). Russia does not seek to dispute the territory of Ukraine, and the ethnic Russians are more reconciled to being citizens of and independent Ukraine, whose troubles now are less relating to nationalism than to maladministration and economic problems.

Constitutions

Russian Federation/Russia (1993)

Preamble

We, the multinational people of the Russian Federation, united in a common destiny ... preserving the historic unity of the state, proceeding from the commonly recognised principles of equality and self-determination of the peoples, honouring the memory of our ancestors, who have passed on to us love of and respect for our homeland ... - reviving the sovereign statehood of Russia.

Article 19 (Equality)
(2) The state guarantees the equality of rights and liberties regardless of ... race, nationality, language, origin ... Any restriction of the rights of citizens on ... racial, national, linguisitic or religious grounds is forbidden.

Article 26 (National Identity, Native Language)
(1) Everyone has the right to determine and state his national identity. No one can be forced to determine and state his national identity.
(2) Everyone has the right to use his native language, freely choose the language of communication, education, training and creative work.

Article 62 (Dual Citizenship)

(1) The citizen of the Russian Federation may have the citizenship of a foreign state (dual citizenship) in conformity with the federal law or international treaty of the Russian Federation.

(3) Foreign citizens and stateless persons enjoy in the Russian Federation the rights of its citizens and bear their duties with the exception of cases stipulated by the federal law or international treaty of the Russian Federation.

Article 65 (Republics)

(1) The Russian Federation consists of the subjects of the Federation: [21 Republics][4] ... Jewish Autonomous Region.[5]

Article 68 (State Language)

(1) The state language of the Russian Federation throughout its territory is the Russian language.

(2) The republics have the right to institute their own state languages. They are used alongside the state language of the Russian federation in bodies of state power, bodies of local self-government and state institutions of the republics.

(3) The Russian Federation guarantees all its peoples the right to preserve their native language and to create the conditions for its study and development.

Article 69 (Indigenous Rights)

The Russian Federation guarantees the rights of small indigenous peoples in accordance with the generally accepted principles and standards of international law and international treaties of the Russian Federation.

Citizenship law (1992)

(a) By birth: if either parent is a citizen of the Russian Federation, and the other is a stateless person, their child shall be a citizen of the Russian Federation, irrespective of the child's place of birth;

(b) By descent: if both parents are citizens are citizens ... irrespective of the child's place of birth;

If one parent is a citizen ... and the other is of another citizenship ... the child's citizenship shall be decided by a written agreement between the parents ... (in the absence of such agreement ... shall acquire Russian citizenship if born on the territory of the Russian Federation.

(c) By registration: persons whose spouse or direct ancestor is a citizen of the Russian Federation; ...

Children of former Russian Federation citizens, born after the termination of parents' Russian Federation citizenship, may register for citizenship within five years after their eighteenth birthday;

Former citizens of the USSR who resided on the territory of the former USSR and who came to reside on the territory of the Russian Federation after February 6, 1992, if they declared their intention to acquire citizenship of the Russian Federation by December 31, 2000.

Stateless persons permanently residing on the territory of the Russian federation ... or on the territory of other republics of the former USSR as of September 1, 1991 ... within one year of enactment of the present Law declare their intention to acquire citizenship of the Russian Federation ...

Foreign citizens and stateless persons, irrespective of their domicile, who themselves are, or one of whose direct ancestors were, a subject of Russia by birth, and who, within one year of enactment of the present Law, declare their intention to acquire the Russian Federation citizenship;

(d) By naturalization: be at least 18 years old and have permanent residence for a total of five years, or three years of continuous residence immediately prior to filing an application. For refugees recognized as such by the Russian Federation, the time periods shall be halved.

Dual citizenship: Recognised, where a pertinent treaty exists with another state.

Belarus (1994)

Preamble

We, the People of the Republic of Belarus, emanating from the responsibility for the present and future of Belarus ...

Article 5 (Political Parties)

(3) The creation and activities of political parties and other public associations that aim at changing the constitutional system by force, or conduct a propaganda of war, ethnic, religious or racial hatred, shall be prohibited.

Article 9 (Self-Determination, Territory)

(1) The territory of the Republic of Belarus shall be the natural condition of the existence and spatial limit of the people's self-determination ...

Article 11 (Equal Rights of Foreigners)

Foreign nationals and stateless persons in the territory of Belarus shall enjoy rights ... on a par with the citizens of the Republic of Belarus, unless otherwise specified in the Constitution, the laws and international agreements.

Article 15 (Heritage, Cultural Development)

The State shall bear responsibility for preserving the historic and cultural heritage, and the free development of the cultures of all the ethnic communities that live in the Republic of Belarus.

Article 17 (Language)

(1) The official language of the Republic of Belarus shall be Belarussian.

(2) The Republic of Belarus shall safeguard the right to use the Russian language feely as a language of inter-ethnic communication.

Article 50 (Ethnicity)

(1) Everyone shall have the right to preserve his ethnic affiliation, and equally, no one may be compelled to define or indicate his ethnic affiliation.

(2) Insults to ethnic dignity shall be prosecuted by law.

(3) Everyone shall have the right to use his native language and to choose the language of communication. In accordance with the law, the State shall guarantee the freedom to choose the language of education and teaching.

Citizenship law (1991)

(a) By birth: (except if born to stateless or unknown parents);

(b) By descent: (if at least one parent a citizen, or permanently residing in Belarus at the time of the child's birth);

(c) By naturalization: can be applied for if person is capable of speaking the language, has resided in the territory for the last seven years, has a legitimate source of income, does not have citizenship of another state, and assumes obligations to follow the Constitution and laws of Belarus. Dual Citizenship: not recognised.

Ukraine (1996)

Preamble

The Verkhovna Rada [Supreme Council = legislature] of Ukraine, on behalf of the Ukrainian people – citizens of Ukraine of all nationalities ... based on the centuries-old history of Ukrainian state-building and on the right of self-determination realized by the Ukrainian nation, of all the Ukrainian people ...

Chapter I (General Principles)

Article 4

There is a single citizenship in Ukraine. The grounds for the acquisition and termination of Ukrainian citizenship are determined by law.

Article 10

(i) The State language of Ukraine is the Ukrainian language.

(ii) The State ensures the comprehensive development and functioning of the Ukrainian language in all spheres of social life throughout the entire territory of Ukraine.

(iii) In Ukraine, the free development, use and protection of Russian, and other languages of national minorities of Ukraine, is guaranteed.

Article 11

The State promotes the consolidation and development of the Ukrainian nation, of its historical consciousness, traditions and culture, and the development of the ethnic, cultural, linguistic and religious identity of all indigenous peoples and national minorities of Ukraine.

Article 12

Ukraine provides for the satisfaction of national and cultural and linguistic needs of Ukrainians residing beyond the borders of the State.

Chapter II (Human and Citizens' Rights, Freedoms and Duties)
Article 38

(i) The establishment and activity of political parties and public associations are prohibited if their programme goals and actions are aimed at the liquidation of the independence of Ukraine ... the incitement of inter-ethnic, racial, or religious enmity ...

Article 53

(v) Citizens who belong to national minorities are guaranteed in accordance with the law of the right to receive instruction in their native language, or to study their native language in state and communal educational establishments and through national cultural societies.

Article 65

(i) Defence of the Motherland, of the independence and territorial indivisibility of Ukraine, and respect for state symbols, are the duties of citizens of Ukraine ...

Chapter III (Elections. Referendum)

Article 73

Issues of altering the territory of Ukraine are resolved exclusively by an all-Ukrainian referendum.

Chapter X (Autonomous Republic of Crimea)

Article 134

The Autonomous Republic of Crimea is an inseparable constituent part of Ukraine and decided on the issues ascribed to its competence within the limits of authority determined by the Constitution of Ukraine. [There follows a list of the powers of the Autonomous Republic, which includes 'ensuring the operation and development of the state language and national languages and cultures in the Autonomous Republic' Education, however, is not specifically included.]

Citizenship law (1991)

(a) By birth: but does not automatically confer citizenship.
(b) By descent: at least one parent a Ukrainian citizen.
(c) By registration: children adopted by citizens; persons who have no other citizenship and at least one parent or grandparent Ukrainian by birth; foreign persons and persons without citizenship under certain conditions (not listed).
(d) By naturalisation: ability to function in the Ukrainian language, knowledgeable of the Ukrainian Constitution, and does not possess any foreign citizenship.

Electoral nationalism

Russian Federation

Liberal Democratic Party of Russia/Liberalno-Demokraticheskaya Pariya Rossii (LDPR) (1990).

The extreme 'Greater Russian' Party chaired by Vladimir Zhirinovsky. As noted in the text above, other parties can be considered nationalist to degree, but are predominantly based on other divisions in politics.

Table 14.1   Presidential elections

	% of vote (1st round)
1991	7.8
1996	5.7
2000	2.7

Table 14.2   State Duma elections (450 members)

	% of vote (PR)	Seats
1993	22.8	64
1995	11.4	51
1999	6.0	17

Belarus

Liberal Democratic Party of Belarus/Liberalna-Demokratychnaya Partiya Belarusi (LDPB) *(1998)*

Fraternal party of the LDPR, and supporter of the Belarus President, Alyaksandr Lukashenka. Is right-wing Pan-Slavic party, in support of close links with Russia. Won one seat in the 2000 legislative elections.

Belarusan People's Patriotic Union/Belaruski Norodna Patryatchny Soyuz (BNPS) *(1998)*

An alliance of 30 conservative parties formed to support Present Lukashenka. Included the LDPB and the White Rus Slavonic Council.

Opponents of union with Russia might be considered Belarus nationalists of a kind. These include the Belarusan Popular Front-Renaissance/ *Narodni Front Belarusi-Adradzhennie (NFB-A)*, the Conservative Christian Party/*Ckonservativnaya Khrystsiyanska Partiya (KRP)* and the National Democratic Party of Belarus/*Natsyianalna-Demokratychnaya Partiya Belarusi (NDPB)*. These parties won no seats, however, and the NFB-A boycotted the 2000 legislative elections.

Ukraine

Popular Movement of Ukraine/Narodny Rukh Ukrainy *('Rukh') (1989)*

The original nationalist movement, which helped bring about Ukraine's independence in 1991, along with the Communist Party of Ukraine *(KPU)*. Its electoral record since independence has been poor (see Table 14.3).

Table 14.3 Supreme Council elections (450 members)

	% of vote	Seats
1994		20
1998	9.4	46

National Front/NatsionalniyFront (NF) (1998)

A right-wing nationalist part alliance of three parties. These parties had won 17 seats in the 1994 election, but won only five seats in 1998.

Forward Ukraine!/Vypered Ukrayino! (1998)

An alliance for the 1998 elections of nationalist parties based in the Uniate Catholic population of Galicia (Western Ukraine). It got only

1.7 per cent of the vote and two seats in the 450-seat Supreme Council.

Various other nationalist or ethnic parties exist in Ukraine, but none has a significant electoral presence. The President, Leonid Kuchma, is a non-party, and can be counted as a kind of Ukrainian nationalist. He was opposed by a Communist Party of Ukraine candidate in the presidential election of November 1999, and won 56.3 per cent of the vote.

Conclusion

The USSR disintegrated into independent states based on the existing republics in 1991. Most of these were 'titular nationalities' in Soviet parlance, that is, they were dominated by one nation or ethnic group. So the legacy of the USSR was a nationalist one, even if there was no intention to encourage national self-determination.

With a few exceptions, the transition to independent nation-states has been peaceful, and relatively successful. This is in marked contrast to the disintegration of Yugoslavia, where a bloody ethnic struggle ensued, and is still unresolved.

The reason for this difference is not easy to establish, but it relates to the distinction, often drawn, between 'civic' or 'inclusive' nationalism and 'ethnic' or 'exclusive' nationalism. Most of the nationalism discussed in this chapter has been of the former variety, as examination of their constitutions and citizenship laws shows. Of course all nationalisms contain both civic and ethnic elements, but the balance between the two differs in each case. Russia, Belarus and Ukraine have tilted towards the civic variety, with some exceptions. In the case of Russia, Chechnya is a failure, and Belarus is drawn back towards union with Russia, which is another failure of nationalism. Ukraine is difficult to assess, because of its multinational tensions which are not yet resolved. But there is an absence of violence relating to national questions, which must indicate an 'inclusive' nationalism at the centre. On the ground, however, Tatars, Russians and others are more ethnic in their claims.

The break-up of the USSR into its components is regretted by many, but it now appears to have been inevitable. The Russian Empire should have disintegrated in 1918, when the rest of Europe was swept by the national self-determination principle, but it was perpetuated by the communists under the USSR. This Union was both undemocratic and repressive of nationality. It could not survive the pressures of the modern world, which in politics is based on the twin pillars of democracy and nationality.

15
Conclusion

The two dimensions of nationalism in Europe discussed in this book have been comparatively neglected in other works on the subject. First, constitutional contexts are rarely looked at, probably because nationalism is seen as an extra-constitutional subject.

At the present time, however, nationalism has triumphed to such an extent that the constitutions of most European states are explicitly national in character. The Preambles of these constitutions (if such exist) declare the national heritage and destiny of the state, and the constitutions spell out the nature of the national language, anthem, flag and so on. They almost invariably define their citizenship in national terms, even if some are more open to 'foreigners' than others. A few are explicitly ethnic in the definition of their citizenship (the *ius sanguinis*), while most adopt a mixture of ancestral qualifications and birth or residence on the soil of the state (the *ius solis*). All have a process of naturalisation, but in most cases this is accompanied by conditions of a long period of residency, knowledge of the language and economic viability. Asylum seekers are sometimes allowed to settle, and in some cases become citizens, but the conditions for these have grown more difficult in recent years everywhere in Europe.

The nation-state is essentially exclusive in nature because of these restrictions. Even in a so-called 'global' era, the fundamental unit of belonging and social and political action is the state. The state provides for social security, health, education, most taxation and public expenditure. Even the advanced forms of supranationalism, such as the European Union (EU), are strongly weighted towards the national end of the national–supranational scale. The EU has expanded its remit into areas formerly occupied by the states, but it has made few inroads into national identities and loyalties. In these, Europeans are nationals first and Europeans second, even if almost half of EU citizens in general today profess both a national and European identity.[1] The reasons for this are partly historical and partly contemporary. History until very recently placed people in nation-states, not in supranational organisations. They are not accustomed to thinking of themselves in anything by national terms. They elect national governments, not supranational ones, their passports are national (even if the EU has a superimposed citizenship for its members), and their language is national, not European (there is no European language as such).

The contemporary reason for the strength of nations is the fact that democracy (in Europe at least) has triumphed over imperialism and various types of authoritarianism, notably fascism, military rule and communism. Some of these were also nationalist, but did not exist in a democratic context. By the 1990s, all but one state in Europe had at least the appearance of democracy, with nominally competitive elections (the exception is the Vatican City State). Of course, the conditions for fair and free elections are difficult to establish and maintain when politicians want to win at all costs. But now international supervision is common in the most unlikely democratic elections, such those in Bosnia-Hercegovina and Kosovo. There are still one or two no-go areas for democracy in European states, such as in Russia (Chechnya) and Belarus, but they are very much the exceptions. Even Albania, Bulgaria and Romania, notoriously undemocratic until 1990, can be considered democratic today.

In this situation of democratic politics, the electoral dimension to nationalism also becomes a key to its character. It was always true that elections in democratic states were the motors of change, and the votes for nationalist parties were one indicator of the strength of nationalism in these. Thus, the progress of Scottish nationalism was plotted by the electoral strength of the Scottish National Party (SNP), and so on. But it was evident in all states that nationalism was expressed by voters in ways that went beyond the votes given to nationalist parties. The clearest examples were the referendums on devolution, when a much wider support for a national parliament was mobilised than ever voted for the nationalist party. While this could be described as support for 'decentralisation', 'regional autonomy', 'good government' and so on, and not for nationalism, there can hardly be any doubt that support for devolution to a nation is an expression of national identity and aspiration for that nation, as distinct from the (multinational) state.

When this is applied generally in Europe, it can be seen that electoral nationalism covers both the support for nationalist parties and support for the nation in general. This can be traced in the histories of those countries, which became independent or united[2] in the early 1990s. The 23 new states, with three exceptions, which achieved national independence, got it by voting in referendums, and for parties or movements which sought independence. Most (the Czechs and Slovaks are exceptions, since they did not hold referendums, nor did the Germans on reunification) voted overwhelmingly to become independent, and supported electoral organisations (not always parties) of a nationalist nature, such as Popular Fronts. Without the advent of democracy in these nations, there would have been no chance of achieving independence.

After independence, many of the Popular Fronts and nationalist parties melted away, as politics became divided over internal matters. Even so, nationalist parties continued, and their strength can be plotted in elections. Nearly all the politicians are nationalist to a degree, for they do not wish to turn the clock back and rescind their nations' independence. Only in Belarus is there a government-led policy of union with Russia, but what this union means is not clear. It might mean something like the EU, but with a stronger form of economic and security integration.

Nations which have not become independent, and which should have done so in a fundamentalist nationalist prospectus, are still found in Europe. The Scots, Welsh, Corsicans, Catalans and Basques are examples, but most of these nations would not vote for independence today in a referendum, if they got the chance, which they usually do not under the present constitutions. Thus democracy does not strengthen secessionist nationalism in many cases, but sustains the official, state nationalism. Some who would probably vote for independence are not given the chance, such as the Chechens in Russia, and the Kosovans in Serbia.

Then there are national anomalies such as the Northern Irish, Corsicans, Flemings, Walloons, Bretons, ethnic Romanian Moldovans, Sami and Roma, who do not really seek national independence or unity with their co-nationals, but who are nationalists nevertheless. Their nationalism is difficult to satisfy, for various reasons. Some are not territorially based, or are spread across the territories of several states (e.g. the Sami and Roma), while others are 'loyal' to the multinational states of which they are members, although that loyalty is not always reciprocated. Many have dual identities, to their nation and to the state. They occupy an uneasy position in a national, democratic Europe.

Where national self-determination has been satisfied, as nearly everywhere in Europe, two nationalist themes continue in contemporary politics. The first, and most virulent, is opposition to foreigners settling in the nation, whether as normal immigrants or as asylum seekers. Every country has tried to restrict immigration more closely in recent years, but the number of resident incomers has grown steadily. Immigrants have been attacked for their non-national ways, whether alleged criminal activities, language, dress, religion or eating habits. Asylum seekers, increasingly spilling out of the trouble spots of the Balkans, North Africa, Turkey and the Asian subcontinent, have highlighted the difficulty of reconciling a national citizenship law with an open inclusive one which is not based on the ethnic or social nation.[3]

Even so, the 'racist' parties in Britain, France or Germany have done very badly in recent elections, with one or two exceptions, such as Le Pen's vote in the first round of the French Presidential elections in April 2002, and the strong nationalist and 'Neo-Nazi' voting in Germany in the mid-1990s. But these were not real challenges to democracy, or to the liberal, inclusive form of nationalism.

The last contemporary manifestation of nationalism in Europe is anti-EU feeling, especially with regard to 'economic and monetary union' and social integration. As the EU has grown more powerful, with a common currency and greater powers for Brussels, so too has nationalism in reaction. All the political elites of the member states have proclaimed that they are not giving away 'national sovereignty' to the supranational body, but the voters have not been convinced. In referendums in Denmark, France and Ireland, for example, proposals for greater integration or enlargement have been rejected or narrowly passed. The Euro currency was rejected by three of the member-states, and is increasingly unpopular in many of the others. Britain has not dared to hold a referendum at all on joining the Euro, and nearly all the parties there have taken a nationalist line,[4] with the exception of the Liberal Democrats (who do not occupy power at the centre).

Given that the EU is not a democratic organisation, that is not surprising. The EU lacks the characteristics of a nation, whether a language, elected government, President or monarch, national history or ethnicity. What it can offer is economic prosperity and convenience for cross-border transactions. Anti-EU feeling is not deeply felt, as long as the EU does not interfere in matters held sacred to the nation. So far, the EU has been usually careful to avoid doing that, but some EU bureaucrats and politicians see nations and nationalism as irritants to be expunged. They in turn have been vilified as typifying 'distant Brussels rule'.

The EU, North Atlantic Treaty Organization (NATO) and the Organization for Security and Co-operation in Europe (OSCE) have been forces for good in central and eastern Europe, where membership has been made conditional on respect for democracy and human rights. The Baltic states, Hungary, the Czech Republic, Slovakia and Croatia have had to moderate their ethnic nationalism to guarantee rights for national minorities in order to satisfy international opinion. Most of these states are now comparatively liberal in character, but with at least one nationalist failing, the poor treatment of the Roma (Gypsies) in the states of central and eastern Europe.

In conditions of liberal democracy, constitutions matter. They lay down the nature of the state, its national character and the rights of minorities and individuals. For secessionists, they provide a peaceful avenue for national self-determinations, although it is true that most states do not countenance the break-up of the state, proclaiming its 'indivisibility'. However, a demonstration of national support in an election or referendum would be difficult for any democratic state to resist.

Elections and voting are thus the key to nationalism in Europe. No nation will achieve independence today without a majority vote of that nation in support. Nationalists who deny this fact – and there are quite a few, notably in Northern Ireland, the Basque country and Corsica – are doomed to failure, even if their actions are able to wring various concessions from state governments. Moderate nationalists are content to operate within the multinational state with national autonomy if they cannot win a majority for independence. This is a realistic strategy, and can lead to independence in certain circumstances, usually the failure of the state to comprehend or satisfy sub-state nationalism.

Nationalism is the dominant political and social force in Europe, and has replaced ideology[5] as the divide between 'East' and 'West'. But European nations are not now hostile to one another, as was the case until 1945, except in the Balkans and parts of the former USSR. Rather, their nationalisms are embedded in democratic ideology, and they are increasingly being satisfied in the context of international institutions such as the EU and OSCE. Only in former Yugoslavia and the Russian Federation is this happy situation not found. Lapses can take place anywhere, and Northern Ireland, Corsica and the Basque Country are continuing locations for violent nationalism. But even these have moderated in recent years, and the central states are usually responsible for provoking violent responses with a violence of their own. Unresolved nationalist claims can be a source for violence, but the democratic solution is for nationalists to produce the votes to support their claims. That is the contemporary way ahead for nationalism in Europe, which is now the companion of constitutionalism and democracy.

Notes

1 States and Nations

1. For the historical atlases used, see Bibliographical Note. It is likely that the names of states and nations found in atlases published in non-English speaking countries will differ considerably from those in these atlases, so too much should not be made of the presence or absence of names in atlases. Nevertheless, standardisation of state names does now occur in international organisations such as the UN and EU, and comparisons across time can be made with these.

2. In this work 'Europe' has been delimited to 44 states: Albania, Andorra, Austria, Belarus, Belgium, Bosnia-Herzegovina, Bulgaria, Croatia, Czech Republic, Denmark, Estonia, Finland, France, Germany, Greece, Hungary, Iceland, Ireland, Italy, Latvia, Liechtenstein, Lithuania, Luxembourg, Macedonia, Malta, Moldova, Monaco, Netherlands, Norway, Poland, Portugal, Romania, Russia-in-Europe (part of the Russian Federation), San Marino, Slovakia, Slovenia, Spain, Sweden, Switzerland, 'Turkey-in-Europe' (north-east of the Bosphorus, although 'Turkey-in-Asia' is an integral part of Turkey, which is an applicant for membership of the EU), United Kingdom, Ukraine, Vatican City State, Yugoslavia. Cyprus, while not usually counted as in Europe, is an applicant for membership of the EU (at least, the southern 'Democratic Cyprus' is). For the main reference works used, see Bibliographical Note.

3. F. Fernández-Armesto (ed.), *The Times Guide to the Peoples of Europe* (London: Times Books, 1994). The 101 sub-headings (some of which include several 'peoples' under one sub-heading) are grouped as follows: *The Maritime North*: Icelanders, Faeroese, Norwegians, Danes, English and Lowland Scots, Northern English, Channel Islanders, Highland and Island Scots, Dutch, Frisians, Normans. *The Atlantic Arc*: Portuguese, Azoreans, Madeirans, Galicians, Asturians and Cantabrians, Canary Islanders, Basques, Bretons, Welsh, Cornish and Manx (three in one group), Irish. *The Continental Northwest*: French, Burgundians, Luxembourgers, Walloons, Flemish, Germans, Rhinelanders, Franconians. *The Alpine Regions*: Swabians, Bavarians, Austrians, Vorarlbergers, Tyrolese, Salzburgers, Carinthians, Styrians, Burgenlanders, Upper Austrians, Lower Austrians and Viennese, Swiss, Piedmontese, Valdaostans and Waldensians, Lombards, Slovenes. *The Western and Central Mediterranean*: Spanish-speaking communities, Navarrese, Aragonese, Castilians, Andalusians, Gibraltarians, Catalans, Valencians and Balearic Islanders (three in one group), Provencals, Corsicans, Sardinians, Ligurians, Veneto-Friulians, Central Italians, South Italians, Sicilians, Maltese. *The Balkans*: Turks, Greeks, Albanians, Macedonians, Bulgarians, Serbs, Montenegrins, Croats, Bosnian Muslims. *The Carpathian Region*: Czechs, Slovaks, Magyars, Scattered Germans, Romanians, Ruthenians, Huitsuls, Boikos and Lemkos (three in one group). *The Northern Plain*: Saxons, Poles, Lithuanians, Latvians (Letts), Sorbs (Wends),

Prussians. *The Northern Baltic*: Swedes, Swedish speaking Finns and Alanders. Lapps, Finns, Karelians, Veps, Estonians. *The Eastern Marches*: Marchland Poles, Belorussians, Ukrainians, Russians. *The Urals and Caucasus*: Volga Tatars, Muslim-Turkic and Mongol Peoples of the Volga-Urals and Daghestan, Non-Muslim Peoples of the Volga-Urals, Peoples of the Caucasus. *Dispersed Peoples*: Jews, Gypsies.

It should be noted that these 'peoples' are not necessarily 'ethnic groups' or 'nations', and that their national consciousness and nationalism is variable and may not even exist. To use this list for the study of nationalism, students would need to consider which of these 'peoples' has in fact developed nationalism. So a corresponding list of European 'nationalisms' would be much shorter, but would also include nations and nationalisms not specified here as 'peoples'. For example, the inhabitants of Scotland are here divided into two groups of 'peoples', 'English and Lowland Scots' and 'Highland and Island Scots', while there is one Scottish nation and one Scottish nationalism covering these 'peoples', with the possible exception of Orkney and Shetland, where some of the inhabitants claim a non-Scottish identity and espouse a political regionalism rather than Scottish nationalism (an 'Orkney and Shetland Movement' puts up candidates in addition to, or instead of, Scottish National Party candidates). All this shows the difficulty of matching an anthropological or historical approach to the political science approach to contemporary nationalism.

4. Several maps give supposed divisions of the languages and peoples of Europe (e.g. Barraclough, *The Times Atlas of World History*, p. 214). From these it is clear that languages and peoples do not always coincide. For example, the German language covers the 'peoples' called 'Germans', and 'Austrians', and the 'Scots' include English, Scots and Gaelic speakers, although these languages are not shown on the map quoted (one language, presumably English covers the 'peoples', English, Welsh, Scots, and Irish). A *Carta Etno-Linguistica D'Europa* was included with the magazine *Ethnica*, Vol. 1, no. 1 (November 1993), published in Milan. The whole of Scotland was called 'Gaelici', although only 1.5% of the population speaks Gaelic. 'Italiani' occupy only the central and southern parts of the Italian peninsula, and Latvians, despite the fact that they were at this time only 52% of the population of Latvia, appear on the map to be overwhelmingly predominant. Another map (*Aproximacio a l'Europa de les Nacions* (Barcelona: Centre Internacional Escarre per a les minories etniques i les nacions, 1990)) explicitly refers to nations. What these maps show is that peoples or nations and languages are not congruous, and that neither are territorially well-defined compared to states. That does not mean that the territorial distribution of languages, peoples and nations is unimportant politically.

Looking at these maps from the point of view of politics rather than linguistics or anthropology, it is clear that the drawing of maps is integral to the state-forming process, and is highly contested in many cases. Contemporary map-drawing political disputes include all the new states of former Yugoslavia except Slovenia. It is obvious that Slovenia has escaped such a dispute because of the near-perfect fit between the Slovenian 'nation' and the state of Slovenia on the map, with a very small (under 10%) non-Slovenian minority. What is not so clear is why cases where the boundaries of nations and states or regions do not coincide and large national minorities are present have not produced map politics of any significance, so far.

5. For a discussion of territorial primordialism in nationalism, see Edward Shils, 'Nation, nationality, nationalism and civil society', *Nations and Nationalism*, Vol. 1, no. 1, 1995, 93–118. Most anthropologists and sociologists reject 'primordialism' , but one anthropologist states that ethnonationalist movements are 'always territorially based'. Thomas Hyland Eriksen, *Ethnicity and Nationalism. Anthropological Perspectives* (London and Boulder: Pluto Press, 1993), p. 14.

6. There is much confusion about this in the literature. Nationalism pertains to nations, and regionalism to regions. Nationalists may support a 'Europe of the Regions', but not because they see themselves as regionalists, rather because such a formula serves the interests of their nationalism. They accept the status of region only in a formal, legal sense to obtain representation for their nation in the EU, or within the state under 'regional devolution' or federalism. Regionalists, on the other hand, make no claim to nationhood for their regions, and accept the legitimacy of the state or official nation, of which regions are arbitrary (state-devised) subdivisions. Regionalists are totally loyal to the state and see themselves as predominantly or totally 'official national' in terms of national identity.

7. States not discussed include Andorra, Monaco, Liechtenstein, San Marino, Vatican State and Malta.

2   The British Isles

1. Linda Colley, *Britons: Forging the Nation 1707–1837* (New Haven and London: Yale University Press, 1992), pp. 374–5.

2. E. Moxon-Browne, 'National identity in Northern Ireland', in P. Stringer and G. Robinson (eds), *Social Attitudes in Northern Ireland* (Belfast: Blackstaff, 1991), p. 25. Figures for Registrar Office marriages from General Register Office for Northern Ireland, *Seventy-Ninth Annual Report of the Registrar General 2000*, Table 7.7 (London: Stationery Office, 2001).

3. For example, David Miller, *On Nationality* (Oxford: Clarendon Press, 1995).

4. Moxon-Browne, op.cit., pp. 23–30. For 1995 survey see M. Duffy and G. Evans, 'Class, community polarisation and politics', in L. Dowds *et al.*, *Social Attitudes in Northern Ireland. The Sixth Report* (Belfast: Appletree, 1997). Ch. 6.

5. Quoted in R. Rose, *Understanding the United Kingdom. The Territorial Dimension in Government* (London: Longman, 1982), pp. 14–15.

6. Commission of the European Communities, *Eurobarometer no. 33 Vol.1: Report* (Brussels, June 1990), p. 2.

7. J. Brand, J. Mitchell and P. Surridge, 'Identity and the vote. Class and nationality in Scotland', in P. Norris *et al.* (eds), *British Elections and Parties Yearbook 1993* (Hemel Hempstead: Harvester Wheatsheaf, 1993), pp. 143–57. For a table comparing surveys on national identity in Scotland from 1979 to 1999, see L. Paterson *et al.*, *New Scotland, New Politics?* (Edinburgh: Polygon, 2001), p. 105.

8. Paterson *et al.*, loc. cit.

9. A. Brown, D. McCrone and L. Paterson, *Politics and Society in Scotland*, 2nd edition (Basingstoke: Macmillan, 1998), p. 213.

10. Federalism and consociational democracy are often used to deal with the problems of multinational states. In Europe, federalism and consociationalism of this type is found in Belgium and Switzerland.

11. Based on the account in *Britain 1992: An Official Handbook* (London: HMSO, 1992), pp. 19–20.

12. Until 1949, when Ireland left the British Commonwealth, citizens of Ireland were also able to hold British passports and those born before then still can. But other British citizens could not hold Irish passports. Even today, Irish citizens who are residents in Britain can receive British social security and vote in British elections.

13. Paterson *et al.*, op.cit., p. 111.

14. B. Taylor and K. Thomson (eds), *Scotland and Wales: Nations Again?* (Cardiff: University of Wales Press, 1999), p. 43.

15. B. Taylor and K. Thomson (eds), op.cit., pp. 65–93.

16. Quoted by Dr Sydney Elliot, 'Finding Out What the People Really Think', *Parliamentary Brief*, Vol. 3, no. 5 (March 1995), pp. 5–6.

17. Quoted in B. O'Leary and J. McGarry, *The Politics of Antagonism. Understanding Northern Ireland* (London and Atlantic Highlands NJ: The Athlone Press, 1993), pp. 279–84.

18. Some grounds for optimism can be gleaned from, for example, B. O'Leary, T. Lyne, J. Marshall, B. Rowthorn, *Northern Ireland. Sharing Authority* (London: Institute for Public Policy Research, 1993), and B. O'Leary and J. McGarry, op.cit.

19. D. McCrone, 'Opinion polls in Scotland, July 1994–June 1995', *Scottish Affairs*, no. 12, Summer 1995, p. 143.

3 France

1. This is the view taken by Hans Kohn in his *The Idea of Nationalism* (1944). He starts the first chapter: 'Nationalism as we understand it is not older than the second half of the eighteenth century. Its first great manifestation was the French Revolution, which gave the new movement an increased dynamic force'. However, 'this did not mark the date of its birth. Like all historical movements, nationalism had its roots deep in the past' (p. 3).

2. Jonathan Marcus, *The National Front and French Politics. The Resistible Rise of Jean-Marie Le Pen* (Basingstoke: Macmillan, 1995), pp. 77–8.

3. There are 22 metropolitan regions with elected general councils, but these have not affected the essentially unitary nature of the French republic. Moreover, the Brittany region offends Breton nationalists, since it is not based on the historic province of Brittany. Jean Ollivro, 'Identité territoriale et réunification de la Bretagne', *Diplomatie Magazine*, no. 2 (Mars–Avril 2003), pp. 51–4.

4. *Time Europe*, 24 June 2002, p. 30.

5. Marcus, op. cit., p. 90.

6. For 1999 figures, see *The Economist*, 2 March 2002, pp. 42–3.

7. Quoted by Christopher Ogden, 'Bombs Away!'. *Time Europe*, 18 September 1995, p. 31.
8. Source: www.uni-wuerzburg.de/law/fr00000_. html
9. Loi Constitutionelle No2003–276 du 28 Mars 2003.
10. Janine Renucci, *La Corse* (Paris: Presses Universitaires de France, 3rd edn., 1992), Ch. I, 'La Corse, Une Colonie'.
11. To qualify for the second round, a party must obtain at least 12.5% of the registered electorate in any constituency. A high abstention rate, as in 2002 (36%) makes that hurdle more difficult to surmount. In 1997 the FN qualified in 132 constituencies, but in 2002 in only 37.
12. Of this total, the Mégret faction won 5.7% of the total, and all 5 seats.
13. *Le Monde, Cahier Résultats*, 23 April 2002, p. 41.
14. Marcus, op.cit., p. 163.
15. *Time Europe*, 6 May 2002, p. 29. For Alex Salmond, see his column in the Scottish *News of the World*, 28 April 2002, p. 26, in which he also attacks the 'loathsome BNP' (British National Party). 'We must defeat hatred, racism, and intolerance wherever it rears its ugly head by standing tougher for the universal values first proclaimed by the French Republic – liberty, equality and fraternity.' Despite this, the Labour Scottish Executive First Minister, Jack McConnell, appeared to link the SNP to the National Front when he said that the 'politics of nation, identity and hatred should be thrown in the dustbin of history'. *Sunday Herald*, 28 April 2002, p. 1.
16. Reuter's News Service.
17. P. Hainsworth, 'The *Front National*: from ascendancy to fragmentation on the French extreme right', in P. Hainsworth (ed.), *The Politics of the Extreme Right* (London and New York: Pinter, 2000), p. 20.
18. *Le Monde*, 24 March 1992.
19. P. Lynch, 'The Scottish National Party and the European Parliament', *Scottish Affairs*, no. 12, Summer 1995, p. 93.
20. *Le Monde*, 8–9 May 1994, 11 May 1994.
21. *Le Monde*, 9 August 1994.
22. *Le Monde*, 2 April 1992.
23. *Le Monde*, 23 March 1993.
24. *Le Monde*, 17 and 24 March 1998.
25. *Le Monde*, 21 March 2002.
26. *Le Monde*, 12 December 1996.
27. Normandy has the Normandy Movement (*Mouvement Normand, MN*), supporting self-government for Normandy in the EU, and the Party for Independent Normandy (*Parti pour la Normandie Indépendante, PNI*) which seeks independence for Normandy, and has set up a 'provisional government'. Occitania has the Occitania Party (*Partit Occitan/POC*) (1987), and Savoy the Savoy League (1994) which seeks to reverse the French annexation of 1860 and re-establish a sovereign Savoy state. Its Secretary-General has been elected to the regional council. Alan J. Day, *Political Parties of the World*, 5th edn (London: John Harper Publishing, 2002), pp. 194–5.
28. A. Nouvel, *L'Occita. Langue de Civilisation Européenne* (Montpellier: Alain Nouvel, 1977), pp. 135–41.
29. F. Fernández-Armesto, *The Times Guide to the Peoples of Europe* (London: Times Books, 1994), p. 74.

30. F. Fernández-Armesto, p. 169.
31. Oonagh O'Brien, 'Good to be French? Conflicts of Identity in North Catalonia', in Sharon Macdonald (ed.), *Inside European Identities* (Providence/Oxford: Berg: 1993), p. 109.
32. *Ibid.*, p. 110.

4   Spain and Portugal

1. In 2002, negotiations took place between Spain and Britain to deal with Gibraltar. Britain proposed shared sovereignty, which was opposed by Spain and by a majority of the inhabitants of Gibraltar, for opposite reasons (the former wanted a transfer of sovereignty, while the latter wanted at least its base to remain under British sovereignty). A compromise giving Britain a secure lease of its naval base and Spain overall sovereignty was proposed by Spain, but not adopted. Curiously, a majority of the people of Gibraltar demanded the right of self-determination, in this case not to go independent but to stay part of Britain. For its part, Britain agreed to hold a referendum in Gibraltar, but made it known that a No vote would entail the cutting of the considerable subsidy from Britain. There was thus a double blackmail, of Britain by Spain, and of Gibraltar by Britain.
2. F. Fernández-Armesto (ed.), *The Times Guide to the Peoples of Europe* (London: Times Books, 1994), p. 64.
3. Paul Heywood, *The Government and Politics of Spain* (Basingstoke: Macmillan, 1995), p. 13.
4. The Spanish Constitution is available on www.uni-wuerzburg.de/law/sp00000_.html
5. The Catalan Government has been criticised for omitting the Spanish flag in public displays, for example, during the Olympic Games in Barcelona in 1992.
6. The Basque Nationalist Party (*Partido Nacionalista Vasco (PNV)/ Euzko Alderdi Jeltzalea (EAJ)*) dates from 1895. The Catalanist Union (*Unió Catalanista*) was established in 1891 to seek self-government. The Regionalist League of Catalonia (*Lliga Regionalista de Catalanya*) contested the general election of 1901.
7. Heywood, op.cit. p. 26.
8. Heywood, p. 24.
9. Heywood, p. 161.
10. Other regions with a nationalist and regionalist party presence are Andalusia (Andalusian Party, with 4/89 seats in the regional election of 1996); Aragon (Aragonese Party, with 10/67 seats in the 1999 election); Asturias (Asturian Renewal Union, with 3/45 seats in 1999); Cantabria (Regionalist Party of Cantabria, 6/39 seats in 1999); Castille and León (Union of the León People, 3/83 seats in 1999); La Rioja (Rioja Party, 2/33 seats in 1999); Valencia (Unity of the Valencian People, 5/89 seats in 1999; Valencian Union (5 seats in 1995 but none in 1999), Valencian Nationalist Party (no seats); Ceuta and Mellila (various regional parties, but supportive of Spanish connection). Alan J. Day (ed.), *Political Parties of the World*, 5th edn (London: John Harper Publishing, 2002), pp. 429–37.

11. In the Senate elections conducted on the same day, by party lists and indirect election by regional legislatures, the Popular Party won 126 seats, the Socialists 62 seats, the Convergence and Union 8 seats, the Basque Nationalists 6 seats and the Canarian Coalition five seats. Thus there were 19 nationalists/ regionalists elected.

12. Survey evidence on support for independence is peculiarly unreliable in Spain. See D. Conversi, *The Basques, the Catalans and Spain* (London: Hurst, 1997), pp. 206–7. Albert Balcells, *Catalan Nationalism. Past and Present* (Basingstoke: Macmillan, 1996), p. 193. These give support for independence as high as 45% in Catalonia (1988) and 74% in the Basque country (1983). These figures can be compared with 24% support for 'self-determination' in Catalonia (1996). John MacInnes, 'Dual Identity in Scotland and Catalonia', *Scottish Affairs Special Issue. Stateless nations in the 21st century: Scotland, Catalonia and Quebec* (2001), p. 118.

5 Italy

1. www.unionvaldotaine.org/mouvement.html
2. www.uni-wuerzburg.de/law/it00000_.html
3. Day's *Political Parties of the World* (2002) lists the following regional parties: Emilia and Romagna Freedom; Autonomous Lombardy Alliance; North-Eastern union; Romagna Autonomy Movement; Sardinian Action Party; Sicilian Action Party; Two Sicilies; South Tyrol People's Party; Union for South Tyrol; Southern League; For Trieste; Valdostan Union; Venetian Republican League. Day lists the Northern League as a 'National Party', although it only contests seats in the north. Worth noting are the Union for South Tyrol (5.5% of vote in 1998 South Tyrol Provincial election with 2 seats) and Ladins-DPS, also in South Tyrol (3.5%, 1 seat).
4. As part of the Freedom Alliance.
5. As part of House of Freedom alliance, which won 368 seats.
6. In the local elections of 16 November 1997, the Northern League came first in the province of Vicenza with 41.4% of the vote (up from 24.5% in 1995), in Varese with 38.1% of the vote (down from 49.3% in 1993), and in the province of Como with 33.1% (up from 20.1% over 1995). In the Province of Genoa it won 7.3% (down from 29.6% in 1993). In the cities up for election, in Alessandria the League won 20.3% of the vote (down from 33% in 1993), in Venice 11.0% (down from 29.9% in 1993) and in Genoa 3.5% (down from 29.2% in 1993). Eleven mayors were elected in small towns. *La Repubblica*, 18 November 1997.
7. Part of House of Freedom group which won 45.4% of vote and 368 seats.
8. A.S. Banks and T.C. Muller (eds), *Political Handbook of the World 1998* (Binghampton NY: CSA Publications, 1998) p. 469.

6 Germany

1. James B. Minahan, *One Europe, Many Nations. A Historical Dictionary of European National Groups* (Westport, Connecticut/London: Greenwood Press, 2000), p. 41.

2. The Basic Law is described in English by Axel Tschentscher, *The Basic Law (Grundegesetz)* (Würzburg: Jurisprudentia Verlag, 2002), also on internet, www.jurisprudentia.de
3. Mary Fulbrook, 'Germany for the Germans? Citizenship and nationality in a divided nation', in D. Cesarani and M. Fulbrook (eds), *Citizenship, Nationality and Migration in Europe* (London/New York: Routledge, 1996), p. 88.
4. Peter Pulzer, *German Politics 1945–1995* (Oxford: Oxford University Press, 1995), p. 21.
5. *Time Europe*, 24 June 2002, p. 30. *Time* gives the following table:

Foreign nationals as a percentage of population (2000)

Country	% of population
Austria	9.3
Belgium	8.3
Denmark (1999)	4.8
Finland	1.7
France (1999)	5.6
Germany	8.9
Italy	2.2
Netherlands	4.1
Spain	2
Sweden	5.5
UK	4

Source: Eurostat, except UK: National Statistics. 'Foreign nationals' are people who do not hold the nationality of the country in which they reside.

6. Loc.cit.
7. *Time Europe*, 24 December 2001, p. 52.
8. Mary Fulbrook, op.cit., p. 102.
9. In the 2002 Bundestag elections it won 7.4% of the German vote, up from 6.7% in 1998.
10. E.g. Susann Backer, 'Right-wing extremism in unified Germany', in P. Hainsworth (ed.), *The Politics of the Extreme Right. From the Margins to the Mainstream* (London/New York: Pinter, 2000), pp. 87–120.

7 The Low Countries

1. There is an important literature on consociational democracy, especially by the Dutch political scientist Arend Lijphart. See for example, Lijphart, *Democracy in Plural Societies: A Comparative Exploration* (New Haven: Yale University Press, 1977).
2. North Holland and South Holland are only two of the twelve provinces of the Netherlands. There is, however, no national question involved here, unlike the use of 'England' for Britain. Curiously, there is also an area called Holland in England, in Lincolnshire.

3. There are 303 000 Frisians in other parts of the Netherlands, and 151 000 in Denmark and East Friesland in Germany. James B. Minahan, op.cit., p. 262.
4. See www.bib.kuleuven.ac.be/english/geschied_e.htm and www.ucl.ac.be/en/institution/history.html
5. A study published in 1987 found that in Flanders only 35.2% identified with Belgium, 39.2% with the Flemish Community/ Region, and 25.6% other. In Wallonia, the figures were 52.7%, 31.7% and 15.5% respectively. In Brussels, 58.0% identified with Belgium, 21.4% with the Community/Region, and 20.6% other. *Complexe Belgique* (Brussels: Cahiers du Centre D'Action Culturelle de la Communauté d'Expression Française (CACEF) A.S.B.L. Bimestriel – 1987 no. 130, p. 13.
6. Consociational (or 'consensus') democracy in Europe is particularly associated with Belgium, the Netherlands, Switzerland and Northern Ireland after 1998. Descriptions of how it works are to be found in several academic texts, especially Arend Lijphart, op. cit.
7. J.B. Minahan, op.cit., p. 255.
8. *Time Europe*, 24 June 2002, p. 30, using the UN High Commissioner for Refugees as source.
9. *Time Europe*, 20 May 2002, p. 30.
10. Neal Ascherson, 'The warning shot', *Observer Review*, 12 May 2002, p. 1.
11. www.eboa.com/fnp

8 Scandinavia

1. Also part of Scandinavia are Greenland, the Faroe Islands, and perhaps Shetland and Orkney. The first two have been under the control of Denmark since the fourteenth century. In 1979 a referendum on autonomy was held in Greenland, which was granted later that year. Nevertheless, Greenland elects two members to the Danish Parliament (*Folketing*). The Faroe Islands were granted autonomy in 1948, but like Greenland, elect two members to the Danish Parliament. Greenland withdrew from the EC in February 1985, after a referendum held in February 1982. The Faroe Islands never joined the EC, but have a special trade agreement with it.

    The parties in these areas are separate from Danish parties, and there are nationalist and unionist parties. The former include the pro-independence Eskimo Brotherhood (*Inuit Ataqatigiit*) in Greenland, and the pro-independence Republican Party (*Tjódveldisflokkurin/Tjfl*) in the Faroe Islands. The former won 20.3% of the vote and seven seats for the Greenland Parliament (31 members) in 1999, but formed a coalition with a non-secession party. The Republican Party won 23.8% and eight seats in the 32-seat Faroes parliament and joined a coalition which promised to hold a referendum on independence in 2012.

    Shetland and Orkney belonged to Norway until 1472 and sometimes claim to be Norwegian, not Scottish. They both have autonomy movements, which are described in Chapter. 2.
2. Quoted by Helge Salvensen in Sven Tägil (ed.), *Ethnicity and Nation Building in the Nordic World* (London: Hurst, 1995), p. 116.

3. James B. Minahan, *One Europe, Many Nations* (Westport, Connecticut: Greenwood Press, 2000), p. 577.
4. Minahan, op.cit., p. 580. Generally see Tägil, quoted above, which is the best source in English about Scandinavian ethnicity and nationalism.
5. Tägil, op.cit., p. 273.
6. Tägil, pp. 276–7.
7. *Economist*, 27 July 2002, p. 39.
8. F. Fernández-Armesto (ed.), *The Times Guide to the Peoples of Europe* (London: Times Books, 1994), pp. 303–4.
9. James B. Minahan, op.cit., p. 24.
10. *Ibid.* p. 305.
11. Minahan, op.cit., p. 27.
12. Most historical atlases call Helsinki Helsingfors until 1918.

9 Switzerland

1. These terms are discussed fully in my book, *The Politics of Nationalism and Ethnicity* (Basingstoke: Macmillan, 1991,1998), Introduction.
2. This information is assembled from various web-sites, notably that of the Mouvement Autonomiste Jurassian at www.maj.ch
3. Swiss citizenship law is extremely complicated, but is being liberalised (2002). Swiss citizenship is 'triple citizenship', with confederal, cantonal and communal levels. At the same time, dual citizenship with a foreign country is allowed. Even the children of a Swiss parent can find it too difficult to become Swiss citizens, if the other parent is a foreigner. Despite the fact that 700 000 foreign residents of Switzerland have been in Switzerland for more than 12 years, and 120 000 for more than 30 years, Swiss nationality law has made it virtually impossible them to get Swiss citizenship. Indeed, the number of naturalisations has been limited to 30 000 per year, although changes in 2002 should make this rise to 35 000 to 40 000. Paul Michaud, 'Switzerland to ease law of nationality', *Dawn the Internet Edition*, 21 June 2002. www.dawn.com/2002/06/21/top19.htm
4. Used: www.oefre.unibe.ch/law/icl © 1994 Dr A. Tschentsches. e-mail axel.tschentsche @ oefre.unibe.ch. There is an official version by the Swiss Embassy in Washington, www.swissemb.org/legal/const.pdf
5. Based in Italian-speaking canton of Ticino. It seeks greater autonomy for Ticino. In 1995, standing alone, it won two seats with 0.9% of the Swiss vote.

10 'Mitteleuropa'

1. Place-names in *Mitteleuropa* make a fascinating study, as many have changed three times in the twentieth century. Most started with German names, since they came under the Hapsburg or German Empires. In 1918, most adopted national (usually Slav) names, except that Russian was favoured in areas ruled by the USSR. After 1990 these adopted national names.
2. The term 'Austria-Hungary' dates from 1867, when Austria and Hungary became a 'Dual Monarchy' under the Hapsburg Emperor as Emperor of Austria and 'Apostolic' King of Hungary. Both countries had separate legislatures and executives, but certain powers were run on an Imperial basis

(e.g. foreign affairs, the army and finance). 'Austria' included Bohemia, Moravia and Silesia (now in the Czech Republic, and from 1918 to 1992 in Czechoslovakia) and Slovenia (after 1918 in Yugoslavia, and since 1991 an independent state) and Bosnia-Hercegovina (administered by Austria under the sovereignty of the Turkish Empire from 1878 and annexed by Austria in 1908. It, then became part of the Kingdom of the Serbs, Croats and Slovenes/Yugoslavia (1918/1929), and since 1992 has been independent). Austria also ruled southern Poland, which had been annexed in 1772, 1793, and 1795. The Republic of Cracow/*Kraków* was given independence in 1815, but was annexed again by Austria in 1846. Hungary included Slovakia (in Czechoslovakia from 1918 to 1992, then independent), Croatia and Vojvodina in Serbia (these last in the Kingdom of the Serbs, Croats and Slovenes from 1918 and Yugoslavia from 1929). Croatia became independent in 1991, and Vojvodina continued as an Autonomous Province within Serbia after the rump Yugoslavia continued in the 1990s.

3. Another source (Banks and Muller, *Political Handbook of the World 1998*), gives the figure as 1.6 million.

4. See W.L. Miller, S. White and P. Heywood, *Values and Political Change in Postcommunist Europe* (Basingstoke: Macmillan, 1998), Ch. 7. The book covers the Czech Republic, Slovakia and Hungary, as well as Russia and Ukraine. Using various measures of nationalism, Hungary was strong on 'external' nationalism, which tested opinion on relations with foreign countries, and Slovakia and Hungary were equally strong on 'cultural' nationalism which stated that only those who spoke the state language should be citizens with the right to vote and that state schools should teach all subjects in the state language (43% agreed). The Czech Republic was weakly nationalist overall (only 26%), which seems to indicate satisfaction with the boundaries of the state (no Czech minorities in other states) and its internal arrangements, for example concerning language.

5. *Ibid.*, p. 127.

6. Bohemia is celebrated in the music of Dvořák, and Moravia in the music of Janáček. Both of these composers are often inaccurately described as Czech nationalists. The former was a Bohemian nationalist, and the latter a Moravian nationalist.

7. Minahan, *One Europe, Many Nations*, pp. 486–7.

8. In particular, Edmund Stoiber, the leader of the Bavarian Christian Social Union, who was the Christian Democratic Union/Christian Social Union presidential candidate in 2002. Stoiber is married to a Sudeten German. Bavaria was the destination of most of the expelled Sudeten Germans in 1945.

9. Named after Edvard Beneš, the President of Czechoslovakia in 1945. The Sudeten Germans amounted to 3.2 million out of a total Czechoslovak population of 13.6 million in 1938. After 1945 there were only a handful left in the Sudeten Lands. Hungarians in Czechoslovakia in 1938 totalled 0.8 million. Around 10.5 million Germans fled to West Germany in 1945, most as a result of being expelled. The biggest number (*c.* 7 million) was from East Prussia and Poland whose territory was expanded to include East Prussia (part of Germany) and a swathe of German territory up to the Oder-Neisse line. The repercussions of this migration are still present in contemporary politics, with claims for restitution or compensation being heard across eastern Europe, and links made with the candidatures for EU membership by Poland, the Czech Republic and Slovakia, which Germany could veto.

10. This figure is taken from *Whitaker's Almanack 2002*. *The Statesman's Yearbook 2003* gives the percentage as 9.7%.
11. Under the Hapsburgs, Crown Lands were the personal property of the Hapsburgs, as compared to Church lands, and aristocratic property. The claim that the Czech state had an ancient existence no doubt refers to the Kingdom of Bohemia, abolished after the Battle of the White Mountain in 1620, but which was already in the hands of the Hapsburgs after 1526.

11 The Balkans

1. Although there is some dispute as to what the term 'the Balkans' covers, here the contemporary states included are Slovenia/*Republika Slovenija*, Croatia/*Republika Hrvatska*, Serbia/*Srbija*, Montenegro/*Crna Gora* (these two joined in the federal republic of Yugoslavia/*Savezna Republika Jugoslavija*), Bosnia-Hercegovina/*Bosna I Hercegovina*, Macedonia/*Republika Makedonija* (Former Yugoslav Republic of Macedonia/FYROM), Albania/*Republika e Shqipërisë*, Greece/*Elliniki Dimokratia*, Bulgaria/*Republioka Bulgarija*, and Romania/*România*. Slovenes may deny that they are part of the Balkans, and prefer to see themselves as part of the ex-Hapsburg *Mitteleuropa*. This is also heard in Croatia, also part of the Hapsburg Empire, and also predominantly (77%) Roman Catholic in religion.
2. Examples of these schools of thought are, for the former, Marcus Tanner, *Croatia. A Nation Forged in War* (New Haven and London: Yale University Press, 1997), and of the latter, Noel Malcolm, *Bosnia. A Short History* (London: Macmillan, 1994). Somewhat in the middle comes Misha Glenny, *The Balkans 1804–1999. Nationalism, War and the Great Powers* (London: Granta Books, 1999). For the point of view of a participant politician, see David Owen's *Balkan Odyssey* (London: Indigo/Gollancz, 1995/96), which has however been criticised for special pleading and poor analysis of the political realities on the ground. The trial from 1999 at the International Criminal Tribunal for the Former Yugoslavia (War Crimes Tribunal) at The Hague of the former Yugoslav President, Slobodan Milošević, and other belligerents, opened a judicial review of these historical events. In fact while there is no totally 'correct' interpretation of history, there is now a rigorous examination of the Yugoslav nationalist war in the Tribunal, even if those on trial claim that it is biased against them.
3. Dusan Kecmanovic, *The Mass Psychology of Ethnonationalism* (New York and London: Plenum Press, 1996). Kecmanovic explains behaviour after the break-up of Yugoslavia thus: '... a lot of the energy that for decades had held people together, enabling them to participate in a supraindividual entity, remained now unbounded, unfettered. The upshot was quite expected: people felt deserted and isolated' (p. 166). 'Over a short time, people changed political allegiances many times. Persons who had been marginalized and, for whatever reason, stigmatized, a few months beforehand, began to figure on the political scene, at times in the role of leaders teaching people what was righteous, what was moral and what immoral Overnight, decades-old friendships were destroyed ... In such a situation the majority of so-called ordinary people saw themselves as incompetent to grasp the meaning of

current events ... Nationalist attitudes and beliefs appeared able to ease the pain and the feeling of infirmity caused by such occurrences. Nationalist ideology has ready-made solutions to all puzzles ... members of a nationalist group take pride in the outstanding qualities and performances of their fellow-nationals. Any feeling of infirmity is simply incompatible with such group membership' (p. 169). This leaves unexplained what caused the political vacuum in the first place.

4. Also spelled 'Herzegovina' in English.
5. James B. Minahan, op.cit., p. 437.
6. These are figures before the 1998 expulsion of Albanians by the Serbs. Most of these returned to Kosovo when the UN took control in 1999.
7. Minahan. op.cit., p. 28.
8. Twenty four seats in the Cyprus Parliament are reserved for Turkish Cypriots, but these are vacant.
9. In this book, on Europe, Turkey is discussed only in terms of 'Turkey-in-Europe' (i.e. the European side of the Dardanelles, amounting to 3% of Turkey's total area) and Cyprus. Turks do not think of themselves as Asian, despite the fact that 97% of the country is in Asia. Fernández-Armesto, op.cit., p. 201.
10. There are 9.6 million Turks in total in Europe (including Turkey itself). Outside Turkey these are spread across Germany (1.8 million), Bulgaria (835 000), the Netherlands (188 000), Cyprus (nearly all in the Turkish Republic of Northern Cyprus) (145 000), France (138 000), Greece (131 000), and so on. The population of Turkey is 66.6 million, of whom 80% are Turks (i.e. speaking Turkish). Religion is less of a divide than language as 99% of the population are Muslim, albeit divided into Sunnis (*c.* 80%)and Alevis (*c.* 20%). Ethnicity is a divide, however, as of the 20% non-Turkish population the Kurds amount to 12 million (10%). The other minorities include Arabs, Circassians, Greeks, Armenians, Georgians, Lazes and Jews.
11. R.C.K. Ensor, *England. 1870–1914* (Oxford: Clarendon Press, 1936), p. 45.
12. The figure in Banks and Muller, *Political Handbook of the World 1998*, p. 402, is 1.6 million.
13. *Worldwide Refugee Information. Country Report: Yugoslavia. 2002.* www.refugees.org/world/countryrpt/europe/yugoslavia.htm
14. Those of Human Rights Watch and Worldwide Refugee Information are particularly useful.
15. International Helsinki Federation for Human Rights Annual Report 1999 on Slovenia. www.ihf-hr.org/reprots/ar99/ar999slv.htm
16. This differs from the 1990 Constitution. The word 'autochthonous' was not present, and the list read 'Serbs, *Muslims, Slovenes,* Czechs, Slovaks, Italians, Hungarians, *Jews* and others' (italics indicate minorities deleted). Germans, Austrians, Ukrainians and Ruthenians were added. Roma (Gypsies) are not included, even if 120 000 were officially registered in Croatia, and probably 250 000 to 300 000 in total, as many did not register.
17. In communist Yugoslavia both Latin and Cyrillic scripts were official.
18. This means that Croats in, for example, Bosnia can vote in Croatian elections, as they mostly took up Croat citizenship when Croatia and Bosnia-Hercegovina became independent states. This was possible even if they had dual citizenship.

19. Citizenship of the Republic of Macedonia Act, Article 2.
20. www.us-english.org/foundation/Greece.PDF
21. This has been used against ethnic Hungarians in Romania, for example, curbing Hungarian language education, and making the display of the flag or singing the anthem of another state a criminal offence. Even the statue of a Hungarian King in Cluj was threatened with removal.
22. The main problem is that at university level, there is no Hungarian-language university, although courses are offered in Hungarian in the University of Cluj in Transylvania. Ethnic Hungarians wanted a Hungarian university, but the Government turned this down and an ultra-Romanian nationalist was elected mayor of Cluj-Napoca in 1992.
23. This law (No. 67 of 15 July 1992) adds the proviso that the share of vote must be at least 5% of the average number of validly cast votes in the entire country for the election of a Deputy.
24. Consisted of 20 parties, one of which (the Democratic Party of Serbia) has been described as nationalist, and one (Social Democratic League of Vojvodina) as regionalist.
25. Included the Democratic Party of Serbia, Democratic Party, Social Democratic Party, Serb Civic Alliance, Social Democratic League of Serbia and two Vojvodina regionalist parties.
26. Figures from www.electionworld.org/election/kosovo.htm
27. www.electionworld.org/election/croatia.htm
28. Day (ed.), *Political Parties of the World* (2002), pp. 390–1.

12 Poland

1. Poland's nationalism can be measured by its national identity, and by its feelings about its neighbours, and about the EU. People in Poland have been almost exclusively 'Poles' since 1945 in terms of national identity, because of the expulsion of foreigners, notably Germans, 'Russians' (including Belarusans, and Ukrianians) and Lithuanians. Dual national identity occurs today if 'European' is included as a national identity. In 2001, 34% gave 'only Polish' as their national identity, with nearly all the remainder adding 'European' to some degree. However, only 1% said they were more European than Polish. Clare-McManus-Czubińska, William L. Miller, Radosław Markowski and Jacek Wasilewski, 'Understanding Dual Identities in Poland', *Political Studies*, Vol. 51, no. 1 (March 2003), p. 124.
2. Thus Stettin became Szczecin, Breslau became Wroclaw and Allenstein became Olsztyn. Posen had become Poznań in 1919.
3. F. Fernández-Armesto, *The Peoples of Europe*, p. 321.
4. J.B. Minahan, *One Europe, Many Nations*, p. 526.
5. There are around 1.2 million Germans in Poland. Thirty per cent of the population of Polish Silesia is German-speaking.
6. B. Swiderek, *Le Mouvement Autonomiste Silésien et L'Europe. Diplomatie Magazin*, no. 2, Mars–Avril 2003, p. 61. Silesian nationalism dates back to the 1930s, when the Silesian (*lasky*) language was constructed from local Slav dialects. The revival of this nationalism in the 1990s also covered the Czech Republic, but there Silesian nationalism merged with Moravian

nationalism. Jaroslav Skupnik, 'Formation and Development of the Czech National Identity' in Shashikant Jha (ed.), *Ethnicity and Nation-building in Eastern Europe* (London: Sangam Books, 1998), pp. 83–4.

7. Silesia first came to attention in the twentieth century in the peace settlements following the First World War, when Poland and Czechoslovakia were formed out of the German, Hapsburg and Russian Empires. Silesia before the War was divided between Germany and Austria. The peace settlement retained the division, now between Poland, Germany and Czechoslovakia. A plebiscite was held on 20 March 1921 in Upper Silesia, in which 65% voted to remain in Germany. Partition followed. The Polish section of Upper Silesia contained round 300 000 Germans out of a total population of 1.3 million. German Upper Silesia contained around 155 000 Poles out of a total of 892 547. These were put under the protection of the League of Nations. Silesia in Czechoslovakia was 40% German, and non-German Silesians identified with the Slav Moravians. Czech Silesia was ceded to Germany by the Munich settlement in 1938, and the Germans were mostly expelled in 1945, when Czechoslovakia resumed control. In 1990, multiparty elections in Czechoslovakia returned several Moravian nationalists, who demanded independence for Moravia. The remaining Silesian nationalists linked up with these Moravian nationalists, but after the independence of the Czech Republic in 1993, Moravian nationalism waned, although it revived somewhat in 1997 with the demand for regional representation in the EU on the accession of the Czech Republic. See Minahan, op.cit., pp. 486–7.

13   The Baltic Nations

1. Miroslav Hroch has expounded this in his *Social Preconditions of National Revival in Europe* (Cambridge: Cambridge University Press, 1985), in which he discusses Estonia and Lithuania as 'belated types'.

2. The best account of these years, and of the history leading up to them, is probably by Anatol Lieven, *The Baltic Revolution. Estonia, Latvia, Lithuania and the Path to Independence* (New Haven and London: Yale University Press, 1993).

3. The Law on the State Language (1995) states that it 'shall not regulate unofficial communication of the population … as well as persons belonging to ethnic communities'. But it makes clear that names (including personal names) and signs and information 'shall be in the state language'. The names of organisations of ethnic communities and their informational signs may be in other languages along with the state language. Signs in other languages cannot be larger than that of signs in the state language.

4. The capital of Latvia, Riga, has more Russian-language schools than Latvian schools.

5. Barry Turner (ed.), The *Statesman's Yearbook 2003* (Basingstoke and New York: Palgrave Macmillan, 2002), p. 601. Other sources give the Russians as high as 31% and non-ethnic Estonians as 37%. US Department of State, *Estonia. Country Reports on Human Rights Practices 2001.* www.state.gov/g/drl/rls/hrrpt/2001/eur

6. A musicologist, Landsbergis now has a ceremonial position in the Lithuanian Parliament.

7. *Baltic Times*, 10–16 January 2003.
8. *Ibid.*
9. *Baltic Times*, 10–16 October 2002.
10. The coalition government consisted of members of the Pro Patria (or 'Fatherland') Union/*Isamaaliit* (*IML*), a 1995 merger with the Estonian National Independence Party/*Eesti Rahvusliku Sõtumatuse Partei* (*ERSP*), the Moderates/*Mõõdukad*, and the Estonian Reform Party/*Eesti Reformierkond* (*ER*). In 2002, the coalition had changed to the Estonian Centre Party and the Estonian Reform Party, with the Prime Minister coming from the Reform Party. The President, Arnold Rüütel, elected in October 2001, came from the Estonian People's Union/*Eestimaa Rahvaliit* (*ERL*). Although a member of the pre-independence Estonian Supreme Soviet, Rüütel had backed independence, and became Estonia's first President.

14 Russia-in-Europe, Belarus and Ukraine

1. Russia is both a European and an Asian country, and its eastern European limits are conventionally set at the Ural mountains, and the Caucasus, including Georgia, Azerbaijan and Armenia. However, these last are not covered here, mainly for reasons of coherence relating to the constitutional and electoral dimensions of nationalism. The USSR consisted of 15 republics, but only seven (including the three Baltic republics) can be considered as European. Three of these are dealt with in this chapter. The remaining one, the Moldavian Republic (now Moldova), is a Balkan state, and has been covered in Chapter 11. The definition of Europe is as much that of geographers' as of political scientists' or historians'. The political scientist Richard Rose, for example, in *What is Europe?* (New York: HarperCollins, 1996) omits Russia, Belarus, Ukraine, Moldova and Turkey-in-Europe. But he also omits countries 'because their position is exceptional or their size marginal' (p. 6). Thus the Baltic states, former Yugoslavia and Albania are not included. On the other hand, James B. Minahan, *One Europe, Many Nations* (Westwood, CT: Greenwood Press, 2000), includes Armenians, Azeris, Georgians, Turks and a variety of minor 'nations' under the rubric of Europe. Felipe Fernández-Armesto, in *The Times Guide to the Peoples of Europe* (London: Tomes Books, 1994) includes various 'Muslim-Turkic and Mongol Peoples of the Volga-Urals and Daghestan' such as Bashkirs, Nogays, Kalmyks and Kumyks', most of whom are in the Russian Federation. Also included are 'Peoples of the Caucasus' in Georgia, Armenia and Azerbaijan, as well as in the Russian Federation. These 'peoples' are usually considered ethnic groups rather than nations, but the distinction falls if and when they demand autonomy or independence from Russia.
2. Most Sovietologists considered the Soviet Union to be a strong and stable political system, when in fact it was on the point of collapse. Many 'experts' followed the official line that the 'nationality question' had been solved through a harmonious development of federalism. There were one or two notable exceptions, such as Walker Connor, *The National Question in Marxist Theory and Practice* (Princeton: Princeton University Press, 1984); Hélène Carrère d'Encausse, *Decline of an Empire: The Soviet Socialist Republics in Revolt* (New York: Newsweek Books, 1979) and Alexander J. Motyl, *Will the*

Non-Russians Rebel? State, Ethnicity, and Stability in the USSR (Ithaca and London: Cornell University Press, 1987).

3. John Breuilly, in *Nationalism and the State* (Manchester: Manchester University Press, 2nd edn, 1993), p. 350, writes: 'However, the main point I would like to make is that one should not see the break-up of the USSR in terms of the rise of nationalist oppositions; rather one should see the rise of nationalist oppositions as a rational response to the breakdown of USSR state power, as the "politics of inheritance" based on the republics'. This is difficult to reconcile with the very strong desire to reconstitute these republics along nationalist lines, with national official languages, education systems, exclusive citizenship laws, and so on.

4. Most of the Republics of the Russian Federation have national or ethnic identities, and some have displayed nationalism since independence. In particular, Chechnya, Dagestan, Ingushetia, North Ossetia (Alania), Tatarstan, have seen ethnic conflicts.

5. The Jewish Autonomous Region (Capital, Birobijan) is part of Khabarovsk Territory in the Far East. Of its population of 208 000 in 1997, however, only 4.2% were Jews, with 83.2% Russians and 7.4% Ukrainians. It was established as the Jewish National District in 1928.

15 Conclusion

1. In the Eurobarometer surveys conducted for the EU European Commission, Public Opinion Analysis sector, there is a series of responses on national and European identities. The identities offered are 'European only'. 'European and Nationality', 'Nationality and European' and 'Nationality only'. Over all the 15 EU members, the last category usually scores from 40–45%, but the first only makes 4–8% (1995–2000). The mixed category putting 'nationality' before 'European' scores 40–45%, and the 'European' before 'nationality' category scores only 6–8%. There is considerable variation among the 15 member-states, with Austria, Greece, Finland, Ireland, Sweden and the United Kingdom having an absolute majority of 'nationality only' respondents in 2000. The most 'European' were Italy, Spain, Luxembourg, France and the Netherlands (all with under 40% 'nationality only'). These responses show little or no trend in the past decade. See *Standard Eurobarometer* 53 (October 2000), pp. 80–1, and *Standard Eurobarometer* 47 (1997), pp. 55–6.

2. Germany became a united nation, not through a referendum, but by a Treaty between the German Federal Republic (GFR) and the German Democratic Republic (GDR), signed on 18 May 1990, followed by a resolution of the GDR Parliament on 23 August 1990 that the GDR should accede to the GFR. A formal unification Treaty was signed on 31 August, and this was ratified by the 'occupying powers', including the USSR, on 12 September. Formal reunification took place on 3 October 1990.

3. These categories were discussed in Chapter 1.

4. Curiously, the nationalist parties (SNP and Plaid Cymru/Party of Wales) are officially in favour of joining the Euro, but their members are uneasy.

5. Of course, nationalism itself may be considered an ideology. The ideologies of socialism/Marxism and capitalism/liberal democracy were the dividing lines in European politics until 1990.

Bibliographical Note

A work such as this, which ranges over almost 100 nations and 44 states, has more the character of an encyclopaedia than a specialised case study. Each of the nations and states discussed is the subject of a small library of works, and it is unnecessary to try to list them here. Even a selection from them would be pointless to compile, as the focus of this book is contemporary constitutional and electoral politics, which is relatively neglected in the literature.

What is necessary, however, is to indicate the main sources used, which can be consulted for further information. These are usually large encyclopedias, dictionaries and handbooks, and they have been heavily used in this book. Also used extensively are the internet web sites on countries, constitutions, parties and elections. These are difficult to list, and many of them are ephemeral. But some are mentioned here.

An important source on internet is the collection of constitutions compiled by the Law Faculty at the University of Würzburg in Germany. These can be accessed at www/uni-wuerzburg.de/law. Other sources on constitutions have been used, usually official sources.

On elections and parties, the main source has been Alan J. Day, *Political Parties of the World, 5th edition* (London: John Harper Publishing, 2002); Arthur S. Banks, Thomas C. Muller (eds), *Political Handbook of the World 1998* [this seems to be the latest edition] (Binghampton, New York: CSA Publications, 1998); Barry Turner (ed.), *The Statesman's Yearbook 2003* (Basingstoke and New York: Palgrave Macmillan, 2002); *Whitaker's Almanack 2002* (London: The Stationery Office, 2001); James B. Minahan, *One Europe, Many Nations* (Westport, Connecticut and London: Greenwood Press, 2000).

Important web-sites are www.electionworld.org and www.parties-and-elections.de.

Works providing data on nations, ethnic groups and states include the books mentioned above, and Felipe Fernández-Armesto (ed.), *The Times Guide to the Peoples of Europe* (London: Times Books, 1994). Historical atlases are invaluable, especially G. Barraclough (ed.), *The Times Atlas of World History* (London: Times Books, 1984 edition), R.R. Palmer (ed.), *Rand McNally Historical Atlas of the World* (Chicago, New York, San Francisco: Rand McNally, 1965); George Goodall and R.F. Treherne (eds), *Muir's Historical Atlas. Mediaeval and Modern* (London: George Philip and Son, 8th edition, 1952); *Hammond Historical Atlas of the World* (Maplewood, New Jersey: Hammond, 1984).

Obviously, a work such as this gets out of date almost immediately, especially with regard to elections. The reader will have to update the material from the sources mentioned. As time passes, the web sites change, but a good search engine should provide the student with all (and more!) of the information required. Analysis is another matter.

Index